Manifesting the Primal Imagination

african christian studies series (africs)

This series will make available significant works in the field of African Christian studies, taking into account the many forms of Christianity across the whole continent of Africa. African Christian studies is defined here as any scholarship that relates to themes and issues on the history, nature, identity, character, and place of African Christianity in world Christianity. It also refers to topics that address the continuing search for abundant life for Africans through multiple appeals to African religions and African Christianity in a challenging social context. The books in this series are expected to make significant contributions in historicizing trends in African Christian studies, while shifting the contemporary discourse in these areas from narrow theological concerns to a broader inter-disciplinary engagement with African religio-cultural traditions and Africa's challenging social context.

The series will cater to scholarly and educational texts in the areas of religious studies, theology, mission studies, biblical studies, philosophy, social justice, and other diverse issues current in African Christianity. We define these studies broadly and specifically as primarily focused on new voices, fresh perspectives, new approaches, and historical and cultural analyses that are emerging because of the significant place of African Christianity and African religio-cultural traditions in world Christianity. The series intends to continually fill a gap in African scholarship, especially in the areas of social analysis in African Christian studies, African philosophies, new biblical and narrative hermeneutical approaches to African theologies, and the challenges facing African women in today's Africa and within African Christianity. Other diverse themes in African Traditional Religions; African ecology; African ecclesiology; inter-cultural, inter-ethnic, and inter-religious dialogue; ecumenism; creative inculturation; African theologies of development, reconciliation, globalization, and poverty reduction will also be covered in this series.

SERIES EDITORS

Dr. Stan Chu Ilo (DePaul University, Chicago, USA)
Dr. Esther Acolatse (University of Toronto, Canada)

Manifesting the Primal Imagination

The Primal Spirituality of Black American Christian Faith

JOSHUA D. SETTLES

Foreword by Gillian Mary Bediako

◆PICKWICK *Publications* · Eugene, Oregon

MANIFESTING THE PRIMAL IMAGINATION
The Primal Spirituality of Black American Christian Faith

Copyright © 2024 Joshua D. Settles. All rights reserved. Except for brief quotations in critical publications or reviews, no part of this book may be reproduced in any manner without prior written permission from the publisher. Write: Permissions, Wipf and Stock Publishers, 199 W. 8th Ave., Suite 3, Eugene, OR 97401.

Pickwick Publications
An Imprint of Wipf and Stock Publishers
199 W. 8th Ave., Suite 3
Eugene, OR 97401

www.wipfandstock.com

PAPERBACK ISBN: 978-1-6667-3829-2
HARDCOVER ISBN: 978-1-6667-9880-7
EBOOK ISBN: 978-1-6667-9881-4

Cataloguing-in-Publication data:

Names: Settles, Joshua D., author. | Bediako, Gillian Mary, foreword.

Title: Manifesting the primal imagination : the primal spirituality of black American Christian faith / Joshua D. Settles ; foreword by Gillian Mary Bediako.

Description: Eugene, OR: Pickwick Publications, 2024 | Series: African Christian Studies Series | Includes bibliographical references.

Identifiers: ISBN 978-1-6667-3829-2 (paperback) | ISBN 978-1-6667-9880-7 (hardcover) | ISBN 978-1-6667-9881-4 (ebook)

Subjects: LCSH: African Americans—Religion. | Black theology. | African American Pentecostals—History. | African American churches.

Classification: BR1644.3 .S48 2024 (paperback) | BR1644.3 .S48 (ebook)

VERSION NUMBER 09/24/24

Scripture quotations marked ESV are from the ESV® Bible (The Holy Bible, English Standard Version®), © 2001 by Crossway, a publishing ministry of Good News Publishers. Used by permission. All rights reserved.

Scripture quotations marked KJV are from the King James or Authorized Version.

Scripture quotations marked NASB are taken from the (NASB®) New American Standard Bible®, copyright © 1995 by The Lockman Foundation. Used by permission. All rights reserved. lockman.org

Scripture quotations marked NIV are taken from the Holy Bible, New International Version®, NIV®. Copyright © 2011 by Biblica, Inc.® Used by permission of Zondervan. All rights reserved worldwide.

Scripture quotations marked NKJV are taken from the New King James Version®. Copyright © 1982 by Thomas Nelson. Used by permission. All rights reserved.

Scripture quotations marked RSVCE are taken from the Catholic Edition of the Revised Standard Version of the Bible, copyright © 1966 by National Council of the Churches of Christ in the United States of America. Used by permission. All rights reserved worldwide.

Dedicated to the memory of my mother,
Irma Nell Reese Settles
(December 25, 1944—December 27, 1999),
and
my daughter,
Reese Akosua Hui-zhen Settles
(May 18, 2014—November 13, 2014)

Contents

Foreword by Gillian Mary Bediako | xi

Preface | xv

Acknowledgments | xvii

Abbreviations | xix

1. Introduction: The "Problem" of the Primal and Race in Euro-Western Christian Civilization | 1
2. From "Barbarian Creed" to "Civilized Faith" | 21
3. Euro-Western Interpretation of Black Peoples | 48
4. Decentering Eurocentric White Supremacy | 82
5. The Primal Imagination in the New Testament | 100
6. Black Pentecostal Churches in Historical Context | 132
7. The Primal in the Pentecostal: A Case Study of the All Saints Holiness Church | 164
8. Primal Spirituality in the St Martins Spiritualist Church | 191
9. Emerging Theological Matters and Concluding Reflections | 216

Bibliography | 243

Foreword

It is rare that one comes upon a book that truly breaks new ground, but this is one such. For it brings together bodies of existing knowledge not hitherto associated with one another in a unique pattern of reflection that sheds new light on old stories and opens up new and redemptive perspectives for a whole range of readers. It not only focuses on the New Testament and Black American Christianity, it also traces the roots of racism in the history of Christian thought and practice in Europe and the Americas, the thread binding these three strands together being the primal imagination, here shown to be of intrinsic importance for the Christian faith, attitudes towards it, and their impact through the centuries.

The first part of the work covers the sweep of Christian history and thought in Europe from earliest times and its extension to the Americas, with a view to demonstrating how the primal worldview that is manifest in the New Testament and the earliest church came to be denigrated and suppressed, how perspectives on Black peoples worsened over time, tracing the roots and emergence of White Supremacy. A most illuminating chapter is chapter 4, "Decentering Eurocentric White Supremacy," which critiques Western methodological approaches so often assumed to be normative, and offers suggestive insights into what indigenous and more specifically Black methodologies might yield. Similarly, Settles critiques Black American religious scholarship and the extent of its imitative or reactive impulses, before preparing the ground for the next chapter, which considers "how the primal imagination underlies and informs the New Testament itself, and how the primal imagination is manifest within it." His conclusion is important:

> The New Testament world is one in which the supernatural does not exist in a conceptual or ideological way, but in which it, and the multitude of spiritual beings and powers emanating from it, impinge on day-to-day life through dreams, cosmic signs, angelic visitations, as well as in other ways. The veil between the living and the dead appears thin and permeable under the right conditions, with the deceased representing potent presences either as revered ancestors or feared demons. Persons, ritual actions, and physical objects are all potential conduits for spiritual power and for the transference of that power from one person to another. In short, the New Testament, and the Christianity reflected in it, is a thoroughly primal text with primal assumptions.

With all this as backdrop, the history of Black American spirituality from the days of slavery to modern times, followed by two case studies of churches in the holiness-Pentecostal/spiritual tradition, takes on new biblical, phenomenological, and theological resonance, situating Black American Christians and the expressions of their faith firmly within the mainstream tradition of Christian spirituality, neither exotic nor heterodox, and to be numbered among "such a great cloud of witnesses" (Heb 12:1 KJV) that surround us.

Before drawing out pointers for further inquiry, Settles's final fascinating chapter explores some implications for embodied theology, that is, "theology expressed *through* the various media of art and the body itself" (emphasis original). It picks up on the fraught question of "multiplicity in the spiritual realm" in relation to ancestors in particular, and in the New Testament, and the "cosmos as a single spiritual system," all of which have a contemporary ring about them.

So, what might this book have to offer us? For a Caucasian Christian, like myself, it helps, in a measured, well-documented, and well-argued way, to unearth the "dark side" of European Christian history, the parts that are not found in standard school textbooks, or curricula of theological education, and yet which have far-reaching impact even into our own times. It thereby forces us to confront our own "cultural demons," as it were. It also brings the New Testament to life in a new way, recovering a depth and vibrancy of spirituality that has tended to be submerged through culture-bound readings down the centuries—the kind of spirituality manifested by the early Irish Christians, who were responsible for re-evangelizing Britain and Western Europe, and which New Age movements in our time feel after—and reconnecting it with the Old Testament in a common worldview.

It also provides a positive lens with which to view Black American Christianity, new knowledge there for us in the case studies of the two churches that takes us sympathetically beyond the Negro spirituals that one may already readily admire, so helping to bind us together in a common humanity as well as a common faith. The book thereby opens up a window of new possibilities in perception, biblical, Christian, and entirely wholesome, for those of us from a more "disembodied" context, uneasy when confronted by primal phenomena.

For Christians worldwide, including African Christians, it illuminates aspects of Christian history that have most probably had a negative impact upon their own contexts and mission stories, given the range and extent of imperial expansion often aligned with Christianity, and likewise provides a liberating interpretative framework through affirming the biblical credentials of the primal imagination and the validity of indigenous expressions of Christian faith. In the case of Christians from the African continent, it offers insight into the distinctive Black American predicament as well as shared experiences.

From what I know of Dr. Settles and other Black colleagues, this study offers Black Americans a perspective that is potentially liberating, in affirming their resilience through a truly melancholy (to say the least) history, and providing solid ground for their intuitive feel for the spirituality inherent in the New Testament and in Christian faith, despite Christianity having been historically overwhelmingly the religion of their oppressors. It also suggests avenues for future fruitful explorations along these lines.

The whole book is well written and documented, easy to read, and with a compelling message. May all who read it be likewise blessed, spiritually challenged and encouraged, as I have been.

Gillian M. Bediako
Akrofi-Christaller Institute of Theology, Mission and Culture
Akropong-Akuapem, Ghana
June 2024

Preface

THIS BOOK EXAMINES ASPECTS of Black American Christianity and the New Testament through the lens of the primal imagination. In this work I redress the widespread notion of Christianity as Euro-Western "civilized" religion and underscore the fact that Christianity itself rests on the foundation of the primal imagination, as indicated in its seminal text, the New Testament. The primal imagination refers to a particular way of seeing and interpreting reality, the fundamental substructure of all subsequent religious and cultural understandings, including Christianity.

The book traces how the conflation of Euro-Western culture and Christian faith, the long history of negative racialist interpretations of Black peoples and religion, and the Enlightenment and post-Enlightenment responses to primal religion have suppressed and obscured the primal features of Christianity in both its expression, and also its apprehension of the New Testament. In it, I examine the historical development of Black American Christianity, its relationship to the primal traditions of conjure, and the rise of the Pentecostal and spiritual church movements, termed the *pneumatic sacramentalist tradition*. Using the primal imagination as a guide, I examine two churches from these traditions, All Saints Holiness Church and St Martins Spiritual Church, as well as aspects of the New Testament to demonstrate both the manifestation of the primal imagination and the indispensability of the primal imagination to Christianity itself.

This book shines a light on new trajectories for theological investigation that go beyond word-based and conceptual forms of expression to incorporate a broader array of religious phenomena, address issues of multiplicity in the spirit realm, and attend to the cosmos as a single spiritual system. All of this requires a broader and deeper engagement with an array of expressive forms and practices, as well as a more robust interaction with African sources, theologies, and methods to illuminate Black American religious experience and enrich Christian theology more fully.

Acknowledgments

SCRIPTURE ADMONISHES US TO "give honor to whom honor is due" (Rom 13:7). Therefore, I first give honor to God, who is the head of my life, the lifter of my head, and the very fount of all wisdom. It is his grace that has made this journey possible. It is simply not possible to name all those who have contributed in ways small and great to my journey and to this project, so I must of necessity limit the list to a very few, while my appreciation of many hundreds of others is engraved forever on the tablets of my heart.

This book is the product of research conducted in the course of my doctoral studies, and so I acknowledge my wonderful and dedicated PhD supervisors, Professor Gillian Mary Bediako and Dr. Ingrid Reneau Walls. Your thoughtful commentary, insights, and encouragements have blessed me throughout this project. To the teaching faculty of the Akrofi-Christaller Institute (ACI) who exemplify the best of Christian scholarship. To my colleague scholars at ACI who have lightened the journey by their comradeship. To my pastors, the Revs. Alaric Omaboe and George Amoako-Nimako, and members of Praise Community Church. To the pastors and congregations of the All Saints Holiness Church and St Martins Spiritual Church. To my many teachers, past and present, and especially Mrs. Gloria McKissack, who was among the first to nurture my love of history and scholarship. To my dear friend Ms. Jeannie Musick, who first introduced me to the scholarship of Kwame Bediako, and with whom I have shared many tears and much laughter through the years. To my father, Fred Sr., and my siblings, Fred, Angela, and David, whose stories are interwoven with my own, and who have always believed in me. To my natural children—Joshua David, Taylor Kweku, Reese Akosua (of blessed memory),

ACKNOWLEDGMENTS

and Emmanuel Nhyira, and my adopted ones—Gideon and Jemima. To my dear wife and friend, Dr. Pauline Settles—words are too few to thank you for all the love, care, encouragement, support, and prayers you have invested in me throughout this process. And finally, to my ancestors, my grandmothers Iona and Flora, and countless others known only to God, and especially my beloved mother Irma Settles of blessed memory; your presences have been a sustaining comfort to me all my life. To God alone be the glory.

Abbreviations

AIC	African independent/indigenous church
AME	African Methodist Episcopal Church
AME Zion	African Methodist Episcopal Zion Church
AmJT	*American Journal of Theology*
ANF	*Ante-Nicene Fathers*
ASHC	All Saints Holiness Church
BECNT	Baker Exegetical Commentary on the New Testament
CBQ	*Catholic Biblical Quarterly*
DSCS	Divine Spiritualist Churches of the Southwest
HTR	*Harvard Theological Review*
JACT	*Journal of African Christian Thought*
JBL	*Journal of Biblical Literature*
JETS	*Journal of the Evangelical Theological Society*
JSSR	*Journal for the Scientific Study of Religion*
JTS	*Journal of Theological Studies*
MSCC	Metropolitan Spiritual Churches of Christ
MSJ	*The Master's Seminary Journal*
NIDNTT	*New International Dictionary of New Testament Theology*. Edited by Colin Brown. 4 vols. Grand Rapids: Zondervan, 1975–78

ABBREVIATIONS

NIGTC	New International Greek Testament Commentary
NPNF2	*Nicene and Post-Nicene Fathers*, series 2
PGM	Betz, Hans Dieter. *The Greek Magical Papyri in Translation, Including the Demotic Spells.* 2nd ed. Chicago: University of Chicago Press, 1996.
SMSC	St Martins Spiritualist Church

1

Introduction

The "Problem" of the Primal and Race in Euro-Western Christian Civilization

KWAME BEDIAKO (1945–2008) DESCRIBES the early church theologian Tatian (120–80) as one whose fundamental outlook demonstrates "the radicality of a Christian self-identity which stubbornly refuses to give credence to the cultural and intellectual superiority which Greeks and Romans claimed for themselves."[1] Tatian's deep apprehension of Christian identity captures something of my own perspective as a descendent of enslaved Africans reared within Black American Christianity, and more specifically within the holiness Pentecostal/spiritual traditions of the Christian faith. Tatian sought a vindication of his own "barbarian" heritage, over against the pretensions of Greco-Roman philosophy, which considered itself superior in every way to the primal religious heritage of the "barbarian" Old Testament that Tatian had embraced upon his conversion to Christ.[2] Black American Christianity presents a similar kind of vindication; it is the reassertion of the essentially primal nature of Christian faith against the

1. K. Bediako, *Theology and Identity*, 67.

2. Tatian begins his major extant work, the "Oration Addressed to the Greeks," by deriding Greek claims to superiority over the barbarians, by pointing out their indebtedness to the barbarians for all they claimed for themselves: "Be not, O Greeks, so very hostilely disposed towards the Barbarians, nor look with ill will on their opinions. For which of your institutions has not been derived from the Barbarians?" ("Address to the Greeks," locs. 27999–8000.

pretensions of Christianity as "civilized" Western religion and the presumption of the normative and norming status of Euro-Western[3] religious expression. The traditions of Black American Christianity, particularly as expressed in the holiness Pentecostal/spiritual church in which I was reared are not a syncretized amalgam of Christianity and African traditional religion, nor do they represent a wholesale rejection of all of the Western Christian tradition. They are instead a demonstrative *reassertion* of the primal imagination, which may be shown, in fact, to be embedded within Christianity itself as it is expressed in the New Testament.

The Problem: Christianity as a Cultural Product of the West

Christianity, despite being a world faith, is frequently thought of as the religion of the West. This characterization of Christianity is puzzling to many, though unsurprising especially among Black Americans who have suffered at the hands of "Christian" America. As a Black American Christian born and brought up in the Black Pentecostal tradition, I am well aware of the disdain with which Pentecostal/spiritual church expressions of Black American Christianity are held, the characterization of Christianity as the "white Man's religion," and the challenges to mission this perception creates. What is more surprising, however, is how this understanding has persisted in academia even in the face of the "shift" in the centers of Christianity from the West to non-Western world,[4] the evidence of which is beyond serious dispute. Within Western culture generally, and the Euro-Western theological academy in particular, Christian faith has often been understood not only as a Western, but also as a "civilized" faith, a term loaded with historical, sociocultural and theological significance. Though few would admit it openly, or put it quite so bluntly, Euro-Western religious expression and theologies are presumed to be both normative and norming for Christianity as a whole, while other expressions and theologies are considered the domain of anthropologists, religious studies specialists, missiologists, or so-called contextual theologians.

The ambivalence with which African Christianity (and by extension Black American Christianity) is viewed by the theological academy,

---

3. *Euro-Western* is used here and throughout the text in reference to the entire constellation of thought and practice emerging from European culture and history, including that of North America.

4. Walls, *Missionary Movement*, 9.

particularly in evangelical scholarship, provides a compelling example of this tendency. It is still considered a specialist genre, with little to contribute to the understanding of the structure or substance of Christianity itself, and regarded as more suited to missiology or religious studies than to theology proper. That Black American Christianity has always manifested a primal imagination foreign to Euro-Western assumptions about the Christian faith and continues to do so makes this ambivalence more than coincidental. The dominant narrative of Christian history and theology continues to reflect the bias that Christianity is "civilized" and European, and that other forms are therefore deviant or sub-Christian.

The Challenge of Race

The ambivalence with which the African/Black American Christianity has been interpreted in the Euro-Western academy is compounded further by the racialist lens through which Black peoples and Black religion have been interpreted in Euro-Western history. Early distinctions between the "civilized" Greeks and the "barbarous" other became exaggerated over time when Europeans encountered others who displayed greater phenotypical differences—hair and skin color in particular—that marked them out as distinct. Stereotypes based on color, and negative associations of Blacks within European culture extend to the early encounters of Greco-Roman society with African and other dark-skinned peoples, and took on greater cultural, and eventually theological significance within Christian Europe. Speculation about such differences eventuated in essentialist theories about race itself. Race, and race-based interpretation of people, became a major, if not dominant, metric for evaluating differences between people groups, and for bolstering claims to Euro-Western civilizational superiority based on racial essentialism. These often gave rise to theological justifications for the enslavement and oppression of Black people, and the denigration of their culture(s) as inherently degraded. Though less prominent than once was the case, racialist ideology remains thoroughly, if subtly, embedded in Euro-Western interpretation of Black peoples and religion down to the present day.

The Limitations of Black Theology in Interpreting Black American Christianity

Given this history, Black American Christianity has primarily been interpreted through the lens of the slavery and oppression experienced by Black peoples. Black theology, which emerged in the context of the social tumult of the 1960s, relies on this formulation. However, this theology is inescapably "bound by white racism and the culture of survival" and thus remains "not only a crisis theology but also a theology in a crisis of legitimation."[5] By placing the challenges of race and race-based oppression as central to the religious experience of Black people, it denies Black Christians' full identity as autonomous theologizing agents in their own right and on their own terms, but instead defines them entirely in relation to oppression and in opposition to the oppressor, rather than in relation to God as their Creator and Redeemer. They thus remain inextricably bound to the oppressor's ontological and epistemological categories and can have no self, nor any knowledge of self, outside those categories. Such a theology cannot transcend itself nor can it "point to any transcendent meaning beyond itself without also fragmenting."[6] It thus becomes easily and inevitably separated from the mainstream of theological discourse, while the insights derived from the primal imagination within Black American Christianity remain inadequately explored.

The Primal Nature of the New Testament

The primal nature of Old Testament religion long presented a problem for Enlightenment influenced scholars, as indeed it did for the Hellenist Christian apologists who found it initially difficult to reconcile with Greek philosophy.[7] However, the New Testament has generally not received the

---

5. V. Anderson, *Beyond Ontological Blackness*, 87.

6. V. Anderson, *Beyond Ontological Blackness*, 92. One possible way of transcending the theological dilemma posed by Black theology is Kwame Bediako's proposal of interpreting the historic and present humiliation of Black/African peoples in terms of a theodicy that does not deny historic injustices, but sees in them the opportunity for "Christians of Africa and of the diaspora . . . to fulfil their discipleship" by "allow[ing] the cross of Christ to shape their theological consciousness and interpret their historical experience" and therefore being in "position to offer a new definition of Christian hope for the world" ("Toward a New Theodicy," 51).

7. K. Bediako describes this as "coming to terms with those elements of the Christian Gospel, teaching and history which were deemed distasteful and unacceptable to

same level of scrutiny as a primal religious text. Instead, the New Testament is often read as if it is entirely devoid of primal religious features. Thomas Jefferson's infamous redaction of the text is perhaps the most extreme example of this desire to excise the embarrassingly primal elements from the New Testament.[8] Quite apart from the supernatural elements present in the New Testament, such as miraculous healings, supernatural gifts of the spirit, demon possession and the like, the underlying primal worldview(s) and overarching cosmological assumptions of the authors and audience of the original texts are infrequently interrogated and often obscured. Or they are pressed into service as background cultural information that must be understood only insofar as it helps us discover the real meaning of the text in our time. These trends are especially apparent in Western evangelical Protestantism.

All that I have just described demonstrates the key problem of the presentation of Christianity as "civilized" religion. It is the adoption and absorption of Greek philosophical concepts into Christian theology, coupled with the cult of reason that emerged during the Age of Enlightenment, which made possible this characterization, but such a classification may not be claimed as intrinsic to Christianity itself, if one considers the origins and early history of the faith on their own terms. Indeed, it was the association of Christianity with European civilization that allowed the enslavement and maltreatment of Africans and especially the denigration of Black religion, whether Christian or non-Christian, to appear theologically justifiable. Yet these same slaves and their descendants upon conversion to Christianity have, through their spirituality, brought to light the fallacy of this assumption. Both the New Testament and Black American Christianity, especially in its Pentecostal manifestations, demonstrate and confirm the deeply primal nature of Christianity—the faith with the closest affinity to the multitude of primal religions in the world. It is one in which what Kwame Bediako terms "the primal imagination" is an inherent feature.

Græco-Roman sensibilities and outlook . . . with the religious history of ancient Israel and the authoritative record of that history, the Scriptures of the Old Testament" (*Theology and Identity*, 32–33).

8. Thomas Jefferson, the third president of the United States, produced a redacted version of Scripture called *The Life and Morals of Jesus of Nazareth* (c. 1819), which eliminated all references to supernatural occurrences. This version can be found online.

The "Primal Imagination" as an Interpretative Key

Kwame Bediako introduces the concept of the primal imagination in his book *Christianity in Africa: The Renewal of a Non-Western Religion*.[9] The *primal imagination*, as Bediako presents it, is the particular "abiding presence of the primal world-view"[10] found within primal religions, but which "transcend(s) primal religions as distinctive religious systems."[11] One may think of prophet William Wadé Harris (1860–1929) of West Africa and Cardinal Milingo (b. 1930) of Zambia, each of whom embraced a "spiritual universe" that was simultaneously "simple and complex" and also a totality,[12] as exemplars of this primal imagination who also functioned within the bounds of a clearly defined Christian theological commitment. The primal imagination is not just the worldview of traditional religious practitioners, but is expressed within the so-called higher religions as well. As Andrew Walls says, "All other believers, and for that matter non-believers, are primalists underneath."[13]

Turner's Six-Feature Analysis of Primal Religion

Bediako's concept of the primal imagination relies on Harold Turner's earlier phenomenological analysis of the world's primal religious found in his article "The Primal Religions of the World and Their Study." Turner identified six features that characterize the worldview of primal religions. Though well known in some scholarly circles, they are listed below for those for whom it may be a new concept and because of their importance in understanding the primal imagination.

First is kinship with nature. By this Turner referred to a "profound sense in many primal societies that man is akin to nature, a child of Mother Earth and brother to the plants and animals which have their own spiritual existence and place in the universe." Engagement with the natural world is therefore conceived in relational terms; "object[s] in the natural environment may enter into a totemic spiritual relationship with men or become tutelary and guardian spirits," while the environment is used, "realistically

---

9. K. Bediako, *Christianity in Africa*, 92.
10. K. Bediako, *Christianity in Africa*, 93.
11. K. Bediako, *Christianity in Africa*, 93.
12. K. Bediako, *Christianity in Africa*, 92.
13. Walls, *Missionary Movement*, 121.

and unsentimentally but with profound respect and reverence and without exploitation." Turner described this as a "profoundly religious attitude to man's natural setting in the world."[14]

The second feature he described is the "deep sense that man is finite, weak, and impure or sinful and stands in need of a power not his own." This is not, as might be assumed by those from technologically sophisticated societies, merely a result of a "lack of technological, economic and political power" but is "an authentic religious sensibility coupled with a realistic assessment of man's condition."[15] The human being stands as a finite creature in as vulnerable a condition as any other creature, ultimately unable to secure his own well-being without external help.

The third feature follows from the second, for the awareness of human finitude brings with it a "conviction that man is not alone in the universe," that is, a belief in the nonphysical, invisible world of "powers or beings more powerful and ultimate than himself."[16] Within this understanding, the universe itself is personalized and "man therefore lives with an awareness of transcendent powers"[17] who are ambivalent and who may be related to.

The benevolent spirit world believed in by primal people is such that humans can enter into relationship with it and "share in its powers and blessings and receive protection from evil forces." This is the fourth feature of Turner's schema. Human frailty coupled with the reality of the spirit world leads inevitably to "a longing for the true life of man . . . that can come only from the gods."[18] It is ultimately from this spirit world and its powers that salvation is sought.

This fourth feature leads to the fifth, which is that death in primal societies "does not represent the end of human existence, but rather a change in its status."[19] As spiritual beings, the participation of humans with the spiritual realm creates the expectation of a continuation of life beyond death. A corollary of this belief in many, though not all, primal societies is the idea that "the ancestors, 'the living dead,' remain united in affection and

---

14. H. Turner, "Primal Religions," 30.
15. H. Turner, "Primal Religions," 31.
16. H. Turner, "Primal Religions," 31.
17. K. Bediako, *Christianity in Africa*, 94.
18. H. Turner, "Primal Religions," 31.
19. Zahan, "African Spirituality," 10.

in mutual obligations with the 'living living.'"[20] Thus those who have died and passed into the realm of spirit beings, continue as present and active agents in the natural realm as well. This feature is particularly prominent within the African primal.

The sixth and final feature is considered by Bediako to be the capstone to the whole primal religious system of belief,[21] for it recognizes that "men live in a sacramental universe where there is no sharp dichotomy between the physical and the spiritual,"[22] and it is within this sacramental universe that all the other features exist as a coherent system. John Taylor expresses this as the conviction that "Nature, Man and the Unseen are inseparably involved in one another in a total community"[23] as an integrated sacred whole. Spirituality and thus religion are not confined to specifically religious events but, the natural world is itself a sacrament and everyday actions are full of divine potentialities.

The six features identified by Turner lead Bediako to discern a special relationship between primal religions and the Christian faith and to suggest that such affinities are not only phenomenological, but have significant theological implications. Bediako asks "how the primal imagination might bring its own peculiar gifts to the shaping of Christian affirmation."[24] Bediako's question is rhetorical, suggesting an affirmative response. This study pursues that affinity and inquires how such gifts may be observed through careful assessment of the witness of the New Testament and Black American Christianity.

Terminology

I want to say something about the terms I employ in this study as it has implications not just for my approach, but also for how this work may be interpreted. First, some may wonder at the choice to use the descriptive category *Black American* instead of African American or African diaspora, especially considering trends in contemporary scholarship. These terms are extremely helpful in conveying the commonalities of religious experience and expression, as well as the historical and cultural links that exist between

20. H. Turner, "Primal Religions," 32.
21. K. Bediako, *Christianity in Africa*, 96.
22. H. Turner, "Primal Religions," 32.
23. John V. Taylor, *Primal Vision*, 64.
24. K. Bediako, *Christianity in Africa*, 96.

INTRODUCTION

Africans on the continent and those in the United States and elsewhere. Though I recognize this, the use of Black American (or simply Black) is intentional and is done for several reasons. The first arises simply from the fact that the term "African American" is not the term by which most Black people in America identify themselves in common speech. It is largely a creation of cultural elites, and carries with it an air of artificiality and has limited currency outside of professional and academic circles. My use of the term "Black" can then be taken as a nod to the primacy of vernacular usage. Second, the term "Black American" keeps before us the painful and uniquely American history of race-based slavery and state-sanctioned White supremacy, a system in part fed by deeply rooted European ideas and negative associations with the term "Black." Finally, it helps distinguish recent first- and second-generation African immigrants to the United States from those descendants of African slaves whose roots in America go back several generations.

Second, the designation *holiness Pentecostal/spiritual church* may seem to confuse and conflate two distinctive strands of Black American religion. There are important differences between the two groups, yet both Pentecostal and spiritual groups share a number of similarities not the least of which is a strong orientation towards the spiritual realm. Most distinctions between the two are more a matter of degree rather than of kind, so I consider them together as part of the same pneumatic sacramentalist strand of Black American religion.

Western scholarship usually separates religious studies from Christian theology; they are considered two different fields of academic inquiry. I am of the view that these narrow and restrictive categorizations cannot do justice to the integrated realties of Black American cultural and religious life, and so I have chosen to eschew them. This work straddles these divides and integrates the insights of at least three areas of scholarship without falling wholly into any of them: Black religion (with particular attention to the Black Pentecostal/spiritual church tradition), New Testament studies, and primal religion (which is a variant of religious studies).

In the Black church testimonial tradition "giving honor to whom honor is due" is an important part of recognizing that all of who I am and what I do is deeply connected to others. I feel it important, then to mention some scholars whose work is vital, and whom I see as complementary to my own. Chief among these is Kwame Bediako's *Christianity in Africa*, which provides the overall structural framework of Christianity articulated in non-Western terms and from a non-Western perspective.[25] Among other things, Bediako identifies the need for Christianity to come to terms with the legacy of colonialism and its associated racism and European ethnocentrism that is so clearly connected with mission history.[26] The "savage heathens" of Africa, and their enslaved brethren in America, constituted a problem for Christian missionaries from Europe steeped in an environment that had serious doubts about the intellectual capacity of African peoples; one in which "it [was] not hard to understand how educated persons would entertain serious doubts about the possibility of 'savage and barbarous' people ever becoming Christians."[27]

The issues Bediako raises in relation to the Christianity in Africa—particularly the legacy of European racism in mission history—are relevant to the current project for many of the same issues emerging from African Christianity are extant in Black American Christianity as well and have led to important advances in theology.[28] In effect, Black American Christianity should be considered a variant of the non-Western Christianity Bediako discusses, yet one that has developed and been sustained *within* the context of Western society. It is therefore best understood as an *extension* of African Christianity rather than one delimited and defined exclusively by the particularities of the unique historical experience of chattel slavery that attended its birth.

Willie Jennings's *The Christian Imagination: Theology and the Origins of Race* is another important work. Jennings shows us that the "diseased social imagination"[29] of Western Christianity inhibits the full flourishing of Christian discipleship in the social sphere, particularly in relation to the range of connections between different persons, societies, and the land. This diseased social imaginary has long hampered a full appreciation and interpretation of Black American Christianity. I share Bediako and Jennings's aim of positing a new vision for theology that moves beyond the imperial imagination that has been heretofore ingrained in the Euro-Western theological academy, and that has imprisoned that theology in a disordered social imaginary. Before moving on, I would like also to mention Judylyn

---

25. Similar themes are sounded in Sanneh, *Whose Religion Is Christianity?*
26. In which history I include the Christianization of African slaves in America.
27. K. Bediako, *Christianity in Africa*, 195.
28. Bediako references the Black theology of James Cone as an example of this (*Christianity in Africa*, 145).
29. Jennings, *Christian Imagination*, loc. 185.

Ryan's *Spirituality as Ideology in Black Women's Film and Literature*. Ryan rejects the normative assumptions of the "paradigm of resistance" that "designates Slavery, racism, colonialism, and other hegemonic practices as determining events and the inevitable starting point of origin for African diaspora cultures and for all related arts."[30] She instead offers a positive vision of Black spirituality—the paradigm of growth—that restores to Black people their full agency as actors, and not only as re-actors. Within this vision, she recognizes the ways in which Black literature frequently affirms the primal sense that "every human activity is an expression of spiritual agency."[31] Her forthright assertion of the positive value of Black spirituality quite separate from the dominant narrative of resistance to oppression is one I share. Ryan's work affirms the decentering of the Euro-Western interpretative framework in elucidating and interpreting Black American religion.

Euro-Western Responses to Primal Religion

The perceived antithesis between the primal and the Christian, between revealed and natural religion, is a by-product of Christian response to the Enlightenment rather than something intrinsic to Christianity. It is from the primal religious environment in which the first centuries of Christianity were lived that "vital elements of the religious experience . . . the sense of total devotion, of being cut to the heart, *katanyxis*, of deep symbolism . . . of participation of the whole person in worship"[32] were taken up into Christian tradition. The earliest Christian theology emerged from the efforts of Greek Christians to relate the gospel to the primal religious concerns of the Greco-Roman world.[33] However, the legacy of the European Enlightenment and Europe's encounter with the wider world has so dramatically shaped Euro-Western biblical scholarship as well as Christian scholarly interpretation of primal religion and spirituality for the past two centuries that that dynamic interaction has been obscured and even denied.

---

30. Ryan, *Spirituality as Ideology*, 16.

31. Ryan, *Spirituality as Ideology*, 29.

32. Yannoulatos, "Growing into an Awareness," 75–76. *Katanyxis* refers to compunction or painful grief for sin.

33. Walls, "Converts or Proselytes," 6.

Implications for Biblical Studies

One important response to the European encounter with religious and cultural diversity was the rise of the comparative study of religion, which was eventually to revolutionize Christian and European self-understanding. The work of Jesuit priest Joseph-François Lafitau (1681–1746) in particular reinforced belief in a progressive scheme of development from lower to higher forms. This had significant implications for the interpretation of the Scriptures generally, and the Old Testament in particular, especially given the prominence of the primal imagination. The empiricist approach advanced during the Enlightenment engendered an anti-supernaturalist attitude towards the Bible and Christianity, evidenced by the development of the historical-critical hermeneutical method. This lack of recognition and consequent irresolution of the relationship between primal religion and Christian faith continues to persist in biblical scholarship. There remains a "profound unease that many Western Christians feel with respect to the religious and cultural world of the Old Testament"[34] and, it may be credibly added, a diminishment and dismissal of the primal features of the New.

Implications for Christian Theology and Worldview

The second key area of impact of the Enlightenment on Christian scholarship lies in Christian cosmology. Shorn of its supernatural and spiritual sense, theology began to be construed as a scientific system of ideas, a way to "police the frontier"[35] between the empirical and spiritual realms, but one that did not challenge the fundamental demarcation between the spheres assumed by the Enlightenment. Anti-Catholic polemics and Enlightenment rationalism were joined to exclude from Protestant Christianity all but the barest possibility of supernatural activity (which was safely locked in the pages of the Bible) and to render any claims of such present activity immediately suspect.

---

34. G. Bediako, "Old Testament Religion," 3. Andrew Walls makes a similar point when he comments, "We need a confident approach to the Old Testament, which Western Christianity finds strange and embarrassing. The Old Testament reflects a primal worldview" (G. Bediako, "Editorial," 3).

35. Walls, "Christian Scholarship," 49.

INTRODUCTION

Disenchanting the World: The Rise of Religious Studies

Perhaps the most enduring legacy of post-Enlightenment Christianity's encounter with non-Christian religion is the very idea of the scientific categorization of religion that emerged from it. Over the course of the nineteenth century, the religious universe inhabited by Lafitau and his contemporaries was reconfigured by an Enlightenment inflected empiricism that confined the supernatural to the heavens and posited natural causes for all phenomena on earth. While the idea of primitive society was being invented as a "distorting mirror" of emerging anthropologists' own societies,[36] the Euro-Western universe was disenchanted, and magic and superstition separated from religion.

The upshot of all this is that religious phenomena, particularly those of a primal nature, were no longer taken to be indicative of reality, except insofar as religious behaviors primarily or exclusively reflect human responses to essentially nonreligious factors. This was especially the case in the American liberal theological academy which largely accommodated itself to the Enlightenment in contradistinction to Europe where the legacy of the Enlightenment led to "the rejection of, or indifference to, the Christianity to which the Enlightenment was largely a dialectical response."[37]

The historical-critical method of biblical studies, the cessationist assumptions of Euro-Western Protestant scholarship, and the naturalistic perspective on religious phenomena all combine to obscure the relationship of the gospel to the primal in the New Testament. It is, as it were, hidden behind the accretions of a post-Enlightenment Euro-Western scholarship that is, on the whole, dubious about the Scriptures, suspicious of claims of the supernatural, and agnostic about the nature of the cosmos. It is difficult, therefore, for Euro-Western scholars, including Christian scholars,

---

36. "Anthropologists took ... primitive society as their special subject, but in practice primitive society proved to be their own society (as they understood it) seen in a distorting mirror. For them modern society was defined above all by the territorial state, the monogamous family and private property. Primitive society therefore must have been nomadic, ordered by blood ties, sexually promiscuous and communist. There had also been a progression in mentality. Primitive man was illogical and given to magic. In time he had developed more sophisticated religious ideas. Modern man, however, had invented science" (Kuper, *Invention of Primitive Society*, 5).

37. Hollinger, "Accommodation of Protestant Christianity," 2. It is from this segment of the academy that much of the scholarship on Black American religion has been produced, and thus frequently reflects a strictly instrumental view of religion, but this is anticipation.

to take primal societies simply on their own terms, and for the expression of religious phenomena arising from these societies to be taken seriously as expressing something fundamental about the nature of reality and of Christian faith. These developments have served to create difficulties in the academic study of the New Testament, and of Black religion—difficulties that must be overcome if the primal features of the Christian faith as seen in the New Testament and manifest within Black American Christianity are to be identified and taken into consideration in the development of a robust Christian theology.

Sources

My sources are divided into two main categories. The first is the New Testament text, particularly those passages in which the primal underpinnings of the text are especially significant. My focus is not on thorough exegesis of selected passages, but rather on discerning how the primal imagination underlies and reflects in them. Thus, significant attention is given to exploring the cultural, religious, and social contexts rather than to textual analysis.

The second source is the tradition itself, and in this regard, this study reflects a recovery or perhaps preservation of memory. When Hans Baer did research in the late 1970s, the spiritual church movement was already marked by instability and significant decline. Many spiritual churches no longer exist or have changed so much that they no longer exhibit some of the distinctive features Baer identified. The study is thus partly historical and partly phenomenological. For my purposes, the focus is chiefly on specific aspects of the tradition, for example, the use of Scripture, ritual and liturgical practices (e.g., laying on of hands, testimony), and the use of symbols or objects. Because my goal is the identification of primal manifestations in aspects of these kinds of churches, I have chosen to use a case study of two churches which are exemplary of the broader tradition. Documentary records from these churches, including photographs, video and audio recordings of sermons and services have been assessed with an eye towards identifying those primal elements which continue to inform their religious practice and worldview. I have, in addition, conducted an analysis of sermons to enable me to identify primal elements, as well as favored scriptural texts. The documentary analysis is supplemented with limited field research consisting of interviews with the pastors and/or other leaders in the churches and participant observation in both congregations.

INTRODUCTION

The final source, and in many respects the most important one from which this study is drawn is my own multiform, decades-long experience in the Black American church, and specifically as one reared within the very tradition(s) being explored. In other words, the knowledge of the primal imagination within these traditions arises in the context of my own relationships—with the churches, the people, the rituals and practices, and with the ideas and concepts being illumined in the course of the study. This is consonant with the indigenous/primal methodology that asserts knowledge itself as a relational entity, and not an arm's-length investigation as if one were peering through a microscope.[38] It accords too with the Pauline sense that human knowledge, always partial—as "through a glass, darkly"—is apprehended within the context of relationship, wherein one knows as he is known (1 Cor 13:12 KJV). There is, therefore, an unavoidable autobiographical element embedded in the research which reflects the Black American cultural context. In this respect I stand within the autobiographical tradition of Black literature which, according to Toni Morrison, become classic within the Black literary form because it enables the writer to present him or herself as representative of the entire community out of which he or she emerges.[39] What is true in its literature is true also within the Black church where the personal testimony has long been a staple of Black Pentecostal piety. The testimony has been described as "the liminal core of Afro-Pentecostal worship."[40] My own journey is therefore part of the witness borne by spiritual and Pentecostal people to the work of God. To exclude it because it is personal would ultimately render the work less authentic and complete than it would be otherwise.

The positioning of Euro-Western culture as the global "centre of legitimate knowledge, the arbiter of what counts as knowledge, and the source of 'civilized' knowledge"[41] is built upon the suppression of the primal imagination explored in this study. Indeed, Western scholarship itself may be considered a locus of imperialism that denies the validity or even possibility of primal sources of knowledge. It is thus unsurprising that scholars in the fields of both New Testament studies and Black religion have generally overlooked, or suppressed their primal features, subsuming them beneath other concerns and interpretative frameworks or in the

---

38. Wilson, "Indigenous Research Methodology," 177.
39. Morrison, "Rootedness," 57.
40. Scandrett-Leatherman, "Can't Nobody Do Me," 283.
41. L. Smith, *Decolonizing Methodologies*, 66.

case of Black church studies, co-opting them for particular sociopolitical agendas. However, the primal needs no sponsor to speak for it, nor should it be conscripted towards another's agenda, but must be permitted to speak for itself. Thus I identify manifestations of the primal imagination when they occur and draw out implications for the meaning and understanding of Christian faith rather than assuming such manifestations must occur in a particular way or assume a particular form.

More specifically, I choose to privilege indigenous approaches to knowledge construction like those that have been identified by such scholars as Linda Tuhiwai Smith and Margaret Kovach and African Christian theologians like Benhardt Quarshie and Kwame Bediako.[42] The methodologies employed by these scholars are premised upon a primal recognition of the relationality of knowledge, that is that knowledge cannot be entirely separated from its source and is transmitted within the context of relationships. In relation to the New Testament, this means adopting a relational approach to the biblical text that considers both content and source, that rejects as artificial the narrative and didactic divide, and that considers the worldview of the author not only as a significant factor in understanding the text, but also an intrinsic part of the divine communication.

As applied to the study of Black religion, I reject the dualistic, dichotomizing approach derived from the Euro-Western academy that has long prevailed in Black religious scholarship and that is premised upon the separation of form and structure from content. Such dualism is antithetical to Black American religious culture that has always perceived an intrinsic link between form and content, and thus serves to obscure the primal African content of Black American religion.[43] Consequently, this study relies on a dialectical approach, that seeks to hold together form and meaning, while privileging the experiential and intuitive sources of knowledge derived from the dynamic context of the Black spiritual/Pentecostal church tradition, the tradition in which I was reared, and which lays great emphasis on attentiveness to the Holy Spirit for insight and guidance in both spiritual and practical concerns.

---

42. Kovach, *Indigenous Methodologies;* Quarshie, "Significance of Biblical Studies"; K. Bediako, "Gospel and Culture."

43. Matthews, *Honoring the Ancestors*, 9–10.

INTRODUCTION

Why It Matters

The shift of Christian centers from the West to the non-Western world is now beyond serious dispute. Christianity, to the extent that it ever was, can certainly no longer be considered to be the religion of White Europeans and North Americans, and there is definitely "no room any more for a Western possessiveness of Christian faith . . . of a sense of superiority over against other peoples."[44] However, the non-Western Christianity that has emerged and still is emerging is not merely a "global Christianity" that merely replicates "Christian forms and patterns developed in Europe"[45] and is exported to the rest of the world, but instead reflects a primal apprehension of reality that is changing and enhancing our understanding of Christianity itself. Though most clearly seen in African Christianity, Black American Christianity likewise reflects this primal orientation, especially within the Black holiness Pentecostal/spiritual church tradition. Thus, as previously mentioned, Black American Christianity is a non-Western faith that emerged and developed *within* Western society. Nevertheless, "the ongoing dehumanization, deculturalization, and dehistoricization of the African world . . . effecting its invisibility in the African-American community, particularly the African-American Christian community," has led to the perception that "African-American religious experience amounts at best to an ambiguously meaningful by-product of a unique and permanent American socio-cultural predicament engineered by the Eurocentric imagination."[46]

The study of Black American Christianity has been constrained almost wholly within the boundaries of *Western* Christianity, leading to an interpretation of any primal manifestations of the faith within the Black religious experience as syncretic accretions, or African retentions without significant epistemic or theological content. It is either perceived as not authentically Christian and thus lacking in theological significance, or else it has been annexed as a subplot to the story of Black resistance to White supremacist claims. Neither of these approaches critically examines the contribution to Christian understanding arising from Black American Christianity as a *non-Western* expression of that faith, manifesting the primal imagination in its beliefs and practices.

44. G. Bediako, "Changing Centre of Gravity," 20.
45. Sanneh, *Whose Religion Is Christianity*, 22.
46. Harvey, "Life Is War," 32.

Within biblical studies the Old Testament has received much more sustained attention as the arena in which the primal imagination is manifest, while the primal elements of the New Testament have either been downplayed or viewed as oppositional to Christian faith. This has contributed to the still pervasive notion that New Testament Christianity represents an evolutionary advance of so-called civilized and ethical religion over the primitive, earthy and materialistic religion of the Old Testament, an idea inextricably tied to a history of Western ethno-cultural elitism. Such a perspective unavoidably privileges "Western civilization" as the culture best suited for the expression of Christian faith, while all others are by definition inferior and/or deficient. I want to remedy that deficit by highlighting ways in which the primal imagination contributed to the theological vision of the New Testament and is intrinsic to Christianity.

This book identifies and offers a new interpretation of existing materials—manifestations of the primal imagination in the New Testament and in Black American Christianity—so that what emerges helps elucidate more clearly and completely the essentially primal nature of Christian faith, further decentering Western religious and theological hegemony, and deepening our appreciation for the primal cultural context of the New Testament.

Implications for Christian Mission and Scholarship

The primal expression of Black American Christianity as seen in the Black holiness Pentecostal/spiritual tradition is a response to the reconciling work of God in the lives of these believers, but it is a response that has mostly been treated as a deviant, syncretic or intellectually unserious form of Christian faith. I emerged from this tradition, and so I am well acquainted with the ambiguity, disdain, and embarrassment with which such churches were and are regarded, by those from more "respectable" traditions and even by some from within the tradition itself. As long as they, and others like them, are perceived in this way, the quasi-elitist assumption of Christian faith as coterminous with Euro-Western civilization remains undisturbed and the reconciling mission of God compromised. A scholarly reflection and interpretation of these traditions enriches Christian scholarship and advances the mission of the church.

A casual survey of the contemporary scene of Black American religious life in the context of the United States, reveals that there are many who have rejected Christianity as a religious imposition alien to Black people and indeed inimical to their full flourishing. This view is bolstered by the checkered history of Christian mission, the complicity of Christians in the transatlantic slave trade and slavery, and Christian theological support for Eurocentric White supremacy. Even in James Cone's time, and in fact, one of his driving concerns, "the black intellectual community . . . [was] becoming increasingly suspicious of Christianity because the oppressor has used it as a means of stifling the oppressed concern for present inequities."[47] This is, perhaps, even more true today, and not only among the Black intelligentsia, but more widely as well. Consequently, it is all the more important from a missiological perspective to disentangle Christian faith from its association with Euro-Western civilization, and to demonstrate the ways in which aspects of Black American Christianity present an authentic and legitimate expression of the primal imagination apart from any racialist concerns.

The first part of this book provides the historical, cultural, and intellectual background to the "problem" of the primal in general, and the primal expressed among Black people in particular. Chapter 2 traces the development of the concept of "Christian" European civilization from its roots in Greco-Roman society. Chapter 3 surveys the Euro-Western Christian interpretation of Black peoples and religion with special attention to the United States context while chapter 4 further explores some methodological issues and the background of Black Pentecostalism.

The book then focuses on the manifestation of the primal imagination within the churches and in the New Testament. Chapter 5 discusses manifestations of the primal imagination within the New Testament including references to how the passages in the New Testament align with the expression of the primal imagination in the use and interpretation of Scripture, and in the religious practice of the congregations. Chapter 6 provides a historical overview of the development of Black American Christianity with special emphasis on the emergence of holiness Pentecostal/spiritual churches and their distinctive features. Chapters 7 and 8 examine the All Saints Holiness of Nashville, Tennessee, and the St Martins Spiritualist Church of St. Louis, Missouri,[48] as case studies of the primal within the context of specific congregations from the Pentecostal and spiritual traditions respectively. Finally, chapter 9 considers theological insights emerging from the study as well as providing a summary and conclusion.

47. Cone, *Black Theology*, 33.
48. These are pseudonyms.

The "Problem" of the Primal and Race in Euro-Western Christian Civilization

My aim is to demonstrate the manifestation of the primal imagination within aspects of Black American Christianity and in the New Testament. This is not in itself a problematic assertion for Christian self-understanding, particularly in light of the evident shift in the centers of Christianity to those people among whom the primal imagination continues to hold sway.[49] It now seems self-evident that "primal religions have had a closer relationship to Christian faith than any other religion" and that "primal religions and Christian faith have a unique phenomenological affinity";[50] assertions to the contrary may thus appear out of place. The simplest approach to this would be to highlight how the primal is manifest in the church traditions under consideration, in their African antecedents, and in the New Testament. However, this would avoid the ugly reality that the rejection and suppression of the primal, and the denigration of those who embrace the primal imagination, especially Black peoples, is embedded in the very structure of Euro-Western Christianity and civilization. It is important therefore to show how Eurocentric White supremacy emerged as the operative system of Euro-Western thought generally, how it worked to solidify the idea of Christianity as cognate with the Euro-Western civilization, and how it essentialized race, thus positioning itself as central vis-à-vis the gospel. Taken together, these lay the foundation for understanding the significance of the manifestation of the primal in Black American Christianity and the New Testament.

---

49. Walls, *Missionary Movement*, 9.
50. G. Bediako, "Primal Religion," 14.

2

From "Barbarian Creed" to "Civilized Faith"

THE "PROBLEM" POSED BY the primal apprehension of Christian faith by Black peoples as expressed in Black American Christianity did not begin with the importation of African slaves into North America during the early modern period. The problem finds its origins within the larger story of Western Christianity, one in which Christianity was gradually transformed from barbarian creed to civilized religion. By the advent of the transatlantic slave trade in which many millions of diverse African peoples were forcibly transported to the Americas and amalgamated into what would eventually become Black American and other diaspora groups, Christianity was seen to be coterminous with White European civilization. By the late nineteenth and early twentieth centuries, the application of evolutionary theories to the study of religion had firmly fixed this idea in place: Christian religion and European civilization went hand in hand, the best and highest of both religion and culture. The United States of America was founded as the exemplary expression of this civilization. In this chapter, I trace the origins and development of this idea beginning with the early church when Christianity was considered a sect within Judaism, into the Greco-Roman era when the perception of Christianity changed from that of a backward, "barbarian" creed to almost complete identification with Roman society. I then follow the church-state symbiosis of Western Christendom and its eventual unravelling, Europe's engagement with the wider world, the beginnings of European racial thought, and finally, the creation of the United States as the epitome of White Christian civilization—the world into which Black American Christianity was born.

Christianity as a Jewish Sect

At its birth Christianity was nothing more than a variant of Judaism, a faith tolerated by the Roman state for its antiquity though disdained for its "peculiar and exclusive religious ideas and practices."[1] Despite the nascent persecution recorded in the New Testament, Christianity attracted little attention from the Roman authorities. Christians, "in so far as they were generally regarded as a Jewish religious sect . . . enjoyed the favour shown to Jews in general."[2] This is not to suggest that Judaism enjoyed anything like a positive reputation in Greco-Roman society. Their religious customs were seen by Tacitus as "impious and abominable," attractive only to "the most worthless rascals . . . [who] learn to despise the gods, to renounce their country, and to think nothing of their parents, children, and brethren."[3] By this, Tacitus denounced Jewish proselytism which he saw as seducing people into a strange barbarian superstition. Yet despite the unmistakable scorn with which he viewed Judaism, he sanctioned the ongoing legitimacy of Jewish religious rites due to their "antiquity."[4] The Jews, though generally despised, were an ancient people with their own history who "might at worst, insurrection excepted, be left to their own devices."[5] So long as Christianity remained within the ambit of Judaism—the events recorded in Acts notwithstanding—"Christians appeared to pose no threat to the Roman system." It is only after the emergence of a Christian identity distinct and separate from Judaism that one begins to see "hostile Pagan [Roman] attitudes . . . hardening into harassment and eventual persecution."[6]

---

1. Markus, *Christianity in Roman World*, 14.
2. K. Bediako, *Theology and Identity*, 19.
3. Tacitus, *Histories* 5.5, locs. 6783–84.
4. Tacitus, *Histories* 5.5, loc. 6776.
5. K. Bediako, *Theology and Identity*, 16.
6. K. Bediako, *Theology and Identity*, 19.

FROM "BARBARIAN CREED" TO "CIVILIZED FAITH"

Primal Religious "Pluralism"

The toleration shown by the Roman authorities to Judaism was more than political pragmatism. Although it was surely politically beneficial for Rome to permit the maintenance of traditional religious practices among its many subject nations, their tolerance stemmed, in part at least, from the primal nature of Greco-Roman religious life itself. These "religion[s] of tradition" had "no underlying idea other than the sanctity of custom hallowed by preceding generations,"[7] rooted in the long tradition of the people, stretching back to time immemorial and without any claim to revelatory authority. They simple existed. In this respect, the Greco-Roman religious system reflected an essentially primal orientation; it was "tolerant of the religions of other peoples and sometimes borrow[ed] certain elements from them"[8] without being fundamentally changed or challenged by the loan. There were "gods many and lords many" and most people cared little about which was worshipped or indeed whether they were false or true. Greco-Roman religion did not generally make the exclusivist claims on their adherents that prophetic religions like Judaism and later Christianity or Islam would. Each of the numerous "primal societ[ies]" under Roman authority were therefore able to maintain "its own religion peculiar to itself,"[9] without disturbing the pax Romana. According to Edward Gibbon:

> The devout polytheist, though fondly attached to his national rites, admitted with implicit faith the different religions of the earth. Fear, gratitude, and curiosity, a dream or an omen, a singular disorder, or a distant journey, perpetually disposed him to multiply the articles of his belief and to enlarge the list of his protectors.[10]

In contrast to these, Judaism and Christianity each called for a decisive conversion—"the reorientation of the soul of an individual, his deliberate turning from indifference or from an earlier form of piety to another."[11] This reorientation was not an envisioned possibility in the religions of much of the Greco-Roman world; there was nothing to turn from nor to, no falsehood to reject or truth to embrace, as the various religions that prevailed throughout the empire "were all considered by the people as equally

---

7. Nock, *Conversion*, 3.
8. Baylis, *Introduction to Primal Religions*, 3.
9. Baylis, *Introduction to Primal Religions*, 3.
10. Gibbon, *Decline and Fall*, 26.
11. Nock, *Conversion*, 7.

true; by the philosopher as equally false, and by the magistrate as equally useful."[12] They were additive, rather than conversionist in nature; gods and goddesses, rituals and practices could be added or discarded as necessary, and respect accorded to the gods of a particular locality whenever the occasion arose.

Though not religiously tolerant in the modern sense of permitting individual freedom of conscience, the pervasive primal religious worldview of Greco-Roman society afforded a remarkable degree of religious plurality in which devotees of different gods lived side by side in relative harmony. This attitude is reflected in St. Paul's encounter in Athens with the altar inscribed "to the unknown god" (Acts 17)—a shrine standing alongside numerous others without any apparent conflict between them. In the Greco-Roman world, it was within philosophy and not religion that conversion was emphasized. It was Greek philosophy which "held a clear concept of two types of life, a higher and a lower" and "exhorted men to turn from the one to the other."[13] Gibbon describes Greek philosophy as often skeptical and indeed dismissive of the claims of popular religion.[14] In his words, "they approached with the same inward contempt, and the same external reverence, the altars of the Libyan, the Olympian, or the Capitoline Jupiter."[15]

The Barbarian Creed

The external reverence to which Gibbon refers was due to an understanding of religion as a civic and social duty and not necessarily a matter of conscious belief or genuine faith. "True religion was marked by dignified and sober piety, fidelity to ancestral customs, reasonableness and civility,"[16] and belonged to Greco-Roman culture. On the other hand, superstition— "marked by excess of emotion and evident in bizarre and irrational

---

12. Gibbon, *Decline and Fall*, 25–26.

13. Nock, *Conversion*, 14.

14. It should be noted here that Gibbon reflected the views of many of his contemporaries by seeking to "admire Greek and Roman philosophers as men of reason like themselves, without having to make any concessions to the general religious beliefs of the society," thus positing a stronger division between religion and philosophy than probably existed (G. Bediako, *Primal Religion*, 68).

15. Gibbon, *Decline and Fall*, 28.

16. K. Bediako, *Theology and Identity*, 26.

practices"—was barbarian.[17] The distinction between the two, and the judgment implicit in that distinction persists, and lies at the heart of contemporary challenges in the interpretation of the primal.

The term "barbarian" was then, as now, a term of derision, a means of distancing oneself from something deemed inferior. It was also a term that not only separated Greek from non-Greek speakers, but also the hellenized urban populations of the empire from those in the countryside. Richard Fletcher describes the attitudes thus:

> The educated and articulate elite of the classical Mediterranean believed that civilization and culture were to be found exclusively in cities. Our daily use of such words as "urbane," "polite" and of course, "civilized" shows what a good job that elite has done in persuading posterity of its point of view.... City dwellers, parasitic upon the surrounding country for their essential supplies, repaid this dependence in the harsh coin of disdain. Most townspeople, most of the time, looked upon the rural peasantry with mingled disgust, fear and contempt. They were dirty and smelly, unkempt, inarticulate, uncouth, misshapen by toil, living in conditions of unbelievable squalor, as brutish as the beasts they tended.... The peasantry of the countryside were beyond the pale, a tribe apart, outsiders.[18]

The attitude of Greek elites towards the countryside is a good example of the general disposition of Greco-Roman society towards barbarism. Judaism was no exception and "Christianity naturally inherited the barbarism of its progenitor,"[19] including its Scripture—what is now known to Christians as the Old Testament.

So long as Christianity remained primarily within the ambit of Judaism, there were few questions raised either inside or outside the group about its identity, the nature of conversion, or the relationship of the group to broader Greco-Roman culture. Preexisting norms refined over centuries provided ready answers to most questions, including how converts were to be integrated into the community. Proselytism itself was not new to Judaism, the parent faith, and thus, that this new Christian sect had "embraced some non-Jews . . . would not be astonishing to anyone."[20] Andrew Walls

---

17. K. Bediako, *Theology and Identity*, 26.
18. Fletcher, *Conversion of Europe*, 16.
19. Markus, *Christianity in Roman World*, 44.
20. Markus, *Christianity in Roman World*, 18.

has noted the "long missionary tradition whereby Gentile proselytes had been welcomed into the fold of Israel."[21] Matthew 23:15 records Jesus's scathing words of condemnation towards Pharisees who "travel land and sea to win one proselyte" (NKJV) and we read in Acts 6:5 of Nicolas who was "a proselyte from Antioch" (NKJV). Many of the early gentile converts to Christianity likely sprang from among the ranks of proselytes, and thus were already assimilated into Jewish cultural life. Yet the inclusion of growing number of gentiles who had no previous association with Judaism raised new and vital questions about the identity of the group and the nature of conversion. Were these gentile followers of Jesus to be treated "as enlightened Gentiles had always been treated in Israel," as "proselytes, stags that had chosen to graze with the sheep"?[22] Or were they something else? The question was one of proselytization versus conversion and the implications of the answer would have profound ramifications for the very nature of Christian faith and identity.

The Jerusalem council recorded in Acts 15 would seem to have resolved the issue by coming down firmly on the side of conversion as against proselytism; gentile believers would not be required to adopt Jewish culture to become Christians. Despite this seemingly clear decision, the question of cultural identity after conversion persisted: "Was Christianity a way of being a Jew or was it something else?"[23] This question was complicated especially by the divide between Greek and barbarian cultures and the disdain with which the former regarded the latter. Christianity would prove distinctive as it sought to hold together the religious and philosophic quest. This was an important factor in the eventual identification of Christianity and Greco-Roman culture, an identification that centered on the critical issues of conversion and integration—conversion of Greek philosophy, and integration of the barbarian religious tradition with Greco-Roman culture.

Engagement of Christian Faith with Greco-Roman Culture

The rise and spread of Christianity raised new issues for the increasing number of higher class and educated Greco-Roman converts to the faith. By becoming predominantly gentile and in breaking with Judaism, the church had created for itself an identity that was "essentially a religious

---

21. Walls, "Converts or Proselytes," 5.
22. Walls, "Converts or Proselytes," 5.
23. Markus, *Christianity in Roman World*, 22.

one, not national, nor cultural, nor social."[24] These converts felt the need to vindicate the Christian faith in ways that were faithful both to Christian teaching and to their Greco-Roman cultural inheritance. Their relationship to Greco-Roman culture could not remain unexamined but had to be reinterpreted in light of their encounter with God revealed in the person of Jesus and the ancient religious texts of a barbarian people, the Jews. Writers like Tatian and Tertullian (c. 155–c. 220) embraced a "radically exclusivist perspective . . . on the relation of Christian teaching to the [Greek] philosophical tradition . . . underpinned by a conviction that the latter amounts to merely human speculation."[25] This was the gospel as the "triumph of barbarism."[26] For Tatian this meant "bidding farewell to the arrogance of Romans and the idle talk of Athenians, and all their ill-connected opinions, [and] embrac[ing] our barbaric philosophy."[27] His embrace of barbarism amounted to a refutation of the claims of Greek philosophy and a repudiation of Greco-Roman cultural assertion of superior status. Accommodation was far from the minds of those who remembered that "the Gospel had after all been preached as foolishness to the Greeks."[28] There was no need to attempt a reconciliation of pagan Greek philosophy with Christian self-understanding. Any such attempt threatened the "diminution of the credentials of the Christian faith . . . reducing Christian teaching to the level of human speculative systems, which lacked any claim to certainty."[29] The two stood apart and opposed to one another: one the wisdom of God, the other the foolishness of man. Perhaps the best-known expression of this approach is Tertullian's cry "What indeed has Athens to do with Jerusalem?"[30]—an indication of the gulf he perceived between the two.

Conversion of the Greco-Roman Past

Tatian and Tertullian each embraced a vision of radical discontinuity with the Greco-Roman past and rejected Greek philosophy as incompatible with a true understanding of the gospel. Other apologists, whose approach

24. K. Bediako, *Theology and Identity*, 36.
25. K. Bediako, *Theology and Identity*, 45.
26. K. Bediako, *Theology and Identity*, 64–136.
27. Tatian, "Address to the Greeks," locs. 23968–69.
28. Markus, *Christianity in Roman World*, 45.
29. K. Bediako, *Theology and Identity*, 43.
30. Tertullian, "Prescription against Heretics," locs. 51899–900.

would ultimately triumph, chose to emphasize the continuity between Greek philosophy and the gospel. One example is Justin Martyr (c. 100–c. 165) who "represented Christianity as summing up all that was best in thought of antiquity."[31] Clement of Alexandria (c. 150–c. 215) is another who, was well acquainted with Greek philosophy and understood the disdain with which educated Greeks and Romans held Christianity, viewing it "as a lower-class superstition from an obscure frontier province."[32] He thus sought to demonstrate, "the relevance and the significance of the Christian Gospel to the quests and aspirations . . . in Hellenistic tradition."[33] His success and that of others such as Origen (c. 185–c. 253) created a new category, that of the "sophisticated Christian scholar who could match any pagan philosopher."[34] As Walls states, this process of engaging "an intellectual environment that combined the influences of Greek philosophy, Roman law, Eastern mysticism and spirituality, and astral science . . . was the highway to a great outworking of creative theological activity . . . [and] the eventual result was Christian theology as we know it."[35]

However, these apologists were primarily concerned with engaging Greek philosophy and not necessarily Greek religion—often derided as superstition by Greco-Roman elites and Christian apologists alike. For example, despite Clement of Alexandria's generally favorable attitude towards what he deems to be good in Greek philosophy, he shared with Greek philosophy a marked disdain towards the religious practices of everyday people. In other words, the apologists, by seeking to "vindicate the Christian faith in ways" that were "faithful to the tradition of Christian teaching and . . . consistent with . . . the cultural dynamics of Graeco-Roman civilisation"[36] subtly created a link between Christianity and Romanism, between the faith and elite Greco-Roman culture, with all its attendant pretensions.

One unfortunate outcome—indeed one diametrically opposed to the perspective of early apologists who saw Christianity as "the vindication of

---

31. Markus, *Christianity in Roman World*, 42.

32. Placher, *History of Christian Theology*, 59.

33. K. Bediako, *Theology and Identity*, 176.

34. Bosch, *Transforming Mission*, 193.

35. Walls, "Converts or Proselytes," 6. See also Pelikan, *Christianity and Classical Culture*.

36. K. Bediako, *Theology and Identity*, 48.

the worth of Barbarian self-identity"[37]—was the development of a tendency on the part of some Christians to embrace the "Hellenistic feelings of superiority, particularly toward the *barbaroi*."[38] They sought to distance themselves from the very cultural identity that writers like Tatian had sought to vindicate. As a comparatively urbanized population, Christians shared in the culture of urban Roman civilization and came to share their biases as well.[39] The link being forged between Romanism with its "confidence in the urban order of imperial Rome"[40] and Christianity would have tremendous consequences as Christianity moved from the margins to the center of Roman society.

Roman Imperial Christianity

The close of the third century saw the last major state sanctioned persecution of Christians in the Roman Empire occur under the reign of Emperor Diocletian. The famed (and disputed) conversion of his successor Constantine marked a significant and permanent change in the relationship of Christianity to the Roman state. However, even before the adoption of religious toleration through the Edict of Milan and the conversion of Constantine, the church "had begun to be a bearer of culture and a civilising presence in society."[41] This is the background against which Constantine's conversion and the later adoption of Christianity as the state religion must be interpreted. While Constantine "did not make Christianity the official religion of the Roman empire" he did "make the Christian church the most-favoured recipient of the near-limitless resources of imperial favour."[42] Converts, both authentic and fake, poured into the church and "Christians suddenly found themselves part of the 'establishment.'"[43] This revolutionary change meant that for the first time, state power was on the side of the church and Christians were faced with the challenge of how to interpret their newfound status. The accommodating approach of earlier apologists

---

37. K. Bediako, *Theology and Identity*, 67.
38. Bosch, *Transforming Mission*, 193.
39. Markus, *Christianity in Roman World*, 78.
40. Fletcher, *Conversion of Europe*, 16.
41. Bosch, *Transforming Mission*, 193.
42. Fletcher, *Conversion of Europe*, 19.
43. Fletcher, *Conversion of Europe*, 22.

provided the template but was "carried to extreme lengths after Constantine's adhesion to Christianity."[44]

The church repaid the generosity of the emperor in the coin of sacred legitimization of the Roman state: "Constantine was the culmination of God's marvellous saving work . . . the head of a unitary Christian society, with a divine mission to rule it as the vicar of Christ and to extend the sway of the Gospel among men."[45] In this formulation, conversion to the Christian faith was seen as part of the mandate of a Christian ruler and the Roman Empire as the "divinely sanctioned socio-political vehicle of Christianity."[46] One begins to perceive the early stages of what Gillian Bediako has aptly termed "a fatal confusion of ideas . . . [the identification of] God with the maintenance of a particular human institution."[47] Though initially Christianity coexisted with other religions within the Roman orbit, later in the fourth century the Roman state began to actively suppress pagan religion and sanction heretical beliefs.[48] Nevertheless, Constantine's conversion and the later adoption of Christianity as the state religion brought about a nearly complete alignment between Greco-Roman culture, Christian faith, and the Roman state. Thenceforth, to be Roman was to be Christian and even more importantly, to be Christian was to be Roman.

Conflation of Roman and Christian Identity

This conflation of Roman and Christian identity was to have significant implications for Christian self-understanding in the Latin West. For one thing it meant that as early as the fourth century "a Catholic bishop could already assume that the Roman and the Christian worlds were coextensive"[49] in both a territorial and a cultural sense. The barbarians outside of Rome were therefore presumed to be outside the Christian orbit and "could be as effectively dehumanized by the educated minority as were the peasantry."[50] Cultural biases took on religious significance. Culturally sensitive evangelization could hardly be deemed proper or even possible among those

---

44. Fletcher, *Conversion of Europe*, 24.
45. Markus, *Christianity in Roman World*, 98.
46. Markus, *Christianity in Roman World*, 141.
47. G. Bediako, *Primal Religion*, 20–21.
48. Markus, *Christianity in Roman World*, 99.
49. Markus, *Christianity in Roman World*, 141.
50. Fletcher, *Conversion of Europe*, 25.

thought to be scarcely better than animals and thus mission, invariably began to be seen as "a movement from the superior to the inferior"[51] and became associated with the suppression or elimination the culture of the latter, inferior group and replacing it with that of the former, superior one, by force if necessary.

The confusion of Roman and Christian identity also meant that Christian conversion became less a matter of renunciation of idolatrous practices and repudiation of sinful behaviors as in the tradition of prophetic religion and much more a matter of conformity to the externalities of rite and ritual. It became a matter of adhesion, of "the acceptance of new worships as useful supplements and not as substitutes."[52] Within the old Roman system religion "was a matter not of personal belief and devotion, but of social duty and ancestral practice,"[53] so one could be a Roman Christian merely by following the prescribed rites and ritual observances. In other words, "though formal and external conformity to Christianity was forced on the Empire, it remained at heart unchanged."[54] The converted "Roman aristocracy . . . did not give up their old pagan interests and habits,"[55] indeed they felt no need to do so because there ceased to exist for them any conflict between the old and the new; in effect, there was nothing to convert from or to. They became Christianized, though perhaps not authentically Christian.

Effectively, Christianity took over the previous role played by paganism within the Empire as a "politically binding force and a means of social control"[56] and Christian theology became an area of imperial policy interest. No longer was Christian orthodoxy and theology a matter only for the church and of fidelity to Scripture and the apostolic tradition, but of imperial power politics to be enforced by the sword. "The Empire of Christ," a notion far removed from that expressed in Jesus's reply to Pontius Pilate, "was an achieved reality, there for all to see . . . and the Church to bless God for."[57]

The barbarian invasions and consequent disruption of Western Roman society discomfited those who saw Rome as the eternal city and raised

51. Bosch, *Transforming Mission*, 193.
52. Nock, *Conversion*, 7.
53. K. Bediako, *Theology and Identity*, 21.
54. G. Bediako, *Primal Religion*, 21.
55. Markus, *Christianity in Roman World*, 140.
56. K. Bediako, *Theology and Identity*, 23.
57. Markus, *Christianity in Roman World*, 142.

theological questions for those who attributed the success of Rome to Christianity. Yet this did not disrupt the conjoining of Christian and Roman identity. Even as the barbarians were conquering Rome, Rome through the church was conquering barbarian culture. As Markus puts it, "Christianity was the Roman faith, and the Roman Empire the Christian society. Barbarians were outsiders to both, and their only way of entry into the one was by entering both."[58] So the adoption of Christian faith by the barbarian aristocracy meant their entry into Christendom, a realm where church, state, and Roman culture, "a literary culture preserved by and through the Church,"[59] were inextricably intertwined. Christendom should therefore be understood as both a geographical expression, denoting those territories under the rule of Christian monarchs, and a cultural one. In this new setting the Western Christian aristocracy saw themselves "as an elite ... called to provide the lead and inspiration in its world, the moral force to dominate its society with a right to impose its will on the recalcitrant."[60]

The Rise and Fall of Western Christendom

Of course, the whole of the Roman Empire did not collapse with the fall of Rome but continued on in the East—where links with classical thought and pagan learning led to "a Christian synthesis both in the realm of thought and in that of social existence"[61]—and would endure for another thousand years. That is a story for another day. I am not here concerned with eastern Christendom and the story of Orthodoxy, or with Christian communities that lay outside the orbit of Rome whether to the east or south, but with the Western Church. There, the gradual collapse of centralized imperial authority left in its wake small barbarian kingdoms increasingly freed from any sense of identification with Christian Rome, and disconnected from the legacy of classical Greco-Roman civilization.[62] The unity of the civilized world under Christian Roman rule had broken down and in its place arose a new social order and a new kind of Christianity—"territorial

---

58. Markus, *Christianity in Roman World*, 143. See also Fletcher, *Conversion of Europe*, 99.
59. Walls, *Missionary Movement*, 69.
60. Markus, *Christianity in Roman World*, 166.
61. Markus, *Christianity in Roman World*, 164.
62. Markus, *Christianity in Roman World*, 162.

Christianity . . . the idea of the Christian nation,"[63] or more specifically, Christianity on the map of Europe. This change "had consequences for the concept of Christendom and European Christian self-understanding reaching into the modern era."[64]

The complete conversion of the peoples of northern and western Europe—what would become the heartlands of Western Christendom—took centuries; it was not until almost the fifteenth century that Lithuania formally accepted Catholic Christianity due to a royal marriage agreement and as late as the seventeenth century, non-Christian burial practices were still being observed.[65] Nevertheless, Europe was, by and large, Christian, a "single people [following] a single code,"[66] presumptively Christian in character. This emerging Christendom was not localized, reflecting only the parochial concerns and customs of this or that tribal group. The lingering heritage of Rome meant that the various local elements were transcended by a shared sense of connection, of sharing in a common cultural legacy—"a single assembly of Christian princes and peoples, a single church, a single sacred language, a single tradition of learning."[67] There was an increasing sense of participation in a distinctively and uniquely Christian civilization, delimited by a common faith and by specific geographic boundaries. This idea was reinforced and solidified by the rise and threat of Islam.

The Emergence of Islam

The eruption of Islam in the seventh century and the rapidity of its spread was a critical element in the consolidation of European Christian identity. Within a hundred years of the death of its founder, "Islamic rule extended from the Pyrenees to the Punjab, from the Atlantic coast of Morocco to the mountains of the Hindu Kush and shores of the Aral Sea."[68] The vast majority of these lands had been the heartlands of Christianity and their fall under Islamic domination had the effect of further isolating the Christian communities of Western Europe from other Christian peoples in Asia and

---

63. Walls, *Cross-Cultural Process*, 35.
64. G. Bediako, *Primal Religion*, 24.
65. Fletcher, *Conversion of Europe*, 507–8.
66. Walls, *Cross-Cultural Process*, 35.
67. Walls, *Cross-Cultural Process*, 36.
68. Fletcher, *Conversion of Europe*, 304.

Africa.[69] It also raised new questions for a people unaccustomed to religious pluralism; Islam was not like the paganism of the as yet un-Christianized populations of Europe—it was monotheistic. Nor was it like Judaism, the religion of those who had been presented with and then rejected the gospel. It appeared most readily to be a heresy, a perversion of Christian faith.[70]

The threat of Islam and the call to crusade by the pope served as an accelerant to the notion of Christendom. The use of force in the expansion of Christendom and as a means of eliminating pagan practices had many precedents and was considered legitimate.[71] Thus military action to reclaim lost Christian territories through the Crusades was undertaken based on an erroneous reading of Jesus's words in Luke 14:23, "compel them to come in that my house may be filled" (NKJV), which appeared to provide scriptural grounds for such an approach. The Crusades represented the height of the Christendom ideal, "holding at that point the allegiance of the majority of Christians in Europe."[72] Yet it may also be said that they were the beginning of the end of Christendom as well.

The Decline of Christendom and the Emergence of Christian Europe

The failure of the Crusades to reach their objectives[73] sharpened the already growing perception of distinction between Christian Europe and the non-Christian, non-European world. The conversion of Lithuania meant that Europe was now fully Christian and the fall of Constantinople to the Ottoman Turks in 1453 increased European isolation from the Christian communities of Africa and Asia. Europe alone now seemed Christian and civilized, while the others were subsumed into a barbarous exoticism.[74] Papal power, which had undergirded and thrived on the Christendom model of society, had been "undermined by the mistakes, pretensions, and worldliness of the papacy itself."[75] This development, coupled with the increased geographical and religious isolation of Western Christians from

---

69. G. Bediako, *Primal Religion*, 37.
70. Fletcher, *Conversion of Europe*, 304.
71. G. Bediako, *Primal Religion*, 32.
72. G. Bediako, *Primal Religion*, 35.
73. The *Reconquista* of the Iberian Peninsula, which culminated in the capitulation of its last independent Islamic emirate in 1492, is the notable exception.
74. G. Bediako, *Primal Religion*, 37.
75. Schaff, *Middle Ages*, loc. 66522.

other Christian expressions meant that "Europe would eventually replace Christendom as [their] integrating focus."[76] The Renaissance rediscovery and appropriation of the legacy of Greek classical civilization, a process hastened by the collapse of the Byzantine Empire,[77] accentuated the sense of a distinctly European civilization, tracing its descent from Greece and Rome. The alignment of state and church implicit in Christendom endured through the Reformation and Counter-Reformation, so that by the onset of the age of European exploration, "Roman Catholics and Protestants were . . . still dedicated to the theocratic ideal of the unity of church and state."[78] The division between various European Christian confessions—increasingly expressed in national terms—became less important than the distinction between European and non-European, whether Christian or not; "Christian identity was located not so much in a particular confession, but in Christianity as European religion.[79] The idea of territorial Christianity continued unabated[80]—it was still Christianity on the map—yet now the map was exclusively of Europe.

European Civilization and the Wider World

The story traced thus far has been exclusively defined by the conditions of European social and religious history with scant reference to the wider world—Asia, Africa, and the Americas. Although there had been thousands of years of commercial and cultural exchange between Europe, Asia, and Africa, most of these, even in ancient times had been indirectly conducted through intermediary peoples.[81] The number of Europeans, even among the elite and educated classes, who had direct contact with or reliable information about Asia or Africa was vanishingly small. It was the direct European encounter with the wider world and her peoples during the early modern era that solidified the idea of Europe and, by extension, Europeans, as a society and people apart from all others: civilized, Christian, and

76. G. Bediako, *Primal Religion*, 37.

77. "The Byzantine scholars and artists who took to Europe principally sought safety on the Italian peninsula. . . . In their luggage, the exiles from Byzantium carried many manuscripts, which preserved the thoughts of the great Greek thinkers and other writers hardly known in the west" (Marshall and Williams, *Great Map of Mankind*, 180–81).

78. Bosch, *Transforming Mission*, 303.

79. G. Bediako, *Primal Religion*, 39.

80. Walls, *Cross-Cultural Process*, 37.

81. Rietbergen, *Europe*, 227.

superior. Of particular importance was the melding of notions of European civilization, Christianity, and race—thinking that would find its culmination in the founding of the United States as a White Christian nation. I shall come to this shortly.

Asia had long exercised a compelling pull on the European imagination. Wealth and wisdom were both associated with the distant lands of the east; the biblical story of Eden, located somewhere in the fabled Orient, only added to the allure.[82] Asia was the birthplace of Christianity and the source of numerous scientific and technological innovations, modern shipbuilding, and navigational techniques salient among them. It was also the home of "the two most revered sources of knowledge: the Bible and the writings of Greek and Roman antiquity."[83] For centuries the Islamic world had "been the essential intermediary between Asia and Europe"[84] and for that matter, sub-Saharan Africa. European knowledge of the two continents was therefore mediated and influenced by Islam, a fact which would particularly color European perceptions of Africa, as shall later be seen.

The Search for an Alternate Route to Asia

The Crusades' failure to dislodge Islam from the Near East and political struggles between the Persian and Ottoman Empires left Europeans searching for an alternate route to the east in pursuit of "gold and slaves in the interior of West Africa . . . the wealth of Asia, for allies in the fight against Islam, and even for a strategic southern detour to the Holy Land."[85] Thus the initial and primary impulse behind European engagement with the wider world was primarily economic and political, rather than religious. The voyages of the Portuguese explorers in the early fifteenth century along the African coasts, and later ones across the Atlantic were motivated by a desire for profit, not souls, for earthly gain, not the kingdom of God. Though Europe was now more fully Christian than ever before, Asia, Africa, and, in due course, the Americas were not seen by most Europeans as societies to be evangelized with the gospel, but as places to be exploited for their material benefits to European society. Columbus's initial journey to America in 1492 was followed two years later by the Treaty of Tordesillas, which

82. Rietbergen, *Europe*, 227.
83. Marshall and Williams, *Great Map of Mankind*, 7.
84. Rietbergen, *Europe*, 231.
85. Rietbergen, *Europe*, 229.

divided the "New World" between Spain and Portugal, thus guaranteeing to each spheres of political and economic dominance.[86] By his second journey, Columbus was already employing systematic terror against American indigenes in order to obtain access to gold.[87] Thus even at the earliest stage, the quest for material gain and political supremacy emerged as a central feature of European encounter with the non-European world. This avaricious spirit was to have disastrous consequences for the peoples of Africa and the newly discovered Americas.

The Christianizing impulse embodied in the ideologies of Crusade and Christendom was not, however, entirely absent. European encounter with America and sub-Saharan Africa was marked by the same "familiar pattern of conquest, subjugation and exploitation, sanctioned by the Pope in the name of Christendom"[88] she had known for centuries. This was to be expected; war and coercion in the name of religion had been embedded in European cultural life for centuries and would remain so until the 1648 Peace of Westphalia brought an end to interreligious wars between European peoples.[89] For the Spanish in particular, the conquest of the New World was simply a continuation of the pattern established in the *Reconquista*. After the defeat of Grenada, the last Moorish kingdom, the Spanish crown began enforcing a policy of conversion or expulsion for Muslims and Jews alike.[90] The Spanish monarchy could not countenance their enduring presence; it was an affront to their idea of Christian Catholic civilization. In the cases of both the old and new crusading impulse, there was a cultural and civilizational clash: the supposed Christian civilization of Europe against the non-Christian barbarous *other*, one increasingly identified not only by religion, but by the color of skin. The encounter between European and non-European peoples led to the development of race as an ideological construct that would play a significant role in the interpretation of that encounter, vis-à-vis European self-consciousness and religious understanding. Observable differences between people groups took on social and theological meaning, with devastating consequences. Though not the primary focus of this chapter, it is therefore necessary to explore, in a

---

86. Dunbar-Ortiz, *Indigenous Peoples' History*, 42.
87. Keillor, *This Rebellious House*, 27.
88. G. Bediako, *Primal Religion*, 40.
89. Cragg, *Church and Age of Reason*, 9.
90. Rietbergen, *Europe*, 226. While the language of "conversion" was used, the policy was one of forced proselytization.

preliminary way, the initial emergence of European ideas about race and its connection with notions of Christian civilization.

The Rise of Race

Roxanne Dunbar-Ortiz identifies how the process of politico-religious purification that occurred in the Iberian kingdoms during this era helped to lay the philosophical foundation of White supremacy, the "essential ideology of colonial projects in America and Africa."[91] This process of politico-religious purification flowed out of the cultural conflation of European and Christian identity that was long in formation but accelerated during the Crusades and European voyages of exploration. Christian identity was positioned "fully within European (white) identity and fully outside the identities of Jews and Muslims."[92] The process to which Dunbar-Ortiz refers was that of determining, for the sake of access to certain privileges, *limpieza de sangre*—purity of blood.[93] *Limpieza de sangre* meant being free of the taint of non-Christian ancestry, particularly that of converted Jews, *conversos*, and Muslims, *moriscos*,[94] who were "seen as deeply suspect in regard to the veracity of their Christian identity."[95] Those so identified would gain legal privileges that "obscur[ed] the class differences between the landed aristocracy and the land-poor peasants and shepherds."[96] The otherwise disempowered and oppressed peasant classes were thus brought into alliance with the aristocracy against those with impure bloodlines on the basis of what Dunbar-Ortiz calls "the first instance of class levelling based on an imagined racial sameness—the origin of white supremacy."[97] This "imagined sameness" was rooted in ancestry, something over which no control could be exercised. It was an inevitability: a predestined, unchangeable, inheritable condition—an idea we shall meet again. Aside the political calculus entailed in this process, there were profound and far-reaching theological implications. It was "a process of discerning Christian

---

91. Dunbar-Ortiz, *Indigenous Peoples' History*, 37.
92. Jennings, *Christian Imagination*, loc. 698.
93. Dunbar-Ortiz, *Indigenous History*, 37.
94. M. Martínez, "Black Blood," 483.
95. Jennings, *Christian Imagination*, loc. 698.
96. Dunbar-Ortiz, *Indigenous Peoples' History*, 37.
97. Dunbar-Ortiz, *Indigenous Peoples' History*, 37.

identity"[98] along ethnic and aesthetic lines such that the ancestral stain of Moorish or Jewish blood could not be fully washed away, even by the waters of Christian baptism. One may discern here a nascent White supremacist theological lens wherein "the body of the European would be the compass marking divine election" even as "the white body would be a discerning body, able to detect holy effects and saving grace."[99] Consequently, physical similarity to Whiteness took on theological significance as a marker of salvific probability.

What began as a religious category in metropolitan Spain increasingly, and inevitably, took on more explicitly racial meaning in her colonies. Conversion to the Christian faith in New Spain and other parts of Spain's overseas empire raised new questions about the legal status of Indians and Africans and their relationship to the Spanish crown. Indian converts to Catholicism were considered pure blooded since they were presumed to have been "descended from Gentiles who had not mixed with 'contaminated' or 'condemned' sects."[100] Their mixture with the Spanish could be seen as a redemptive process wherein whatever negative attributes accrued on the basis of Indian blood would be purified by the infusion of Spanish blood, an idea that "echo[ed] the notion that Jesus took on the sins of humanity in order to purify it."[101] There was power in the blood—the blood of "Whiteness"—to define the parameters of human existence, and to redeem it when it fell short.

For Africans, no such possibility existed. There was a long-standing Iberian prejudice against blackness, rooted in its association with servitude and derived in part from Islamic perspectives,[102] yet this is not entirely sufficient to explain the disparate legal treatment they received. American indigenes and enslaved Africans were both treated quite brutally in the Spanish and Portuguese colonies. More important than rank prejudice was the fact that, unlike the natives who were, theoretically at least, considered "free vassals . . . in a kind of contractual relationship with the Spanish crown,"[103] Africans were considered foreigners brought under the dominion of the

98. Jennings, *Christian Imagination*, loc. 705.
99. Jennings, *Christian Imagination*, loc. 713.
100. M. Martínez, "Black Blood," 484.
101. M. Martínez, "Black Blood," 485.
102. For more on Islamic antecedents to Spanish racial thought see Sweet, "Iberian Roots."
103. M. Martínez, "Black Blood," 488.

Spanish monarchy involuntarily. This affected their legal status.[104] Enslaved Africans were thus caught in a bind. On the one hand, by virtue of their ancestors having been forcibly enslaved, they could never, except in rare cases, be legally granted the rights that accrued to subjects of the Spanish crown; "blacks were, by definition, impure because of their connection ... with slavery."[105] The impurity that attached itself to them was due to their forefathers' enslavement—an extension of the principle established during the Crusades that "all persons captured in [the Crusade] were consigned to servitude." On the other, those Africans who had been converted to Christianity prior to their capture were also enslaved. Thus, "Africans' willingness to accept the Christian faith had no bearing on the ... decision to seize them as human property."[106] Though they might be redeemed by the blood of Jesus, they remained in the bonds of slavery.

Race as a Legal Construct

In theory at least, the Iberian powers distinguished between African slaves and others based solely on convoluted legal doctrines centered around issues of lineal descent, and not on the basis of a supposed ontological inferiority stemming from race; "efforts to relegate [Native Americans] to a sub-human category were, for the most part, resisted."[107] In practice, however, the Iberian powers "were undoubtedly influenced by the attitudes of their Muslim trading partners along the Saharan littoral,"[108] in their views and treatment of African captives. Tragically, what Muslim powers had practiced inconsistently and in violation of extensive Islamic

---

104. "Castilian legal thought placed a great deal of weight on voluntarism; blacks had been forcibly integrated into the Hispanic world, thus essentially precluding the possibility that they could have a communal contractual relationship with Castilian monarchs. Hence, their redemption was possible, but only through individual meritorious deeds that demonstrated their deep loyalty to the Christian faith, their masters, and, by extension, the larger community of Old Christians.... Another factor that made the status of blacks in the Spanish colonial world problematic was their foreignness, or, rather, their African ancestral origins, which within Spanish political theory meant that, unlike the 'natives' (*naturales*), they had no natural love for the territories that now belonged to the crown of Castile and were therefore more likely to side with Spain's enemies" (M. Martínez, "Black Blood," 489).

105. M. Martínez, "Black Blood," 491.
106. Sweet, "Iberian Roots," 157.
107. Marshall and Williams, *Great Map of Mankind*, 26.
108. Sweet, "Iberian Roots," 162.

jurisprudence, the Christian nations of Iberia took up and transformed "into a coherent ideology"[109] used to legitimize the enslavement of Africans, whether Christian or not. Ancestry, not creed, became the key determinant of the social position of Black peoples within the Iberian metropole and overseas empires. All else was secondary.

In the Iberian states, slave ancestry, not religion or culture, provided the theoretical legitimation for discrimination against non-Europeans. Notwithstanding the prejudices held by the Iberian Catholic powers against African and American indigenes and the legal disabilities enacted against them within their colonies, Catholic orthodoxy mitigated against them being viewed as subhuman; "whatever else might be said of non-Westerners, they were officially human beings and potentially Christians with full spiritual equality."[110] The official Catholic position that "African slaves were supposed to be baptized or at least exposed to some basic Catholic principles before they arrived in the Americas"[111] was a reflection of this principle. Their freedom, but not their humanity, was taken away and their maltreatment officially proscribed; Portuguese slavers who mistreated slaves could be, and sometimes were, reported and punished.[112]

Distinctions between Emergent Iberian and Anglo Racial Ideology

Protestant England was bound by no such restriction or ideology. Indeed, in England a belief in the inherent inferiority of a people, as exemplified by their uncivilized state, was growing. The position of the Catholic powers implies only a situational disability subject to legal or social modification, while the latter suggests a fundamental unalterable condition. England's seventeenth-century politico-religious subjugation of Catholic Ireland contributed to the strengthening of this idea. The strategies employed in their

---

109. Sweet, "Iberian Roots," 162. Sweet notes, "The crucial difference between Muslim and Portuguese variants of racial ideology was that Muslim racism was constantly subject to scrutiny by jurists and scholars. In addition, Islamic law prohibited the enslavement of other Muslims, including blacks."

110. Curtin, *British Ideas and Action*, 33.

111. M. Martínez, "Black Blood," 488. This is not, however, to suggest altruistic motives or adherence to Christian principles by the Spaniards and Portuguese. "Despite papal endorsement and a policy of conversion, the Catholic Church neglected the spiritual well-being of the Africans. Christianization of blacks was merely a convenient excuse for enslaving them" (Sweet, "Iberian Roots," 159).

112. Monrad, *Description of Guinea Coast*, 223.

conquest presaged what was to happen to the indigenous people of North America—the systematic attack on the ancient Irish social system, the forbidding of traditional songs and music, the extermination and brutalizing of whole clans[113]—though without the explicitly racial basis that would later come to characterize America colonization. These brutalizing tactics were not new; they had a long history of employment in the Crusades against both Islam, the external cultural threat to Christian civilization, and against heretical groups of Christians, the internal threat to that same civilization. The atrocities committed in the course of English domination of Ireland were based on the Christendom idea of "an elite . . . called to provide the lead and inspiration in its world, the moral force to dominate its society with a right to impose its will on the recalcitrant."[114] Yet in this case, the elite was not a Romanized military aristocracy participating in a Catholic, and by implication, a nonnational, multiethnic, Christendom, but English Protestants contending for a particular social order—a Christian church and society "cleansed of corruption."[115] Color did not enter into it; the Irish were as white as the English.[116]

The "persecuting impulse" demonstrated by the English was born from an enduring belief that the Irish were "a species of wild people"[117]— their supposed barbarity was evidence of their natural inferiority, and their inferiority the grounds of their suppression. The subjugation of the Irish people based on their alleged barbarity suggests a link between barbarism and ontological inferiority in the consciousness of the English people. As England expanded her overseas empire into North America, the inferiority ascribed to the white Catholic Irish was applied even more to the indigenes of North America and to Black Africans, both of whom were thought to live without "religion, government or even social structure."[118] The English

---

113. Dunbar-Ortiz, *Indigenous Peoples' History*, 38.

114. Markus, *Christianity in Roman World*, 166.

115. Horsman, *Race and Manifest Destiny*, 10.

116. Interestingly, despite the color difference, savagery among the Irish was later held to be evidence of their supposed African origins. See Jahoda, *Images of Savages*, 226–27.

117. Blackburn, "Old World Background," 76. Blackburn here refers to a view of the Irish dating from the early feudal period around the twelfth century, but Dunbar-Ortiz argues that "the Irish under British colonial rule, well into the twentieth century, continued to be regarded as biologically inferior" (*Indigenous Peoples' History*, 39). See also Horsman, *Race and Manifest Destiny*, 73, 141.

118. Marshall and Williams, *Great Map of Mankind*, 27.

experience in Ireland made it easier for them to consider any uncivilized people—that is, people living in any way different from the standards of Protestant English society—as inherently inferior.

Dunbar-Ortiz contends that Calvinism, the religious background of many of the settler colonialists in Ireland and later in the United States, provided the ideological basis for White supremacy because of its emphasis on election and on material prosperity as a sign of divine favor while misfortune and dark skin were evidence of damnation.[119] The suggestion that the distinctive Calvinist theologies of election and divine determinism was a contributory factor to the development of White supremacy in the United States is an interesting one, but it cannot fully account for other, nonreligious factors that contributed to this derogatory perspective on non-Western peoples. Having said that, it does appear that Protestantism, by breaking free from the bounds of Catholic orthodoxy and replacing the universal authority of the pope with the limited and national authority of the monarch, created an environment where religious concerns could more readily be subordinated to political or economic ones—slavery included. While both Catholic and Protestant powers participated in the slave trade and harbored racial prejudice, "in the lead-up to the formation of the United States, Protestantism uniquely refined white supremacy as part of a politico-religious ideology."[120]

The United States: White Christian Civilization Exemplified

Laying aside for now the issue of race, I return to the central theme of this chapter. By the time of the American Revolution, Christianity was thoroughly identified with European civilization and ideologies of conquest and compulsion. The subjugation of indigenous American and African peoples was widely regarded as the divinely appointed means by which these populations would be brought into the Christian fold.[121] The English colonization of North America began in earnest in the early seventeenth century and was supported by the same idea—Christian England civilizing and Christianizing the native.[122] Yet unlike the Spanish and Portuguese whose motives for colonization of the Americas were primarily inspired by

119. Dunbar-Ortiz, *Indigenous Peoples' History*, 48–49, 52.
120. Dunbar-Ortiz, *Indigenous Peoples' History*, 39.
121. G. Bediako, *Primal Religion*, 40.
122. G. Bediako, *Primal Religion*, 43.

the quest for wealth, with Christianity an ancillary concern, the propagation of Christian faith was a much more prominent motive for the English colonists who settled the eastern seaboard of North America.

Christianity as a Contributor to American Identity

The religious motivations of many of the immigrants to England's North American colonies are well known. The Calvinist Puritans "saw themselves as 'poor exiles of Christ' seeking refuge from persecution.... They came to New England to preserve their idea of pure first-century Christian worship and church order."[123] They sought to continue what they believed to be the uncompleted task of the English Reformation: "purifying church, society, and self"[124] in a new land "from which the renovation of the world would begin."[125] Maryland too was founded in order to "offer religious freedom to English Protestants and Roman Catholics," and to "serve as a rebuke to the religious wars tearing England apart,"[126] while Rhode Island was settled by religious refugees—"unorthodox Puritans exiled from Massachusetts Bay."[127] Even Virginia, though founded on a more explicitly commercial basis,[128] emphasized conversion of the native population in her propaganda.[129] In every case, the vast and supposedly empty American wilderness[130] provided the opportunity to begin anew, to inaugurate a perfected Christian civilization, possessed of "a unique national destiny and purpose," cleansed of all the corruptions of old Europe, and populated by "a special chosen people, a people destined to change the world for the better."[131] The ideal of Christendom, though perhaps not the exact form, was renewed along the American shore.

123. Keillor, *This Rebellious House*, 61.
124. M. Noll, *Rise of Evangelicalism*, 53.
125. Horsman, *Race and Manifest Destiny*, 83.
126. Jones, *Dreadful Deceit*, 8.
127. Keillor, *This Rebellious House*, 68.
128. Keillor, *This Rebellious House*, 49.
129. G. Bediako, *Primal Religion*, 43.

130. Dunbar-Ortiz identifies this idea as part of the "founding myth" of the United States: "the colonist acquired a vast expanse of land from a scattering of benighted peoples who were hardly using it—an unforgiving offense to the Puritan work ethic" (*Indigenous Peoples' History*, 46).

131. Horsman, *Race and Manifest Destiny*, 82.

By the late seventeenth century, the restlessness born of disenchantment with Puritan idealism and religious coercion gave way to a growing spirit of religious toleration. William Penn's colony set the pattern: "No group could claim official status; none could therefore apply coercive measures, and the American pattern of wide diversity within a framework of full toleration began to appear."[132] By the dawn of the eighteenth century, strands of English Puritanism, Continental Pietism, and high-church Anglicanism combined to fan the initial flames of an evangelical revival that would sweep first England and then her colonies in what is known as the First Great Awakening.[133] Even while religious revival was taking shape, another movement was also emerging that would exercise as great, if not greater, influence on the direction of the emerging American nation.

The Enlightenment Contribution to American Identity

European intellectuals, thrilled by the pace of scientific discovery and disenchanted with the claims of revealed religion, were turning decisively from divine revelation to human reason as the ultimate source of knowledge and as the basis upon which to organize society. It was a movement that "gradually dissolved the intellectual and religious patterns which had governed European thought since St Augustine."[134] Just as religious reformers saw America as an opportunity to begin anew, so too the educated elites who were to lead the American Revolution "saw a chance to break through the crust of tradition and establish a new social order consistent with the most Enlightened ideas."[135]

Unlike their Continental counterparts however, American Enlightenment thinkers were generally not anti-Christian in their views, though many were not orthodox in their religious beliefs. There was room within their Enlightenment vision of government for a broadly Christian understanding of society. Like the Puritans who preceded them, American intellectuals looked to antiquity for inspiration, but to classical Greece and Rome rather than to the primitive church. These two movements, one religious and marked by "an intensely emotional quality,"[136] and the other

132. Cragg, *Church and Age of Reason*, 179.
133. See M. Noll, *Rise of Evangelicalism*, 50–75; Keillor, *This Rebellious House*, 74–78.
134. Cragg, *Church and Age of Reason*, 234.
135. Keillor, *This Rebellious House*, 84.
136. Cragg, *Church and Age of Reason*, 184.

secular, rationalistic, and at points anti-Christian, would together lead to the development of a uniquely American civil religion—what Steven Keillor terms *political Protestantism*.[137] This civil religion linked "the enjoyment of British liberty and the proclamation of freedom in Christ to a republican analysis of the political world" and partly explains the active support by American Evangelicals for the American War of Independence.[138] Political Protestantism enabled the creation of an alliance between American Enlightenment thinkers and orthodox Christians to persist long enough to insure the successful founding of the United States.[139] The constitution produced by these men was republican in structure, and modelled on the ancient examples of Greek democracy and the Roman Republic.

Despite the lofty Enlightenment influenced language of the Declaration of Independence—all men are created equal and endowed by the Creator with inalienable rights—the US Constitution introduced into American political and social life an element of White supremacy; slavery was retained and citizenship restricted on the basis of race.[140] Its retention stood as a glaring contradiction to the principles of Enlightenment thinking embedded in the Declaration of Independence and to the Christian morality that animated the founders, but would eventually be justified on the basis of racial essentialism. The United States, though secular in its political arrangements, was broadly Christian in its ethos. The overwhelming majority of its citizens saw themselves as heirs of a Christian heritage and the United States as the bearer of Christian civilization. For many, Christians and non-Christians alike, it was the exemplar of Christian civilization, destined to spread the twin blessings of republican governance and Christian civilization across the continent.

Conclusions

I have in this chapter journeyed from the earliest origins of Christianity as a sect within Judaism and traced its path through gradual acceptance to state religion under the late Roman Empire. I have shown how the early

---

137. Keillor, *This Rebellious House*, 87.

138. M. Noll, *Rise of Evangelicalism*, 186.

139. Keillor, *This Rebellious House*, 87–89.

140. Douglas Sharp, citing Ian Lopez, notes that though the 1789 constitution does not specifically address citizenship, descendants of Africans were not enfranchised as citizens until the 1860s and American indigenes until 1924 (*No Partiality*, 77).

apologists paved the way for an association of Christian faith with the elite culture of Greco-Roman society and how this culture, disdainful of outsiders and of rural peasants, created the idea of Christianity as a cultural good associated with a particular kind of civilized life, one that was Roman in its essence. This cultural alliance eventuated in Christendom, as the church filled the vacuum left by the collapsing Western Roman Empire and how barbarian elites conquered Rome while simultaneously being assimilated into the culture of Christian Rome. Western Christendom found its apex in the Crusades, which brought Europe face to face with Islam, cutting European Christianity off from other expressions of faith and cementing the identity of Europe as the Christian continent. The failure to dislodge Islam from the Near East was the proximate cause of the European voyages of discovery that brought Europe into encounter with the wider world. It was this encounter, more than any other factor, which melded the notion of Christianity, European civilization, and race—a new element in the matrix of European self-understanding. I discussed briefly how race emerged as a key issue within the context of Europe's engagement with the wider world and how the ethos of forcible conversion found its way into that encounter. Finally, I examined the emergence of the United States, initially colonized by religious people in a quest to build a society upon Christian principles, but eventually founded upon a combination of Enlightenment ideas and Christian cultural values—the ultimate expression of White Christian civilization. It is from within this society that the enslaved Africans, torn from their homelands and forced to forge a new identity for themselves, came face to face with the Christian gospel. Many were converted and from these small seeds grew the tree that is Black American Christianity.

3

Euro-Western Interpretation of Black Peoples

THE ENCOUNTER BETWEEN EUROPE and the non-European world during the early modern period brought European peoples in contact with a vast number of peoples, societies, and religious practices previously unknown to them: peoples, societies, and practices far different than their own, and from those with which they were familiar. The conceptual maps of Europe had to be redrawn to accommodate and interpret this new information in a way that cohered with existing religious beliefs about the world and its peoples. Additionally, the rise of scientific rationalism in European society during the seventeenth and eighteenth centuries introduced new criteria by which non-European peoples could be understood and ultimately judged. Differences between fair-skinned, "civilized" Christian Europeans, and dark-skinned, "primitive" heathen Africans (and others) became worthy of investigation. It is within the context of this encounter that these descriptors—civilized, primitive, Christian, and heathen—acquired new definition and clarity as Europeans sought to make sense of the world around them. Efforts to understand this new world of information led to the eventual development of anthropology and religious studies, among other fields, as academic disciplines to be approached on a scientific basis. The idea of race, too, emerged through this process, as a means to categorize, evaluate, and ultimately rank human beings. At the earliest stages, however, no such scientific approach could be discerned. Much of what was asserted and propagated by European scholars was not based on empirical data but rested on long-standing prejudices and ideological assumptions that guided the selection and interpretation of their world. Black peoples and religious practices were seen and interpreted through the lens of deep-seated cultural, theological, and intellectual antecedents that it is the business of this chapter to explore.

African-European Encounter: Ancient Days

The European experience of African people did not begin with the transatlantic slave trade, but extends back into biblical times. The Old Testament world was a dynamic one that included many diverse peoples—Semites, Black Africans, and Indo-Europeans, among others—few of whom likely looked anything like the modern Whites whose images dominate popular media presentations.[1] Almost all of the Bible is set in Africa and Western Asia, with scant reference to Europe or European peoples, and interaction between the diverse peoples of Asia, Africa, and Europe was commonplace. In the Greco-Roman world of the New Testament, society was divided into two broad groupings: Greeks and barbarians, while the Jews added themselves as a third category.[2] Echoes of these distinctions are found in Gal 3:28—"there is neither Jew nor Greek, there is neither slave nor free, there is no male and female" (ESV). The primary basis upon which Greco-Roman society was divided was cultural and religious, not ethnic. "Greekness" was not an ethnic category as such, but rather a function of participation in a lingua-cultural elite, entered "via education and not birth,"[3] and was, as mentioned earlier, a means of distancing oneself from barbarism—anything that "did not belong to the sphere of Greek (or later, Roman) civilization."[4]

Nothing like the contemporary understanding of race or ethnicity existed at any time in biblical history. That was a later development. Black Africans were found among every rank and category of society, with many hailing from the kingdom of Meroë in Nubia, outside the boundaries of the Roman Empire and known to the Greeks as Ethiopia. *Ethiopia* itself was an expansive geographical category, encompassing all of what is now termed sub-Saharan Africa:.

1. Hays, *From Every People*, 45.
2. Hays, *From Every People*, 143, 145. See also Buell, *Why This New Race?*
3. Hays, *From Every People*, 143.
4. Markus, *Christianity in Roman World*, 44.

> The Roman world encountered Black Ethiopians as merchants and traders, soldiers, slaves, and former slaves who had become freedmen. Indeed Black Ethiopians appeared in Roman society at all levels: soldiers, slaves, freedmen, officials, nobles. . . . Blacks were continuously being assimilated into the genetic melting-pot of the Roman world.[5]

Within the boundaries of Rome were many other cultural groups with varying degrees of dark and black skin, spread across what is now North Africa.[6] These too were part of the sundry peoples that made up the Roman world. On the face of it, that Black people occupied diverse positions within the Greco-Roman world suggests color was not an obstacle to social advancement within society, or that color prejudice did not exist. This is, however, an overly simplistic assumption. One must look deeper to understand the origins of these deeply rooted European ideas and negative associations of the term "black."

Blackness in European Thought: Greco-Roman Antiquity

The presence of Black people within various strata of Greco-Roman society tells us nothing of the moral, aesthetic, or social meaning Greeks and Romans ascribed to skin color. It cannot be taken as given that any such meaning would be found; the search itself reflects contemporary assumptions that would appear alien to the Greeks and Romans. Indeed, contemporary "preconceptions about 'blacks' in predominantly 'white' societies have distorted modern visions of the ways in which [blacks] were perceived in Roman society."[7] Race simply did not exist as a concept in classical antiquity, hence in assessing attitudes about blackness one must avoid over-simplification and reading modern ideas into ancient societies. With this caveat in mind, the high regard for classical antiquity in Enlightenment and post-Enlightenment Europe and America makes knowledge of Greco-Roman views of Black and African peoples essential to understanding later developments in European interpretations of Black peoples and religion.

---

5. Hays, *From Every People*, 147, 148–49.
6. Hood, *Begrimed and Black*, 26.
7. Thompson, "Roman Perceptions of Blacks," abstract.

Greek Views of Black African People: The Exotic and Erotic "Other"

Greek accounts of African people, including the Egyptians, with whom they had direct interaction, and of the "Ethiopians" who lived beyond Egypt, vary. Homeric accounts of Ethiopians blend elements of mystery, legend, and myth. In Homer's stories, the myth of the noble savage appears in embryonic form, a recurrent motif in Euro-Western consciousness. Ethiopians are described as people living in a world "beyond the range of civilized Mediterranean life, untrammeled by the vices of Greek urban life . . . inhabit[ing] lands of bucolic abundance and fantastic profusion of natural resources" and "occupying a space where the human met the divine."[8] This idyllic vision was coupled with another, less picturesque one. These lands were also believed by the Greeks to be the abode of wild and monstrous races, notably the sexually depraved Garamantes, stories about whom circulated and influenced European ideas about Black people for centuries.[9] *The Histories* by Herodotus provides a somewhat more realistic account than Homer's, but still "perpetuat[es] [and] in fact enhanc[es], the representation of the Ethiopian as the noble savage."[10] Herodotus presents the Ethiopians as both "the tallest and the most beautiful of all men" and as exceptionally long-lived, "the greater number of them reach[ing] the age of a hundred and twenty years, and some surpass[ing] even this."[11] Yet alongside these laudatory remarks, Herodotus too sounds the theme of sexual depravity among dark-skinned people. He suggests that Indians, whom he likens to the Ethiopians, were animalistic in their sexuality and exhibited peculiar bodily traits:

> The sexual intercourse of all these Indians of whom I have spoken is open like that of cattle, and they have all one colour of skin, resembling that of the Ethiopians: moreover the seed which they emit is not white like that of other races, but black like their skin; and the Ethiopians also are similar in this respect.[12]

For Herodotus, dark skin overrode any other physical feature, and tied the otherwise culturally distinctive Indians and Ethiopians together.

---

8. A. Johnson, "Blackness of Ethiopians," 168.
9. Jahoda, *Images of Savages*, 30–31.
10. S. Johnson, "Blackness of Ethiopians," 169.
11. Herodotus, *Histories* 3.20, 3.23.
12. Herodotus, *Histories* 3.101.

Dark skin was the most notable feature of the Africans encountered by the Greeks. They sought to explain it by reference to the heat of the sun, which was believed to have scorched them, given to them bandy legs, dark eyes and curly hair.[13] These physical attributes differed from those of the Greeks—who considered themselves the normative somatic type—and thus required explanation. However, skin color was not only an external trait, but was considered indicative of inward qualities as well. Those from more northerly climes were similarly judged.[14] For example, some accounts consider Ethiopians as cowards, citing their dark skin and woolly hair as evidence.[15] Yet in others, dark skin was not associated with cowardice. Robert Hood notes that "among the Greeks the most memorable trait of the dark-skinned Ethiopians, Egyptians, and Colchians were their courage and skill as warriors. Hence, a dark complexion featured as a sign of courage and a warrior."[16] Early antiquity gives us no consistent view. Classical Greece "did not have a fixed developed aesthetic for abstract words like color," but employed "fluid paradigms for light and darkness [that] shaped an emerging aesthetic about whiteness and blackness in the West."[17] Light and darkness did not, however, take on the kind of oppositional qualities associated with combat between good and evil; this was a later development.[18] Generally, as dark-skinned peoples, Africans were described by the Greeks in ways that emphasized their exotic origins and supposed eroticism, though with little pejorative sentiment attached to these descriptions.

Roman Views of Black African People: Diverse Perspectives

The Romans, too, were fascinated with the dark skin color of the Africa as they had "assimilated Greek ethnocentric beliefs about the rest of the world"[19] yet substituted themselves in place of the Greeks as the ideal rulers of the world.[20] This had nothing to do, however, with their skin color or

13. Isaac, "Proto-Racism," 36.

14. "Northern peoples have grey eyes and this is explained by the influence of the temperature on the balance of moisture in the body" ("Proto-Racism," 36).

15. A. Johnson, "Blackness of Ethiopians," 169.

16. Hood, *Begrimed and Black*, 31–32.

17. Hood, *Begrimed and Black*, 30.

18. Hood, *Begrimed and Black*, 31.

19. Hood, *Begrimed and Black*, 31.

20. Isaac, "Proto-Racism," 36.

those of their subject nations, but with geographical location; Rome was in the "right place" on the map. The heterogeneity of the Roman Empire and the comparatively commonplace presence of dark and black-skinned Africans in Roman cities made them appear less exotic than they had in classical Greece. Consequently, one finds a variety of images of Black people:

> Some positive and others (the majority) negative . . . images of Aethiopes as sharp-witted and crafty southerners; or as "lustful, darkly mysterious and sexually fascinating" people; or as backward barbarians "addicted to horrid practices"; or (in the post-Severan era) as brothers of the militant Sudanese warriors and marauders who were then causing havoc on the southern frontier of Egypt; or as members of a far-distant, exotic, noble-natured and pious nation of which Homer had sung in praise; or, again as strangers with a natural tendency to evil who were also harbingers of bad luck and disaster.[21]

What emerges are disparate and situational depictions of Black people, none of which can be reasonably said to constitute a "type" in the Roman consciousness. But there was a growing association of Black people with eroticism and sexual prowess,[22] one that has continued to persist in Euro-Western thought through the centuries. However, black skin, though a remarkable feature, lacked any predominant moral association. Blackness had no particular social meaning, though it must be admitted that "a negative symbolism of the colour black . . . fed a superstitious belief that a chance meeting with a black stranger was an ominous presage of bad luck or disaster."[23] What emerges instead is the beginning of a fluid "mythic structure" of color consciousness that associated blackness with "curiosity, carnality, and negativity" and which would later be given "a moral category by Christians as they tried to make sense of biblical notions of sin and evil."[24]

Blackness in Early European Christian Thought

The formative years of Christianity within the Roman Empire saw the reconfiguration of existing Greco-Roman concepts of color in a way that

21. Thompson, "Roman Perceptions of Blacks," 3.
22. Hood, *Begrimed and Black*, 39–41.
23. Thompson, "Roman Perceptions of Blacks," 4.
24. Hood, *Begrimed and Black*, 43.

strengthened the negative association of darkness/blackness with sin/evil. This reconfiguration can be partially traced to the influence of Persian cosmology on Judaism during the Hellenistic period.[25] Persian Zoroastrianism embraced an essentially dualistic cosmology wherein equally powerful uncreated good and evil deities operate in active opposition to one another. Thus, plurality and diversity in the world were believed to be divergences from the ideal, realities that had emerged "only because of the existence . . . of evil divinity," Angra Mainyu, who stands in opposition to Ahura Mazdā, the divinity within whom "all divine goodness [is] comprehended."[26] The literature of Qumran, a Jewish ascetic sect, likewise emphasizes a cosmic struggle between the forces of light and the forces of darkness. This cosmic struggle, led by the devil, is seen in the opening lines of the War Scroll of Qumranic literature: "The first attack of the sons of light will be launched against the lot of the sons of darkness, against the army of Belial."[27]

Dualistic Spirituality and Emerging Color Associations

The dualistic perspective on spirituality expressed in these texts came to exercise a compelling pull on the Christian theological imagination, but, more importantly, placed darkness and light in stark opposition to one another and clearly associated darkness with the demonic: "the supreme adversary of God and his people is the devil"[28]—a devil that was increasingly personified as black. One finds the idea powerfully reflected in Athanasius's *Life of Antony*. In it, the devil is described as coming to Antony in the guise of a black boy, "taking a visible shape in accordance with the colour of his mind" and identifies himself as "the friend of whoredom . . . the spirit of lust."[29] Evil power and sexual immorality are conjoined and given expression through the body of a black boy, the incarnation of illicit sexuality and demonic depravity. The "spirit of lust" is embodied in the form of a black *boy*, which introduces a homoerotic element to the story and is suggestive of unrestrained sexuality. The black body emerges as the locus of an alluring, yet perverse and illicit, eroticism.

25. Hood, *Begrimed and Black*, 73.
26. Boyce, *Early Period*, 192.
27. 1QM I, in F. Martínez and Tigchelaar, *Dead Sea Scrolls*, 1:113.
28. Barrett, *New Testament Background*, 246.
29. Athanasius, *Life of Antony*, loc. 530509.

That Antony's demon took "visible shape in accordance with the colour of his mind" echoes an idea found in Greco-Roman society, namely that "blackness . . . does not appear 'natural,' either spiritually or physically,"[30] and therefore wants explanation. Black was seen as a deviation from what is normal or natural. This was not yet, a racialized notion, but the seedbed of later racist thought is clearly present. The writings of Origen are particularly significant in this regard, as he provides the most thorough engagement of any of the early Christian thinkers on the place of Blacks in the Scripture.[31] The majority of his commentary renders Blacks as nothing other than "symbols of sinful souls," because of their dark skin, and Ethiopia itself "a figure of demonic forces."[32] Little positive imagery is found there. Mark Scott's commentary on Origen confirms this and is worthy of quoting at length:

> Origen's exegesis of Song 1:6 evinces the most racially offensive material in his commentary, although he does not expressly disparage black skin. While expounding on the allegorical meaning of this verse, he parenthetically discusses the natural origin of physical blackness. He comments that "the Ethiopian race" became black through prolonged exposure to the intense rays of the sun. Originally, he tacitly argues, white Ethiopians became black, departing from their natural hue, only after being "scorched and darkened." Once darkened, the Ethiopians transmit their "congenital stain" to their progeny.[33] To classify blackness as a natural deformity rather than as an expression of divine creativity reveals a parochial view of blackness. In these deliberations Origen presupposes whiteness as the natural condition of humanity and blackness as an anomalous state that arises afterwards. These assumptions make black pigmentation an ailment that one must overcome, if one can invert the analogy to spiritual blackness to apply to physical blackness.[34]

Blackness is here construed as a congenital stain, a heritable trait, likened to sin, and in fact, indicative of it. One senses here the earliest intimations of blackness as a sign of divine disfavor or curse, an idea that would later find fuller expression in the curse of Ham myth. Though Scott seeks to downplay the derogatory nature of Origen's commentary, he is forced to

30. Scott, "Shades of Grace," 74.
31. A. Johnson, "Blackness of Ethiopians," 172.
32. A. Johnson, "Blackness of Ethiopians," 172, 175.
33. Scott here cites Origen, *Homilies on Jeremiah*.
34. Scott, "Shades of Grace," 79.

admit that his "symbolic associations between blackness and sin carry over to the physical realm and engender negative racial attitudes."[35]

Though Origen's derogatory interpretation of blackness is not the sole voice of Christian antiquity, it may be considered a representative one. His allegorical interpretation of biblical Ethiopians provided the scriptural support for already existing negative views of blackness and Black people in Greco-Roman antiquity and eventually came to "dominate [their] portrayal in Christian literature of the late antique period."[36] His analysis also served to enforce a binary color distinction between black and white wherein whiteness is the "counterpoint to all that is earthly physicality—that is, as all that is rational, enlightened, and spiritual—or of the mind,"[37] and is thus to be aspired to. Blackness is the opposite and is, therefore, to be escaped. As the classical period drew to a close, the association of blackness with the demonic, with sinful degradation, and with illicit eroticism, and the belief in black skin as a mark of depravity or an ill omen, had begun to be firmly etched in the consciousness of European Christendom.

Blackness in European Thought: Medieval and Early Modern Period

Throughout the Middle Ages and into the Early Modern period, blackness continued to be associated with both carnality and the demonic. Popular iconography pictured demons with black skin,[38] while children were frightened with the image of the devil portrayed with black skin.[39] In the visions of Saint Hildegaard of Bingen her womb is "invaded by little black demons" whose black skin is torn off by the Christ child who "disposes of [the skin] and then clothes them in white garments that open to them the serene light of Christ."[40] Beyond these, however, in largely preliterate medieval Christendom where few had access to the Bible and where oral and pictographic sources of information dominated,[41] was the curse of Ham myth—a myth that has proven to be exceptionally pernicious. This long-standing idea,

---

35. Scott, "Shades of Grace," 81.
36. A. Johnson, "Blackness of Ethiopians," 186.
37. Pfeifer, "Deconstructing Cartesian Dualisms," 529.
38. Hood, *Begrimed and Black*, 96.
39. Vaughan and Vaughan, "Before *Othello*," 28.
40. Hood, *Begrimed and Black*, 97.
41. Braude, "Sons of Noah," 106.

perhaps more than any other, lent theological legitimacy to the subjugation of Black people.

Emergence of the "Curse of Ham" Mythology

The curse of Ham myth is based on a passage in Gen 9:18–27 recounted here as follows:

> At the end of Genesis 9, Noah and his family are settling down after the flood. Noah plants a vineyard, drinks wine from the vineyard, becomes naked, and then lies uncovered in his tent (9:20–21). His son Ham, explicitly identified as "the father of Canaan" (9:22), sees his father's nakedness and then tells his two brothers Shem and Japheth. The two brothers take a garment (lit., "the" garment) back into the tent, and cover Noah without looking at him. When Noah awakes and finds out what his youngest son Ham had done to him (9:24), he pronounces a curse on Canaan, the youngest son of Ham (9:25), stating: Cursed be Canaan! The lowest of slaves will he be to his brothers."[42]

For medieval European Christendom, this passage "explained the inherited trait of enslavement"[43] and provided a justification for it. However, the identity of the cursed Canaan and his descendants was not initially or solely fixed upon Africans, of whom medieval Europeans had little knowledge and with whom they had even less direct contact. At different times the passage was used to justify the rule of one European tribe over another, or the right of aristocrats to dominate others.[44] Although the biblical genealogies of Gen 10 place some of the descendants of Ham within what is now called Africa, identifying Ham, Shem, Japheth and their respective offspring is less straightforward than the mythology surrounding the passage has assumed:

> Cush, the son of Ham, whom most, but by no means all, commentary has identified with Ethiopia, fathered a people who speak Semitic languages. Furthermore, Cush's son Nimrod . . . is located by almost all in the Asiatic and presumably Semitic stronghold of Mesopotamia. Many of the sons of Japhet, the so-called European, can be linked to Asia Minor and Central Asia. . . . Neat and

---

42. Hays, *From Every People*, 51.
43. Blackburn, "Old World Background," 91.
44. Blackburn, "Old World Background," 94.

clear-cut continental divisions among the three sons are not only completely alien to the biblical text, they are also incomprehensible to the ancient and medieval mind.[45]

Consequently, the territories ascribed to the descendants of each of Noah's sons varied significantly, and the curse associated with Ham was interpreted in diverse ways—as well as the peoples to whom the curse presumably applied.[46] Though the Bible provided medieval and early modern Christians an authoritative reference for belief in the common descent of all peoples from the three sons of Noah, the text itself provides no direct support for the permanent subjugation of African peoples that was to be later derived from it, or for the belief still held by some that Black people are cursed.[47]

It was the revival of slavery by Islamic slavers during the early modern period that led to an increasing association of slavery with Black people, and ultimately to the curse being identified exclusively with Black people. Some scholars have directly linked the revitalization of the myth in fourteenth century Europe to Islamic sources, even though the story of Noah recorded in the Qu'ran 11:25–49 omits the relevant portions from which the myth is derived.[48] Others have attempted to trace it to Jewish rabbinic traditions, but this idea is strongly contested.[49] Whatever its origins, the idea found ready ground in preexisting European association of blackness with sin and evil. Belief in the curse of Ham provided European Christians

45. Braude, "Sons of Noah," 108–9.
46. Braude, "Sons of Noah," 131–33.
47. The persistence of this myth is easily attested, but one distressing example is found in a recent book by popular Ghanaian pastor and evangelist Dag Heward-Mills. In his book *How to Pray* he writes, "The curse on Ham is a punishment on Ham, the dark son of Noah. This punishment explains the difficult conditions under which black people struggle all over the world. It is a curse that is played out in every continent on this world. Black people everywhere have the lowest levels of wealth, health, education and standards of living. It can be the only explanation for the state of the black man in every part of the world" (*How to Pray*, 28).
48. Sweet, "Iberian Roots," 149; see also Hood, *Begrimed and Black*, 155; Blackburn, "Old World Background," 92. Though the Qu'ran itself makes no mention of the story, it is clear from the literature that the curse of Ham was an established feature of Islam by the fifteenth century.
49. Frequent references are made in the literature to rabbinic texts as the source of the curse of Ham myth, but David Aaron contends that this is a misreading of the relevant texts, consequently, "the existence of a Hamitic Myth within Judaism has yet to be verified. . . . Christians . . . were not in need of midrashic parables on the descendants of Noah to find a theological justification for slavery" ("Early Rabbinic Exegesis," 752).

the requisite biblical sanction for holding Black people in perpetual slavery, contrary to prevailing norms of European slavery, which was dying. As the African slave trade expanded in the sixteenth and seventeenth centuries, so too did the frequency with which the myth was deployed.[50]

> Only with the growth of the slave trade and the increasing reliance on sub-Saharan Africa as a source for slaves did the curse's role as a justification for racial slavery eclipse its function as a scriptural explanation of either "blackness" in particular or servitude in general.[51]

By the time of the founding of the United States, and throughout the nineteenth and twentieth centuries, the myth was employed, often by clergymen, first as a defense for slavery and later as justification for the permanent subordination of Black people to Whites.[52]

The Emergence of a Unified Euro-Western Conceptual Framework

Taken together, negative European beliefs about blackness and Black peoples, including the pernicious curse of Ham myth, provide the cultural background against which new ideas about race and religion were developed and advanced in Enlightenment and post-Enlightenment Europe and America. Without existing cultural biases against Black peoples, the association of blackness with evil and sexual perversion, and the biblical curse of Ham, it is difficult to see how the ideological architecture of White supremacy could have been erected or sustained within the context of Christendom. Indeed, the theological constraints of Christendom delayed its establishment. While the curse of Ham myth may have assigned the descendants of Ham a subordinate position within the family of nations, they were still considered as fellow men, bearers of a common humanity and heirs to a common destiny. Though cultural and religious biases were present, they were insufficiently robust to overcome allegiance to biblical orthodoxy; they awaited the application of nonreligious, naturalist theories of humanity to blossom into a full-fledged racial ideology.[53] It was this ide-

---

50. Blackburn, "Old World Background," 95.
51. Haynes, *Noah's Curse*, 7.
52. Hays, *From Every People*, 52–54.
53. Augstein, *Race*, xxv.

ology, born from the alignment of scientific theories with existing cultural and religious prejudices, that ultimately placed Black people—designated as primitives—and primal religions at the bottom of a hierarchical evolutionary scale, while White people and Christianity were placed at the apex. Gillian M. Bediako has helpfully delineated three components of the Euro-Western conceptual framework under which primal peoples and religion were considered—cosmic, historical, and cultural. I here follow her designations, with one key modification in the area of culture to take into account dynamics unique to the American context.

The Cosmic Framework: The Great Chain of Being

The great chain of being had a "decisive influence in the seventeenth and eighteenth centuries on the European understanding of primal peoples."[54] It was, as Gustav Jahoda observes,

> a comprehensive hierarchical order, instituted by the Creator, in which the varieties of objects of creation are arranged in infinitely small gradations, from minerals via plants, animals and humans right up to the angels in increasing degrees of perfection. It embodied the "principle of continuity" which emphasized the inter-connectedness of all things . . . [and] it also embodied that of "plenitude," implying that there is no specifiable limit to the varieties of creation. Humans were regarded as occupying a middle position between the lower animals and the angels and other higher beings. It was seen as the task of scholars, and later also science, to discover the right slot into which any particular organism was to be inserted.[55]

The genesis of the idea can be traced to neo-Platonic Greek philosophy, later modified and taken up into Christian thought, primarily through the influence of Saint Augustine (354–430). Each of the constituent principles of the great chain of being—plenitude, continuity, and gradation[56]—had a profound influence on European interpretations of the peoples of the world. It was not a scientific theory as much as it was a unfalsifiable doctrine to which all kinds of evidence could be twisted to conform,[57] and yet it

---

54. G. Bediako, *Primal Religion*, 49.
55. Jahoda, *Images of Savages*, 32.
56. Lovejoy, *Great Chain of Being*, 52, 55, 59.
57. Jahoda, *Images of Savages*, 38.

provided "a satisfactory key for interpreting the universe as a whole and the diversity of phenomena within it,"[58]—in a manner which could, in principle, be harmonized with Christian thought and yet appeal to non-Christians as well. It attained its greatest influence in the eighteenth century, not because of any direct influence of Greek or medieval philosophy, which had fallen out of favor in any case, but due to the emphasis placed on it by Locke (1632–1704) and Leibniz (1646–1716) in the late seventeenth century.[59]

Plenitude

The principle of plenitude[60] carried within it the necessity of a fixed and hierarchical scheme. Just as "shadows were as needful to the Sun of the intellectual heavens as the Sun to the shadow,"[61] so too it was necessary that some occupy lower and some higher positions on the scale of being. Inherent too was an optimistic view of the universe satirized by Voltaire (1694–1778) in *Candide* that this is the best of all possible worlds, with evil itself a necessary constituent.[62] The compatibility of these ideas with the Calvinist theology of election—a theology that heavily influenced many of the settler colonialists in the United States as noted above—is not difficult to discern; divine determinism is directly deducible from it.[63] Compatible too was treatment of non-European people as inferior, as demonstrated in Edward Long's 1774 *History of Jamaica*.[64]

---

58. G. Bediako, *Primal Religion*, 49.
59. Lovejoy, *Great Chain of Being*, 183–84.
60. Lovejoy, *Great Chain of Being*, 51.
61. Lovejoy, *Great Chain of Being*, 52.
62. Lovejoy, *Great Chain of Being*, 64.

63. Nick Trakakis identifies the principle of plenitude as the "traditional" response to theodicy for the divine determinist ("Does Hard Determinism," 244).

64. Long divided man into three species: Europeans, Negroes, and "orang-outangs," with Africans arranged on an ascending scale with the Jagas of Angola at the bottom and the Wolof and the Ethiopians, presumably the high type of African man, on the top. He argued, "The system of man will seem more consistent, and the measure of it more complete, and analogous to the harmony and order that are visible in every other line of the world's stupendous fabric. Nor is this conclusion degrading to human nature, while it tends to exalt our idea of the infinite perfections of the Deity; for how vast is the difference between inert matter, and matter imbued with thought and reason" (Long, *History of Jamaica*, 2:371, quoted in Curtin, *British Ideas and Action*, 44–45).

Continuity

The principle of continuity, directly deducible from that of plenitude, held that "if there is between two given natural species a theoretically possible intermediate type, that type must be realized."[65] Scholars considered it their task to discover the right slot into which any particular organism was to be inserted, "to examine, classify, and arrange the whole order of nature in a rational pattern."[66] The "beastly" African[67] was readily conscripted as the missing link between man and animals. As more empirical approaches to the study of natural phenomena gained ground, information from travelers' accounts were pressed into service by biologists as evidence to support their preexisting ideas. In other words, "the eighteenth-century biologist began with a system"—in this case, the principle of continuity—"and used empiricism to make it as accurate as they could."[68]

Gradation

The third principle of gradation—"that all living things could be classified and fitted into a hierarchy"[69]—meant that human beings too could be ranged from the lowest to the highest type. As Gillian Bediako says, "It became not simply the lowest quality of man-in-general that approximated the highest in the animals, but specific groups of people, who formed the link."[70] Europeans did not, of course, question their own place within this hierarchical system. It was assumed that when God made man in his image, the image was that of the European man.[71] They presumed themselves to

---

65. Lovejoy, *Great Chain of Being*, 58.
66. Jahoda, *Images of Savages*, 32; Curtin, *British Ideas and Action*, 36.
67. Vaughan and Vaughan summarize the report of a 1564 voyage attributed to Robert Gainsh: "In '*Trodlogitica*' (according to ancient authors) the people inhabit caves or dens, eat serpents, and 'have no speache, but rather a grynnyng and chatteryng. There are also people without heades, called *Blemines*, havyng theyr eyes and mouth in theyr breste.' Africa houses satyrs, too, Gainsh told his readers, 'which have nothing of men but onely shape,' and in '*Ethiopia Interior*' are '*Anthropophagi* that are accustomed to mans fleshe'" ("Before *Othello*," 25; citing Richard Eden and Richard Willes, *The History of Travayle in the West and East Indies, and Other Countreys Lying Either Way*).
68. Curtin, *British Ideas and Action*, 36.
69. Curtin, *British Ideas and Action*, 37.
70. G. Bediako, *Primal Religion*, 52.
71. Curtin, *British Ideas and Action*, 41.

be the normative type against which all other peoples, degraded from the original stock, were to be measured; European man was the measure of all things. All other 'types" were believed to fill the gap between themselves and the apes. Mankind could therefore be subdivided "between civilised and savage, 'polished' and 'monstrous,'" without breaking the principle of continuity.[72] Much later, the various European "races" would be subjected to a similar scrutiny wherein people of Anglo-Saxon blood—the English and their American descendants—deemed themselves innately superior to other European groups.[73] For now, however, it was enough to demonstrate that Whites sat at the apex of humanity while Blacks occupied the lowest place.

The classificatory scheme of Carl Linnaeus (1707–78) was perhaps the most influential of efforts to categorize human beings in line within the framework of the great chain of being, but also represents a watershed in its intellectual influence. Linnaeus's scheme was a "monstrously confused" effort to classify man that included mythical creatures like the "Wild Man" of the woods alongside subcategories of humans like American, European, Asian, and African.[74] The criteria he used were challenged as arbitrary, while his grouping of men with apes in the same order "relinquish[ed] man's special station within creation,"[75] and thus fell afoul of more pious critics. Linnaeus's classification disclosed the great chain of being as primarily a creedal framework under which creation could be examined and classified, yet one that was not falsifiable and therefore not truly scientific.[76] In addition, the rigid hierarchy of the system left no real prospect for hope or for the amelioration of evil in the present world. Evil was, as we have seen, considered necessary to the perfection of the whole cosmic system. Furthermore, evidence gathered by empirical observation increasingly contradicted the principle of continuity. The great chain was breaking. Johann Friedrich Blumenbach (1752–1840), considered the founder of

---

72. Marshall and Williams, *Great Map of Mankind*, 215; G. Bediako, *Primal Religion*, 52.

73. By the mid-nineteenth century, "in Western Europe and America the Caucasian race became generally recognized as the race clearly superior to all others; the Germanic was recognized as the most talented branch of the Caucasians; and the Anglo-Saxons, in England and the United States, and often even in Germany, were recognized as the most gifted descendants of the Germans" (Horsman, *Race and Manifest Destiny*, 43–44).

74. Jahoda, *Images of Savages*, 41.

75. Augstein, *Race*, xii.

76. Jahoda, *Images of Savages*, 38.

physical anthropology, had scant regard for it, or for Linnaeus's classifications, and instead relied on the empirical studies he pioneered to categorize racial groups.[77] By 1799, Charles White's essay "An Account of the Regular Gradation in Man and in Different Animals and Vegetables," an essay that employed the great chain as its operative theory, was being met not with approbation, but with disdain.[78] In the face of these challenges, the chain of being was temporalized, yet in its essence remained a key component of European cosmology.[79]

The Transmutation of the Great Chain

The transmutation of the chain of being "into a historical, developmental and evolutionary series"[80] was a consequence of the implications of its own claims to comprehensiveness. The preservation of the principle of continuity in the face of observable discontinuities led to the idea that all things must be assumed to "have some degree or measure of any quality which is possessed by anything," with the implication that there must be a prototype from which all things developed.[81] An evolutionary progression from the imperfect to the perfect was a necessary implication of the temporalization of the great chain of being. The evolutionary idea could readily be applied to human beings and human society as well and, when applied, would provide a compelling explanation for the vast array of different people and societies and their supposedly primitive condition as compared to that of European civilization. The "racialization" of the chain of being that eventually led to the burgeoning of race theories later in the nineteenth century is clearly anticipated.[82]

The Historical Framework: Four Stages Theory

The same latent evolutionary ideology present in the great chain was evident in other areas of human inquiry. The chain of development from lower to higher species seen in biology was presumably mirrored in human societies

77. Jahoda, *Images of Savages*, 64.
78. Anonymous, "On Charles White's *Account*."
79. Lovejoy, *Great Chain of Being*, 242–87.
80. G. Bediako, *Primal Religion*, 53.
81. Lovejoy, *Great Chain of Being*, 276–77.
82. Jahoda, *Images of Savages*, 54.

as well. Mankind could thus be expected to live in a variety of states, from the original primeval setting up to civilized European society, which was presumably the apex of human culture.[83] In this schema, non-European peoples represented an earlier stage of development of society. "Savage" societies were envisioned as a kind of living museum in which European people could figuratively travel backwards in time and observe the earliest stages of human social organization, to see their own forebears mirrored in the present. The native inhabitants of America were especially subject to this kind of treatment.[84] Thinkers like Rousseau (1712–78) saw in them a manifestation of the ideal state of liberty, people living in "the golden age of individual liberty and happiness . . . as yet unfettered by formal laws and government . . . no private property, no division of land or wealth."[85] The supposed innocence and liberty of primitive man stood in favorable contrast to the decadence and tyranny of the European. This was the revival of the utopian ideal of the noble savage in the American woods.[86]

Concurrently, another thesis was emerging which was to have significant influence on subsequent anthropological thought: the four stages theory. This theory was most coherently articulated by Adam Smith (1723–90) in his Glasgow lectures of 1762–63. Smith posited four stages through which mankind passes, each building on the other in succession. The idea that societies progressed through stages based on modes of economic production meant that each stage was in fact an advance on the previous one—a view counter to the "primitivist appeal to the virtues of the simple life" espoused by Rousseau.[87]

There were, however, inconsistencies in the application of the theory—inconsistencies that always rebounded to the detriment of non-European, and especially African, people. For example, European ideas of property—seen as essential to progress—and commercial manufacture, were directly tied to progression through the various stages. The lack of these, as among the indigenes of North America, was taken to be an indication of their social immaturity.[88] However, the societies of Asia, so clearly well cultivated,

---

83. G. Bediako, *Primal Religion*, 54.

84. Marshall and Williams, *Great Map of Mankind*, 191.

85. Marshall and Williams, *Great Map of Mankind*, 213.

86. Sinclair, *Savage*, 64–9c; see also Curtin, *British Ideas and Action*, 48–51; Jahoda, *Images of Savages*, 49–50.

87. Marshall and Williams, *Great Map of Mankind*, 214.

88. Marshall and Williams, *Great Map of Mankind*, 215.

with advanced arts and manufactures, clearly fit the fourth stage, yet they too were not considered to be on the same level as European societies. Smith considered them to be atrophied and stagnant.[89] On the other hand, African societies, whose highly developed agriculture should have placed them *above* the indigenous peoples of America on Smith's scale, were still generally considered to occupy the lowest place.[90]

Despite these glaring inconsistencies, "the scale of economic and social development seemed to provide tangible criteria for measuring the hitherto rather vaguely defined categories of 'savage,' 'barbarous' and 'civilized,' and to reinforce scientifically value judgements already held on other grounds."[91] The four stages theory offered a progressive, though paternalistic, alternative to the static determinism implied in the great chain of being. If non-European societies were primitive and reflective of an early stage of social development, there was, at least, hope for their eventual progress to European levels of civilization. Consequently a "largely benevolently tolerant view of savages" prevailed throughout much of the eighteenth century.[92] However, this progressive vision, already dim, was further tempered by theories of climate and by the polygenetic/monogenetic debate among scholars, both of which hampered prospects for any improvement; neither climatic nor genetic factors were subject to human intervention. These ideas contributed to the later development of scientific racism.

Environmentalism and Human Diversity

From ancient times, climatic conditions had been held to be influential in the development of human diversity. Climatic conditions were believed to influence the development of human societies as well. Those people fortunate enough to live in the "right" conditions—that is, those Europeans living in the latitudes between Rome and Paris[93]—would consequently attain the highest levels of physical and social perfection. Comte de Buffon's environmental theories were widely admired and influential, as they provided an explanation of human diversity that upheld European supremacy without running afoul of unorthodox polygeneticist claims, that is, the

89. Marshall and Williams, *Great Map of Mankind*, 147, 149.
90. Marshall and Williams, *Great Map of Mankind*, 247.
91. G. Bediako, *Primal Religion*, 57.
92. Jahoda, *Images of Savages*, 49.
93. Marshall and Williams, *Great Map of Mankind*, 246.

claim that different human populations have different origins. "In his view, the human mind and physicality were a result of environmental influences: a savage tribe transported to Europe and fed on European food would gradually become not only civilized, but white,"[94] that is, they would revert to their original prototypical form, the European somatic type. However, despite Buffon's own allegiance to monogeneticism (a single origin for all human groups), his work in comparative anatomy opened the door to polygeneticist arguments by demonstrating the similarity in physical structure between animals, especially men and apes.[95] Most environmental theorists like Buffon remained within the framework of monogeneticism and thus, within the bounds of broad Christian orthodoxy. Others, however, were not so constrained.

Monogeneticism vs. Polygeneticism

Those scholars willing to risk unorthodox claims went further, however, and posited that Africans and Europeans were so distinctive in their physiognomy and innate characteristics as to belong to different species with different origins. David Hume (1711–76), for example, rejected the environmental hypothesis altogether, famously stating:

> I am apt to suspect the Negroes to be naturally inferior to the whites. There scarcely ever was a civilized nation of that complexion, nor even any individual eminent either in action or speculation. No ingenious manufactures amongst them, no arts, no sciences. . . . *Such a uniform and constant difference could not happen, in so many countries and ages, if nature had not made an original distinction between these breeds of men.*[96]

Hume's assertion was fully concordant with the emerging nonreligious temper of the European philosophes who were unconcerned with adherence to Christian orthodoxy. His statement linked race and culture, color and achievement in a causal relationship, with reference neither to God nor biblical revelation. Lord Kames's polygenetic theory, on the other hand, included environmental factors. He held that "as there are different climates, so there are different species of men fitted for these different

---

94. Augstein, *Race*, xv.
95. Curtin, *British Ideas and Action*, 42.
96. Hume, *Essays Moral, Political, Literary*, "Essay 21: Of National Characters," n10; emphasis added.

climates."⁹⁷ It was, however, Edward Long's *History of Jamaica*, published the same year as Kames's *Sketches of the History of Man* (1774), which lent the greatest evidential support to the polygeneticist cause.

Edward Long's residence in Jamaica lent an aura of scientific credibility to his work, as it was supposedly backed by direct observation of enslaved Blacks in Jamaica. His language, crude and abusive, reduced Blacks to the status of animals and he opposed those who argued that Africa was simply in an earlier stage of development, insisting instead that Blacks' supposed genius, "consists alone in trick and cunning, enabling them, like monkeys and apes, to be thievish and mischievous, with a particular dexterity. They seem unable to combine ideas, or pursue a chain of reasoning."⁹⁸ Consequently, their societies could not ever be expected to develop, and the discipline of slavery was necessary to prevent their reversion to utter barbarity. Drawing on beliefs going back to antiquity of the sexual perversity of Blacks, Long suggested that "amorous relationship between [orang-utans and Negroes] may be frequent ... it is certain, that both races agree perfectly well in lasciviousness of disposition."⁹⁹ In another pamphlet, he states, "the lower class of women in *England*, are remarkably fond of blacks, for reasons too brutal to mention"¹⁰⁰—which reasons were the larger genitalia of Black men and the physiologically unexplained greater sexual desirability of Black women.¹⁰¹ One is struck by the constancy of this particular theme in European thought.

Long's polygeneticism was too radical for an age when the dominant assumption remained that all men, of whatever color, were created in God's image and endowed with reason. Yet although most were unwilling to follow his polygenetic thesis, his writing gave expression to existing European xenophobia by cloaking it in scientific garb. It consequently became accepted as a standard work on Jamaica, the largest and wealthiest of Britain's

---

97. Home, "Preliminary Discourse," 18.

98. Long, *History of Jamaica*, 2:377, quoted in Jahoda, *Images of Savages*, 55.

99. Long, *History of Jamaica*, 2:370, quoted in Jahoda, *Images of Savages*, 56.

100. *Candid Reflection upon the Judgement Lately Awarded by the Court of King's Bench in Westminster-Hall, on What Is Commonly Called the Negroe-Cause by a Planter*, quoted in Curtin, *British Ideas and Action*, 46; emphasis original. See also Jahoda, *Images of Savages*, 56, who extends the quote thus: "They would connect themselves with horses and asses, if the laws permitted them." Thus, Long directly equates interracial sex with bestiality.

101. Curtin, *British Ideas and Action*, 47.

West Indian colonies.[102] Not only that, but the 1788 publication of parts of his *History of Jamaica* in the United States provided "a set of ready-made arguments for any publicist who wanted to prove the 'fact' of African inferiority."[103] His work anticipated, and helped lay the groundwork for, the scientific racism that would soon come to dominate Euro-Western discourse on non-White peoples.

The dissonance between British willingness to believe the most outlandish statements about African people in Africa or in the colonies, and their experience of the many black servants, both slave and free, within Britain itself, is remarkable. Long's imprecations against racial intermixture among the "lower classes" were no doubt based on their frequent occurrence. That the estimated fifty thousand Africans resident in England during the eighteenth century apparently assimilated and disappeared into the white population, without being segregated into ghettos, bears this out.[104] Despite this, the image of Blacks was shaped "by accounts of his existence in Africa," or in Long's case, Jamaica, "and remained undisturbed by the evidence of men's own eyes of the black presence in England."[105] The lengths to which European thinkers were willing to go "to justify the mistreatment of Africans as animals and savages" demonstrates how readily its "philosophy [became] the whiting on the sepulchre of bad behaviour."[106]

The Cultural Framework: Eurocentric White Supremacy

Culture is the last and most important component of the Euro-Western conceptual framework for it underlay both the cosmic and historical aspects already described. Bediako labels this aspect Eurocentrism, which she defines as a "cast of mind which, when exposed to other peoples and their world-views, presumed European superiority and responded with a comprehensive effort to subdue all new phenomenon under existing European frames of reference in order to reinforce them."[107] Eurocentrism pervaded the overall conceptual framework of European peoples, influencing both what they saw and how they interpreted it: the place of Europeans in the

---

102. Marshall and Williams, *Great Map of Mankind*, 250.
103. Curtin, *British Ideas and Action*, 45.
104. Sinclair, *Savage*, 83.
105. Marshall and Williams, *Great Map of Mankind*, 34.
106. Sinclair, *Savage*, 82.
107. G. Bediako, *Primal Religion*, 58.

great chain of being (at the top), the place of European societies in the four stages of history (the highest), and the optimal environmental conditions for the development of culture and civilization (Europe).[108] In every way Eurocentrism served as the operative cultural lens through which Europeans perceived and interpreted the new and overwhelming diversity to which they were exposed.

Eurocentrism helps explain the assumptions underlying the Euro-Western worldview in this period. However, Eurocentrism alone fails to adequately capture the uniquely American aspects of Euro-Western thought that emerged from the encounter between European and non-European people. One must go a step further to acknowledge not only an amplified ethnocentrism—something of which all ethno-cultural groups may conceivably be found guilty—but an emerging racialist ideology, White supremacy.[109] The need for such an ideology rested on several factors. First, unlike in Europe, Europeans in America coexisted with a large resident population of enslaved Africans who had been imported expressly for commercial purposes as slaves. For example, by the mid-eighteenth century Blacks comprised fully 20 percent of the population of the thirteen American colonies that became the United States.[110] An even higher percentage is recorded in the West Indies and more Africans than Europeans entered the Americas overall in the period before the 1830s.[111] Second, by the close of the eighteenth century, the labor of the millions of enslaved Africans forcibly transplanted to the Americas had become integral to the burgeoning global capitalist economy. The first centers of industrialization in England depended in large part on the slave trading port city of Liverpool.[112] "The slave trade not only was profitable in itself, but gave rise to numerous industries in Great Britain and other countries," including

108. G. Bediako, *Primal Religion*, 58–61.

109. By *racialist* I mean the reification of race as a primary and essential category of being. This is in distinction to *racism*, which ascribes value and significance to differences, real or perceived, between people groups, and enshrines and enforces such distinctions via law, custom, economic practices, and cultural norms of behavior.

110. U.S. Department of Commerce, *Historical Statistics of the United States*, as cited in Conniff and Davis, *Africans in the Americas*, 126.

111. "Indeed, in every year from about the mid-sixteenth century to 1831, more Africans than Europeans quite likely came to the Americas, and not until the second wave of mass migration began in the 1880s did the sum of net European immigration start to match and then exceed the cumulative influx from Africa" (Eltis, "Free and Coerced Transatlantic Migrations," 255).

112. Rodney, "How Europe Became Dominant," 7.

finance.¹¹³ Lloyd's of London and Barclays Bank are but two examples, as both got their start as financial powerhouses on the profits of slave trading.¹¹⁴ In the United States early industrialization and capital accumulation were built on both the slave trade and on slave-produced cotton.¹¹⁵ Foreign trade was, in fact, the cornerstone of American economic development until the mid-nineteenth century, and slavery was pivotal to that trade.¹¹⁶ Third, and perhaps most consequentially, there was in America an absence of strong cultural institutions to mediate relationships, both economic and personal, between enslaved Blacks and their White masters:

> Traditional guaranties of order had become superfluous. Its religion was so dynamic that it needed no church; its wealth and opportunity were so boundless that a center of financial power could lose its meaning; and in its need for politicians and lawyers by the thousands it could do without a governing class and ignore many an ancient tradition of bench and bar. Thus for the American of that day [the early nineteenth century] it was the very success of his society—of capitalism, of religious liberalism and political democracy—that made it unnecessary for him to be concerned with institutions.¹¹⁷

This last factor is key to understanding the larger picture of Euro-Western interpretation of Black peoples and the cultural architecture of White supremacy in the United States. It therefore requires some exploration before returning to the central theme.

Formative Factors of American Expression of Eurocentric White Supremacy: Protestantism and Ecclesial Fragmentation

I mentioned before that Protestantism, by replacing the universal authority of the pope with the limited and national authority of the monarch, created an environment where religious concerns, such as those around slavery, could more readily be subordinated to political or economic ones. The fragmentation of Christendom freed Protestant monarchs from the constraints of papal authority and greatly minimized any loss of political legitimacy for

---

113. Tannenbaum, *Slave and Citizen*, locs. 213–14.
114. Rodney, "How Europe Became Dominant," 8.
115. R. Bailey, "Slave(ry) Trade," 375.
116. Rodney, "How Europe Became Dominant," 9; see also Inikori, "Slave Trade," 295.
117. Elkins, *Slavery*, locs. 250–54.

disregarding the censure of the church. This fragmentation was even greater in the United States which had in its founding disestablished the church: "No group could claim official status; none could therefore apply coercive measures."[118] Though the evangelical revivalists of the late eighteenth century in the United States often spoke out against slavery and in favor of abolition, the voluntarist nature of Evangelicalism itself mitigated against manumission—"when evangelical voluntarism took the place of earlier coercive establishmentarian Protestantism . . . the possibility of using undemocratic coercion to do what 'the people' could or would not choose to do for themselves" was also lost.[119] Slaveholders did not fear expulsion from religious bodies due to their slave holding, nor could churches effectively enforce exhortations against slavery. As an institution, the church in the United States was politically impotent in the face of slavery.

Formative Factors of American Expression of Eurocentric White Supremacy: Republican Governance

What Protestantism did to the authority of the church, republican governance did to the authority of the American state. The founders of the United States cast off the authority of the British crown and substituted democratic republicanism based on the models of classical Greece and Rome. Yet the structure and ethos of the American political system was based on a constitution that not only recognized slavery's persistence, but also "created a defiantly independent citizen suspicious of authority and protective of individual rights, including the right to hold slaves."[120] Counterintuitively, the republican political structure of the US Constitution led to a system that was conservative and resistant to change. Political reform of the slave-based US economy was therefore nearly impossible after its ratification. Other, less republican regimes ended slavery peacefully. Aristocratic monarchical Britain ended slavery peacefully in the West Indies in 1833.[121] Although it took imperial Brazil until 1888 to fully abolish slavery, by the 1860s, when more than 90 percent of the total Black population of the American slave states were still enslaved, "in Brazil at the same time, more than half were already free, and the proportion of free to slave, which had been steadily

---

118. Cragg, *Church and Age of Reason*, 179.
119. M. Noll, *Rise of Evangelicalism*, 255.
120. Keillor, *This Rebellious House*, 131.
121. Keillor, *This Rebellious House*, 129.

rising since the eighteenth century, would continue to do so over the ensuing 28 years."¹²² On the contrary, slavery was ended in the United States only by the violence of the Civil War at the cost of 620,000 lives.¹²³ These all demonstrate the comparative weakness of US political institutions on the issue of slavery.

Formative Factors of American Expression of Eurocentric White Supremacy: Deficiencies in Legal Frameworks

Unlike the Catholic Iberian powers that regulated slavery within an existing framework of Christian doctrine and law, England and the United States had no such framework. In Iberian legal tradition "the slave had a body of law, protective of him as a human being, which was already there when the Negro arrived and had been elaborated long before he came upon the scene."¹²⁴ The personality of the enslaved person was legally distinct from his status as a slave and the difference between the slave and the free man was accidental not ontological.¹²⁵ He had certain rights, protected by law and backed by church and social custom.¹²⁶ In contrast, the identity of Blacks in North America very early became so thoroughly associated with slavery that even the terms "Negro" or "black" came to mean slave.¹²⁷ "Because the Negroes were brought in as slaves, the black color raised the

---

122. Elkins, *Slavery*, locs. 3084–85.
123. Keillor, *This Rebellious House*, 129.
124. Tannenbaum, *Slave and Citizen*, locs. 506–7.
125. "The slave, as a human being, is derived from the same source, and will finally come to the same end, as other men. The distinction between slavery and freedom is a product of accident and misfortune, and the free man might have been a slave" (Tannenbaum, *Slave and Citizen*, loc. 481).
126. "In effect, slavery [in Latin America] under both law and custom had, for all practical purposes, become a contractual arrangement between the master and his bondsman. There may have been no written contract between the two parties, but the state behaved, in effect, as if such a contract did exist, and used its powers to enforce it. This presumed contract was of a strictly limited liability on the part of the slave, and the state, by employing the officially provided protector of slaves, could and did define the financial obligation of the slave to his master in each specific instance as it arose. Slavery had thus from a very early date, at least in so far as the practice was concerned, moved from a 'status,' or 'caste,' 'by law of nature,' or because of 'innate inferiority,' or because of the 'just judgment and provision of holy script,' to become a mere matter of an available sum of money for redemption." (Tannenbaum, *Slave and Citizen*, locs. 577–83).
127. Jones, *Dreadful Deceit*, 44.

presumption of slavery ... in many states this presumption was enunciated by statute, putting on [Blacks] the onus of proving that they were free."[128] The combination of these factors meant that relationships between Blacks and Whites in the United States were based on the Black person being enslaved, potentially enslaved, or formerly enslaved. He thus had no identity independent of the institution of slavery, which cast its shadow on enslaved and free, Black and White alike. The inferiority of Blacks was dictated by economic necessity and presumed by law and custom, while Black personhood was entirely negated.

The high population of Blacks in the United States as compared to Europe, the embeddedness of slavery in the global economic system generally and the US economy specifically, and the absence of mediatory cultural or customary institutions within the United States made issues of intercultural interaction between Blacks and White a practical economic and political matter, rather than the largely theoretical concern it was in Europe. This eventuated in the erection of an ideological architecture that could both explain and sustain the permanent sociopolitical subordination of Black people. Accordingly, White supremacy, the sociocultural, political, and economic dominance of White people over others, especially Blacks, became the operative cultural and institutional framework of Black-White relations within the United States. This racialist ideology—Eurocentric White supremacy—functioned as both an interpretative lens through which Black people were assessed, and a hegemonic system under which they were forced to live. This ideological system is especially important to keep in mind when it comes to the development of Black American Christianity.

Race and Religion

The broader Euro-Western perception and response to primal religion is considered elsewhere. In general terms, the demarcation between Euro-Western perceptions of primal peoples and their perceptions of primal religion is a somewhat artificial one. These were considered together—"primitive religion merely illustrated and confirmed the primitive mentality that expressed itself in, and explained the 'low' and 'savage' state of culture."[129] Though I consider Black American Christianity to be an expression of the primal imagination, and a species of African Christianity, its

---

128. Tannenbaum, *Slave and Citizen*, locs. 716–17.
129. G. Bediako, *Primal Religion*, 63–64.

origination *within* the larger framework of American Christianity requires a somewhat different treatment than the primal religions of Africa, Asia, or the non-European world more broadly. This is not to suggest anything about the nature of Black American religious experience itself, nor does it refer to either the persistence or elimination of African primal elements within Black American Christianity. I refer only to its development in the context of history, a story that will be taken up in detail in another chapter. My concern here, however, is the link between the emerging racialist ideology of Eurocentric White supremacy, and Euro-Western Christian interpretation of religious phenomena. This relationship is critical to understand, as the racialist pattern of interpretation informed and continues to influence responses to Black religion generally and Black American Christianity specifically. One need only recall Hurston's assertion "that the Negro has not been christianized as extensively as is generally believed. The great masses are still standing before their pagan altars and calling old gods by a new name,"[130] to discern a view of Christianity as a product of civilized Euro-Western culture against whose norms Black American Christian expression fell short.

Co-opted Christianity

Christianity did not stand apart from the sociocultural order of Euro-Western societies but was imbedded and institutionalized in them. It is therefore inaccurate to assert that Christianity per se was the *cause* of the racialist system that developed within those societies. It is more accurate to say that Christianity was conscripted in support of it.[131] I have noted above the "process of discerning Christian identity"[132] along ethnic and aesthetic lines that begin during the European journeys of exploration and continued throughout the colonial period. This process, wherein "Europeans reconfigured Christian social space around white and black bodies,"[133] was a theological one, and was part of the entire reconfiguration of Euro-Western civilizational thought in consequence of the encounter with non-European lands and peoples. The epistemological limits of existing European Christian theology had been reached, and indeed breached by

---

130. Hurston, *Sanctified Church*, 103.
131. Sharp, *No Partiality*, 164–65.
132. Jennings, *Christian Imagination*, loc. 758.
133. Jennings, *Christian Imagination*, loc. 758.

this encounter,¹³⁴ resulting in the need for a reconfiguration of that theology. This reconfiguration proceeded along racialist lines:

> Theology . . . [became] the trigger for the classificatory subjugation of all nonwhite, non-Western peoples. But that classificatory subjugation began simply as the reassertion of a doctrinal logic—that God created the world.¹³⁵

Many, perhaps most, Christians readily embraced the racialist consensus of the day, validated it in scriptural terms, and vigorously defended it as being divinely prescribed. Inasmuch as Europe was "Christian" so too the racialist systems developed in Euro-Western societies were also expressed in Christian terms, given Christian justifications, and supported by Christian churches.

Importantly for those nations dominated by Protestantism, the Bible was claimed to have ordained a particular pattern of racial supremacy and subordination. In these nations, the Bible was increasingly presented and perceived as "foundational to civilization . . . as culture-constituting,"¹³⁶ with culture here understood not in the anthropological sense, but as "nam[ing] that essential core of a nation unaffected by material and mechanical progress . . . comprehend[ing] all of the virtues that were hidden inside the national mind."¹³⁷ Slavery and Black subordination were seen by their defenders as inextricably linked to biblical authority. Eurocentric White supremacy was intertwined with the post-Enlightenment defense of biblical authority. To reject it would be "an implied rejection of the authority of Christian revelation."¹³⁸ The lengths to which scholars were willing to go to substantiate the claim of racial supremacy and subordination were extensive. Race-based slavery, for example, was supposed to not only be described in the Bible, but was attributed to divine decree:

> Thornton Stringfellow, a Baptist minister in Culpeper County, Virginia, claimed, on a careful reading of Genesis, that God himself was the begetter of slavery. . . . This [Gen 9:25–27] led Stringfellow to wonder, indeed, whether it might "not be said in truth, that God decreed this institution before it existed; and has he not connected

---

134. Jennings, *Christian Imagination*, loc. 2046.
135. Jennings, *Christian Imagination*, locs. 1968–70.
136. Jennings, *Christian Imagination*, loc. 3025.
137. Sheehan, *Enlightenment Bible*, 253.
138. Kidd, *Forging of Races*, 143.

its existence with prophetic tokens of special favour, to those who should be slave owners or masters?"[139]

Stringfellow's reading of Gen 9 is but one example of the kinds of scriptural exegesis deployed in support of these assertions and was, by no means, exceptional. Noah's curse in Gen 9 played a "central role . . . in the antebellum proslavery arguments."[140] Pro-slavery apologists held that, as putative descendants of the biblical Ham, "literal slavery [was] necessary to prescribe and enforce temperance among [Blacks], to restrain them, and to restore them to reason and order,"[141] or stated differently, to civilize them— an argument we have met before in Edward Long's treatment of slavery in Jamaica.[142] Biblical arguments in support of Euro-Western White supremacy persisted into the postbellum period as well, as typified in the thinking of clergyman and scholar, Benjamin Palmer, considered by Haynes to be "the "founding father" of the Southern Presbyterian Church.[143] Before and during the Civil War, Palmer wielded the Bible to "remind Southerners that the preservation of slavery was a divine trust,"[144] and in the aftermath of defeat, to support racial separation as a means of upholding what was believed to be a divine mandate for the preservation of racial purity, based on his reading of the dispersion in Gen 11.[145]

Religious Scholarship and the Ideology of Race

Arguments about race reached their apex during the nineteenth century, though they extended into the twentieth. However, notwithstanding the ongoing debate between monogeneticists and polygeneticists concerning the origins of man, unanimity began to emerge concerning the salience of race as an organizing principle. It is no exaggeration to say that race became the dominant theme of Euro-Western thought during this era since "a scientific understanding of race seemed to promise a more authentic narrative based upon the facts of nature, the biological differences that existed

139. Kidd, *Forging of Races*, 140, citing Thomas Stringfellow, *Scriptural and Statistical Views in Favor of Slavery*.
140. Haynes, *Noah's Curse*, 70.
141. Haynes, *Noah's Curse*, 98.
142. Long, *History of Jamaica*, 2:377, quoted in Jahoda, *Images of Savages*, 55.
143. Haynes, *Noah's Curse*, 125.
144. Haynes, *Noah's Curse*, 131.
145. Haynes, *Noah's Curse*, 137.

between racial units."[146] "Race" it was said, "is everything."[147] The zeal to develop a "rationally reformed Christianity" in step with the spirit of the Enlightenment meant that the Bible was subjected to empirical analysis in order to "re-establish [the Christian faith] on firmer foundations,"[148] yet the analysis was filtered through the lens of racialist assumptions and the conclusions arrived at were almost invariably supportive of the White supremacist status quo. The racialist analysis that underlay so much of nineteenth-century scholarship was especially prominent in the arena of Protestant biblical studies. The Bible was enlisted to provide the needed "evidence for the dispersion of races and the beginnings of racial divisions and patterns."[149] A corollary to this was an emerging anti-Semitism that revealed itself in an increasing discomfort with the Old Testament and Semitic religion. It was claimed, for example, that Christianity—though originating among the Semites—was "beyond the comprehension of the Semitic mind."[150]

Christians joined the growing consensus that "human morphology is indicative of ability and that differences in characteristics and sociocultural expressivity are explained by biology,"[151] and race came to be considered a defining factor in religious expression. The study of religion thus became racialized, and biology the key to understanding variation in religious practices and modes of expression. This categorization extended beyond distinctions between Whites and non-Whites but subdivided and ranked Whites into various racial types as well, with Teutonic Anglo-Saxons being considered (by themselves at least) as the highest of European type and the ones best suited for a full apprehension of Christian truth. Some scholars believed that "the type of religion to which an ethnic group adhered was

---

146. Kidd, *Forging of Races*, 121. In his chapter "Monogenesis, Slavery, and the Nineteenth-Century Crisis of Faith" (121–67), Kidd provides a detailed overview of the complexities that surrounded questions of racial differences, particularly the difficulties encountered by monogeneticists who sought to maintain allegiance to scriptural orthodoxy concerning the single origin of mankind while simultaneously justifying the subjugation of people of African descent.

147. Robert Knox, *The Races of Man*, as quoted in Augstein, *Race*, xxx.

148. Kidd, *Forging of Races*, 83.

149. Kidd, *Forging of Races*, 168.

150. Kidd, *Forging of Races*, 172. Discussion of the Old Testament and the broader discomfort with the "primal religion" of the Bible is discussed in ch. 4.

151. Sharp, *No Partiality*, 123.

deducible from its cranial formation."[152] Charles Kingsley in England promoted the idea that "God had fitted the Teutonic race to become the ruling race of the world" and that Anglo-Saxon expansion was an extension of God's kingdom on earth; "the reign of world peace, order, and morality was to be established by the Anglo-Saxon Teutonic Christians and if necessary was to be founded on the bodies of inferior races."[153] Others held that Christianity itself would be perfected and receive a "glorious embodiment" through its "reciprocal penetration with the noble German nature."[154] As late as 1915, S. H. Digg could confidently assert that Teutonic people, who, according to him could be identified by the "physical formation of the head and face," embraced religion that was "individualistic and intellectual . . . emphasizing freedom of belief," that is, "the more Teutonic in blood the more *protestant* in the full, non-emotional sense is their religion."[155] These were not fringe beliefs, but mainstream views.

In contrast to the supposedly inherent capacity of Aryan people for high religion, the black races had a "psychic weakness" and were believed to lack the aptitude "for the appreciation of theological concepts and for religious and moral development."[156] Blacks had nothing of value to contribute to Christianity and even their ability to fully understand it was lacking. In its more favorable, though equally paternalistic, manifestation, religious racialism perceived an inherent gentleness and unselfishness in Black people that might serve as a useful counterweight to the "Caucasian ability to govern and achieve domination at any cost"[157] in the development of true Christian civilization. Though "inferiority in intellect, energy, and selfishness" of Black people was assumed, an article in *The North American Review* speculated that their practical religious potential might be greater than that of Whites: "Does the dark race in all its varieties possess the capacity for understanding and living out the deep meaning of the World's ruler, Christianity, as the offspring of the followers of Odin never did, and never can, understand and act it?"[158] Beneath the complimentary words, however, one notes the enduring presumption of Black inferiority and

152. Kidd, *Forging of Races*, 172.
153. Horsman, *Race and Manifest Destiny*, 76, 77.
154. Pfleiderer, "National Traits of Germans," 39.
155. Digg, "Race to Thought Expression," 357.
156. Kidd, *Forging of Races*, 172.
157. Horsman, *Race and Manifest Destiny*, 265.
158. "Men and Brutes," 267.

subordination. If Blacks were to contribute anything to Christianity, it could not be in the arena of intellect or governance, but rather something in line with their inherently submissive and humble nature. Within nineteenth-century racialized religion, there was no consideration of Black peoples as equal contributors and interpreters of the Christian faith either in the present or the future.

Conclusions

In this chapter I examined how Europeans viewed and interpreted Black peoples. It has been demonstrated that the interactions between African and European peoples in the Old Testament and in the period of classical antiquity were not marked by racial animosity. Greeks and Romans largely viewed black skin with fascination and associated Black people with the exotic and erotic—associations that would persist for centuries. The intrusion of dualistic schemes of good/evil into Greco-Roman and Judaism consciousness introduced a dichotomous association of black with sin and evil that was expanded upon by early Christian scholarship, notably that of Origen. In medieval Europe, these associations continued while the introduction of Black slavery in concert with the Crusades added servitude as an additional associational category. The emergence of the curse of Ham myth added to these existing associations, creating in the minds of European Christendom at the dawn of the early modern era, definitive links between Blackness, slavery, sin, exoticism, and the erotic.

I discussed also the threefold conceptual framework under which Black people were considered: a cosmological one—the great chain of being; a historical one—the four stages theory; and a cultural one—Eurocentric White supremacy. Each of these concepts served to advance the notion of Black people as inherently subordinate and inferior to Whites and provided legitimation for their debasement. I highlighted particularly the unique strands of Eurocentric White supremacy that emerged within the United States and discussed some of its religious and cultural bases—notably the comparatively high population of Blacks in comparison to Europe, the embeddedness of Black slavery in the economic system of North America, and the absence of mediatory cultural, religious, or customary systems within the United States. From thence follows a brief examination of the racialized approach to the study of religion developed in the nineteenth century. What emerges from this exploration is a Euro-Western belief in the ontological deficiency of Black peoples. Belief in this deficiency was rooted in ancient prejudices, compounded by a history of Black enslavement and subjugation, and justified based on biological essentialism and biblical authority. It was therefore almost impossible for Euro-Westerners to perceive anything of value in Black people or their religious practices, which must, of necessity, be equally regarded as deficient and degraded.

4

Decentering Eurocentric White Supremacy

THE DEROGATORY GAZE CAST upon Black people and Black religion was amplified where those traditions most obviously departed from the assumed norms of Euro-Western Christianity and/or were aligned with the primal sensibilities of Africa, as in Pentecostalism. Such religion was facilely dismissed as "sound instead of sense,"[1] characteristic of those considered to be in a "low stage of culture. . . largely controlled by their feelings."[2] The racial construct of Eurocentric White supremacy, and responses to that construct, have been the primary lens through which Black religion has been assessed within studies of religion. Useful though these paradigms may be, they have ultimately served to reduce Black people to reactors, recognizable only in their role as responders to the coercive power of Eurocentric White supremacy, and consequently devoid of any imagined life or meaning outside that framework. They have thus been rendered marginal players within their own stories. Now, however, the focus shifts from the exterior gaze to the interior self-understanding as more recent, and indeed personal aspects of the study come into view.

---

1. "Fanatical Worship of Negroes Going On at Sanctified Church" (*Commercial Appeal*, May 22, 1907), quoted in Sanders, *Saints in Exile*, 31.
2. Henke, "Gift of Tongues," 199.

Methodological Issues

Before proceeding to the assessment of the churches, and of the New Testament, the difficulties imposed by Eurocentric White supremacy on Euro-Western scholarship specifically, but on the larger theological academy in general, in comprehending the relationship of the primal to Christian faith must be addressed. In order to privilege the internal voice and definition of the primal, it is important to first identify how Eurocentric White supremacy has led to the development of methodologies that have distorted and obscured the primal within the academic study of the New Testament and of Black religion. It is therefore important to address certain methodological issues that arise in any attempt to engage the New Testament from the perspective of the primal. Just as the "new worlds, new wealth and new possessions"—including the indigenous and primal peoples of these new lands—encountered by Europeans were subjected to scrutiny, exploitation, and control, for the benefit of European societies, so too the "imperial imagination"[3] turned towards the Bible, interprets the Scriptures as a kind of undiscovered country from which religious truth(s) can be extracted in a way that alienates those truths from their primal context and modes of expression and are made to buttress Euro-Western cultural and political hegemony. Furthermore, the presuppositions of Euro-Western civilizational superiority suggests that "the Eurocentric way of interpreting the text is the normative way by which all other approaches are to be tested . . . tacitly implying that the Eurocentric approach is without cultural bias,"[4] while others' are inherently suspect. While this is deeply problematic in any field, in the arena of biblical studies and theology, it is extraordinarily so, for it makes God the ally of Eurocentrism.

This approach is, to an extent, understandable given the long residency of Christianity in European lands and the influence of Christianity on European culture, and philosophy. Yet it must be recognized as a category error. Europeans assumed that since they belonged to Christ, Christ—and the Bible through which he was revealed—belonged to them. Thus, in a twist of irony, the Bible, or rather Euro-Western interpretation of the Bible, became a tool for the suppression and delegitimization of the very primal setting from which it is derived, "an instrument of domination" wielded in

---

3. L. Smith, *Decolonizing Methodologies*, 23.
4. Myers, "Hermeneutical Dilemma," 42.

the conquest and colonization of indigenous peoples,[5] including Africans transported to the Americas as slave labor. The biblical authors were people operating from within a primal worldview, no less in the New Testament than in the Old, and this places the imperial imagination in contrast and opposition to the primal imagination in reading and understanding the Bible. The difficulties encountered by European Christian scholars as they attempted to reconcile the ancient primal world of the Bible with their own assumptions of European Christian civilizational superiority reflects this tension.

I want to note that the Euro-Western interpretative tradition has not only been cut off from the primal world of the Bible, but also from other Christian interpretative traditions that align more closely with the New Testament era. I speak here of the Eastern traditions of the Syriac and later Arabic speaking Christian communities of the Middle East who "share the broader culture of the ancient Middle East, and . . . are ethnically close to the Semitic world of Jesus than the Greek and Latin cultures of the West."[6] Among other deficiencies arising from this disconnection is a poverty of thought around the doctrine of inspiration, which was a process "that took thirty to fifty-plus years to complete"; and involved not only the particularities of Jesus's life and teaching—which were probably in Aramaic—but also the Aramaic testimony about his life, the translation of that testimony into the Greek language, and the compilation of that testimony into what is called the Gospels.[7]

Indigenous Methodology

As mentioned in chapter 1, to allow the primal to speak for itself requires a methodological approach that decenters Euro-Western civilization as the keeper and arbiter of legitimate Christian theology. Simultaneously, it requires a privileging of primal epistemologies and expressions to create space for an alternative hermeneutic in biblical interpretation. The decentering of Euro-Western norms and the privileging of the primal is aided by recent developments advanced by scholars who themselves hail from indigenous communities which largely maintain a primal orientation. These methodologies arose in opposition to the reification of Euro-Western reality, the

---

5. Tamez, "Bible and Five Hundred Years," 18.
6. K. Bailey, *Jesus through Middle Eastern Eyes*, 12.
7. K. Bailey, *Jesus through Middle Eastern Eyes*, 19; see also 18.

assumption that "Western ideas about the most fundamental things are the only ideas possible to hold . . . and the only ideas which can make sense of the world, of reality, of social life and of human beings."[8] As such they are well positioned to help illumine a text that is neither Western nor modern.

African Christian scholarship has provided new lenses through which to assess and interpret the Scriptures in ways that remain faithful to historic orthodox Christianity, while resisting the claims of the Euro-Western academy to normative status. These scholars generally accept the divine inspiration and authority of the Bible, considering it "a sacred book meant to determine their beliefs and regulate their relationship with God and their fellow human beings," but interpret it in ways that both make the Bible meaningful to the African Christian and legitimize African Christian theology.[9] These scholars ground their orthodoxy in the assertion that the gospel is conveyed as much in the messenger as in the message, and thus cannot be reduced to a particular scriptural formulation like John 3:16 or the Four Spiritual Laws. The gospel is, rather, "a person, Jesus Christ of Nazareth, Son of God, Saviour of the World,"[10] who is himself the communication of the divine nature in human form. The gospel, therefore, should be considered separately from the history of its proclamation, that is, from Christianity as it has been understood and interpreted within the historical framework of Euro-Western Christianity. The essential claim is that "Christ and him crucified with its theocentric base within a monotheistic framework,"[11] is the true integrating center and reference point for all Christian theology, not standards derived from Euro-Western culture. African Christian theology thus stands fully within the tradition of historic Christian faith, even as it resists Euro-Western pretensions of authority, and charges of syncretization are misguided.

One of the key insights emerging from indigenous methodology is an understanding of the relationality of knowledge. This stands in contrast to the dominant Euro-Western paradigm of knowledge as an individual entity—something to be searched for, gained, and owned[12]—yet is consonant with the sense of knowledge conveyed, for example, in Phil 3:10.[13]

8. L. Smith, *Decolonizing Methodologies*, 58.
9. Quarshie, "Significance of Biblical Studies," 17.
10. K. Bediako, "Gospel and Culture," 8.
11. Quarshie, "Significance of Biblical Studies," 22.
12. Wilson, "Indigenous Research Methodology," 176.
13. "That I may know [Christ] and the power of His resurrection, and the fellowship of His sufferings, being conformed to His death" (NKJV).

This implies also a subjective, rather than objective treatment of text, subjective chiefly in the sense that Scripture is encountered as the "living and active" word (Heb 4:12 ESV)—the personal *logos* through whom all things came into being (John 1:1). The relationality of knowledge further suggests that knowledge, especially oral tradition, cannot be disentangled from its source; "stories can never be decontextualized from the teller. They are active agents within a relational world, pivotal in gaining insight into a phenomenon."[14] Consequently, the biblical tellers—though they committed the oral tradition to writing[15]—feature as active conversation partners— "living dead" ancestors of the Christian faith who continue to speak and from whom we are enjoined to learn.

African philosophy is helpful in this regard as generally speaking, "it is an essential element in African belief that 'living' and 'dead' live in symbiosis, interdependent, capable of communicating one with another."[16] Those who have died and passed into the realm of spirit beings continue as present and active agents in the natural realm as well. They are considered "living members of the community . . . responsible for channelling the life force within the community and thus exert an influence on the vitality of the community."[17] In a similar way, Kwame Bediako draws on the traditional African worldview, to assert that knowledge, particularly of the Scriptures, is inseparable from being, and is shared not only with the living, but with the living dead. He affirms a deeply primal apprehension of the Scripture as "a story in which we participate" alongside our ancestors.[18]

> Scripture is not just a book existing independently of us. Scripture is life, like our Christian life itself, that gives us the record of the word of God made life in the incarnate Son. Scripture is the living testimony to what God has been about and continues to be about, *and we are part of that testimony* . . . the characters of Scripture are our contemporaries, *they are our ancestors.*[19]

---

14. Kovach, *Indigenous Methodologies*, 94.

15. This is not to suggest that primal equates to pre- or nonliterate. The religious adherents of Greece and Rome, though literate, were primal. See G. Bediako, "Primal Religion," 12.

16. E. Smith, *African Ideas of God*, 24.

17. Nichols, "African Christian Theology," 27.

18. K. Bediako, "Scripture as the Hermeneutic," 5.

19. K. Bediako, "Scripture as the Hermeneutic," 6; emphasis added.

This is further articulated in the notion of vital participation wherein it is understood that "it is participation in a common life and in its resources and powers that constitutes community"; a common life "constituted in Christ and actualized through the Spirit . . . [thus] includ[ing] both living and dead."[20] I will say more about how relationship with ancestors reflects in the New Testament itself, but for now I briefly cite Heb 12:1, which calls attention to the righteous dead as "a great cloud of witnesses" (NIV) who surround the faithful in their quest to persevere in the race marked out for them, existing not simply as memory but as presence.[21]

Indigenous methodology does not entirely displace other forms of biblical hermeneutics in this study, nor is it necessarily employed in opposition to them. I use it as a means by which to bring to the fore and illuminate the primal imagination as it is manifest in the New Testament in ways that other methods may not. There are some practical considerations that arise in consequence of its use: 1) the rejection of the distinction between narrative and teaching passages, and 2) careful consideration of the worldviews of the writers. Harold Turner's six features, and especially the sixth one, the sacramental universe, provide an integrating hermeneutic throughout.

The Narrative/Didactic Divide

The distinction made between the theological value of narrative or historical passages and those which are most explicitly didactic is frequently affirmed in classic evangelical Protestant New Testament hermeneutics, the rule of thumb being that didactic texts take precedence over narrative ones. This evangelical caution is rooted in the quest for epistemological certainty that it shares with post-Enlightenment modernity. By their nature, narrative texts lack the precision that yields this degree of certainty and therefore lend themselves to subjective interpretations that may dismiss authorial intent. Yet to ignore these texts because of an inability to "integrate the texts into a hermeneutic that calls for strict literalism in the propositional texts"[22] is to develop a canon within the canon, or, to borrow Orwell's phraseology, to assert that all Scripture is God breathed, but some is more God breathed than others. It concedes the primacy of post-Enlightenment modernist epistemology, an epistemology "based on a rationalist, secular

20. K. Bediako, *Christianity in Africa*, 103.
21. See Kabasélé, "Christ as Ancestor," 120.
22. Weathers, "Leland Ryken's Literary Approach," 116.

paradigm [which] discounts the possibility that knowledge arises from happenings that cannot be explained through reductionist means."[23] The tools of science are used not only in the interpretation of Scripture, but also to practically exclude from Scripture those texts for which science proves an unreliable guide. This exclusion debars the "inseparable relationship between story and knowing"[24] that is so integral to the primal framework in which the biblical authors operated. It also denies "the way any significant history is remembered and recorded."[25]

In the primal understanding, narrative is not understood simply as background information that "frames" the truths, which are to be found in explicitly didactic portions of the story. Rather, the stories themselves "are vessels for passing along teachings, medicines, and practices . . . [and] reveal a set of relations comprising strong social purpose,"[26] including, I would add, relations with the supernatural realm. Thus, stories have an inherently didactic purpose and value. Scripture confirms this perspective when it insists that "all Scripture is inspired by God and profitable for teaching, for reproof, for correction, for training in righteousness" (2 Tim 3:16 NASB), and that "whatever was written in earlier times as written for our instruction" (Rom 15:4 NASB). In both cases, no distinction is made between narrative and other forms of Scripture as sources of teaching/instruction (διδασκαλίαν/didaskalían). For example, in 1 Cor 10:11, Paul explicitly references the story of Israel's complaint and rebellion in the wilderness. The whole honor roll of the faithful recorded in Heb 11 is likewise an example, as the stories of their lives are listed as a source of both encouragement and instruction.

Given that the narrative of Luke-Acts alone comprises fully 25 percent of the New Testament, the exclusion of narrative as a source of theological insight is irresponsible. Pentecostal scholars have long contested the primacy of didactic passages in theological interpretation, alleging that it compromises Luke's independence as a historian-theologian in his own right, with perspectives that are equally valid to those of Paul.[27] It must be admitted that some evangelical scholars have advanced in their willingness to use biblical

---

23. Kovach, *Indigenous Methodologies*, 78.
24. Kovach, *Indigenous Methodologies*, 94.
25. K. Bailey, *Jesus through Middle Eastern Eyes*, 19.
26. Kovach, *Indigenous Methodologies*, 95.
27. Stronstad, *Charismatic Theology*, 10–13.

narrative to establish theological norms,[28] though other, more conservative ones, continue to insist that narratives are unreliable guides to doctrine and thus cling to traditional grammatical-historical hermeneutics.[29]

The Black American religious tradition however has always evinced a tendency to "represent black experiences and perspectives by means of a diverse selection of biblical texts and themes"[30] with biblical narrative playing a leading role in those representations, thus situating narrative at the center rather than the periphery of Black American theology. In any event, my aim is not primarily exegetical in the sense of the extraction of conceptual knowledge for its own sake or for the sake of applying this decontextualized knowledge to our own or other's lives. My concern is a holistic appreciation of the author's communication, including his underlying worldview, and with what the text reveals about the nature of reality and consequently about theology. This leads to the second methodological consideration.

Worldview

As I already indicated, my method entails a special attentiveness to the authors and to their ontological assumptions and perspectives as revealed in the biblical text. The biblical writers are not two-dimensional characters whose worldviews are to be acknowledged and then set aside or simply pressed into service as background cultural information that must be understood only insofar as it helps us discover the real meaning of the text in our time. Their worldview is rather considered as part of their essential witness to Christ.

B. J. van der Walt's definition of *worldview* as an "integrated, interpretive set of confessional perspectives on reality which underlies, shapes, motivates and gives direction and meaning to human activity"[31] is good, but it is bound to Euro-Western epistemological categories. It therefore cannot adequately describe all that this study seeks to uncover about the biblical authors and text. In the first place this is because the terms "religion," "spirituality," and "worldview" can equally be used when referring to the conceptual universe of primal people, for whom such categories are not nearly so distinct. Second, "the subject-object distinction implicit in

28. Larkin, "Recovery of Luke-Acts," 409.
29. See Thomas, "Hermeneutics of Noncessationism."
30. T. Smith, *Conjuring Culture*, 21.
31. Van der Walt, *Liberating Message*, 39.

the term "confessional perspectives on reality" does not exist in the same way,"[32] if by "confession" one means belief, solely in the cognitive sense. The strong divisions of which modern Euro-Western thought is so fond, fail because "it is post-Enlightenment Western thought that neatly separates belief, assumed to be localised within an intangible thing called mind, from the external reality assumed to be independent of the belief itself and upon which the mind operates."[33] Nevertheless, if confession is understood in the sense of bearing witness to an extant reality of which one has become aware, then the definition is acceptable for the purposes of this research. An example is Rom 1:19–20 wherein Paul emphatically states that God has made himself known, and that God's invisible attributes are clearly seen and understood from creation itself. These are not statements about belief in God in an abstract or conceptual sense, but about the reality to which the created order bears witness and of which all can be presumed to be aware; statements with which many primal peoples would readily assent. As the Akan of Ghana would put it, *Obi nkyerɛ abɔfra Nyame* (No one teaches a child God). Worldview thus includes both divine self-disclosure (revelation) and participation as epistemological categories.

Assessing the Primal: Methodological Issues in Black American Religious Scholarship

When it comes to articulating the legitimacy of the primal expression of Christianity within Black American religion, the methodological issues are compounded by the long history of biased and negative interpretation of Black peoples and religion within Euro-Western culture. On the one hand, this history made it almost impossible for Whites to perceive anything of value in Black people or their religious practices, which were equally regarded as deficient and degraded. The overly demonstrative nature of Black religion rendered it barbaric in the eyes of White observers,[34] and consequently inherently sub- or un-Christian. These views were not restricted to Whites but were adopted by many educated Blacks as well. African Methodist Episcopal (AME) Bishop Daniel Alexander Payne (1811–93) denounced demonstrative practices in strong language:

---

32. Settles, "Primal Spirituality and Identity," 29.
33. Settles, "Primal Spirituality and Identity," 29.
34. Raboteau, *Slave Religion*, 74.

I attended a "bush meeting," where I went to please the pastor whose circuit I was visiting. After the sermon they formed a ring, and with coats off sung, clapped their hands and stamped their feet in a most ridiculous and heathenish way. I requested the pastor to go and stop their dancing. At his request they stopped their dancing and clapping of hands, but remained singing and rocking their bodies to and fro. This they did for about fifteen minutes. I then went, and taking their leader by the arm requested him to desist and to sit down and sing in a rational manner. *I told him it was a heathenish way to worship and disgraceful to themselves, the race, and the Christian name.* In that instance they broke up their ring; but would not sit down, and walked sullenly way.[35]

Payne's assertion that such behavior was "disgraceful" to "the race" and his use of the term "heathenish" demonstrates both his concern for respectability and a belief that these practices were innately un-Christian. Payne could not, therefore, permit them to persist. The primal imagination manifest in these practices was, for him and others, evidence substantiating Euro-Western belief in Black inferiority; a degraded and barbaric people must necessarily have a degraded, uncivilized, and sub-Christian religious understanding.[36]

On the other hand, within the Black American theological academy, scholarship has long been dominated by debate about the extent to which Black Christianity has been "accommodative to white-dominated society or emancipatory for the Black masses,"[37] with liberation being a key theme. This debate was not merely academic but came to the fore in the tensions among Black clergymen and churches over the aims and methods of the civil rights movement of the 1960s. This was most strikingly demonstrated in the acrimonious schism in the then largest Black American denomination, the National Baptist Convention, USA when 'supporters of church-based civil rights activism walked away to create their own denomination, the Progressive National Baptist Convention (PNBC)," a split which "was fundamentally rooted in a deep *theological* divide over Christian identity and the church's role."[38] This theological divide preceded the publication of James Cone's landmark work *Black Theology and Black Power* by several

35. Daniel Alexander Payne, *Recollections of Seventy Years*, quoted in Anyabwile, *Decline*, 224.
36. Kidd, *Forging of Races*, 172.
37. Baer and Singer, *African American Religion*, xviii.
38. S. Johnson, "African American Christian Tradition," 69.

years, and set the trajectory of Black American academic religious discourse for many years.

The ensuing years have seen the emergence of a number of other voices, most notably womanist scholars, who have challenged the assumptions of Black theology, which has failed, in their view, to interrogate the "patriarchal architecture of meanings and social power" that has been an "enduring aspect of the Christian tradition"[39] even while seeking to address and overthrow racism, thus eliding issues of sexism. These scholars used the liberationist themes of Black theology to launch a trenchant critique, and began to "query the ways that heteropatriarchal norms of the Christian tradition were being replicated in black churches and in African American liberation theology."[40] Despite this critique, the theme of liberation, both spiritual and sociocultural/political, has remained a key axis around which various strands of Black theology, and indeed biblical scholarship generally within the Black theological academy has revolved. The extent to which this is true is revealed by Thomas Hoyt's assertion that "for blacks the Bible attains its authority as that authority *conforms to the black story through experience and culture*," thus placing the authority of Scripture in subjection to the particularities of the sociocultural liberation of Black people, without reference to divine revelation. Hoyt views this approach as "fundamental to any black biblical hermeneutic."[41] This is a political hermeneutic that goes beyond the idea of Scripture as a "story in which we participate,"[42] in which Black people find themselves and the realities of their current and historical situation interpreted in light of the larger story of God's movement in history, but instead places *liberation* in general, and the liberation of Black people in particular, as *the* axis around which biblical history, and, in a derivative way, world history, revolves. However meaningful this theme of liberation may be in understanding Black Christianity within the sociocultural/political context of Euro-Western White supremacy in the United States, or even in illuminating supposedly sexist presuppositions within the Christian tradition—Black or otherwise—it "represents a forced dichotomy of the African American religious process solely along obvious

---

39. S. Johnson, "African American Christian Tradition," 76.

40. S. Johnson, "African American Christian Tradition," 78.

41. Hoyt, "Interpreting Biblical Scholarship," 33; emphasis added. In fairness to Hoyt, he does acknowledge the need for a more expansive, imagination-based reading of the text that goes beyond the constraints imposed by the historical-critical method.

42. K. Bediako, "Scripture as the Hermeneutic," 5.

political lines,"[43] and forecloses meaningful engagement with Black religion strictly in religious terms. When the primal is excluded, all that remains is the political. Consequently, "black religious experience maintains its integrity as a meaningful phenomenon only to the extent that the existence of African-Americans continues to be defined by racial oppression and a perennial struggle for social and political emancipation,"[44] an interpretation that tends to circumscribe Black religion entirely within the ambit of Eurocentric White supremacy.

This reductionist reading of Black religious experience stems, at least in part, from the dualistic separation of "form from function, structure from meaning, and style from content" derived from Euro-Western epistemological assumptions "that favors literate over narrative means of expression" and "denies the legitimacy of non-Western cultural forms."[45] However, Black American cultural tradition rejects the disjunctive "either/or" thinking that predominates in Euro-Western thought, and instead "prefers the conjunctive 'both/and' of archaic and oral cultures in which ambiguity and multivocity are taken for granted."[46] Euro-Western dualism is, therefore, inherently antithetical to the primal "grammars of knowing"[47] operative within Black American culture that recognize an intrinsic link between form and content, and consequently serves to obscure the primal African content of Black American religion. By severing the *forms* of Black American Christianity from any connection to its African *content*, Black theologians have unwittingly contributed to the racist denigration of "all things black or African"[48] and "set 'Christian' and 'non-Christian' traditions against each other"[49] in a way that inevitably privileges one—generally Euro-Western Christianity—over the other, and which denies the primal foundation that underlie them both.

The imposition of this dualistic, disjunctive framework on Black American religion has led to Africa being considered by religious scholars

---

43. Matthews, *Honoring the Ancestors*, 8.
44. Harvey, "Life Is War," 18–19.
45. Matthews, *Honoring the Ancestors*, 10, 11, 14.
46. T. Smith, *Conjuring Culture*, 143.
47. According to Harvey, "grammars of knowing" refers to "modes of meaning construction that constitute epistemologies and are rooted in particular conceptual repertoires and approaches to analyzing and interpreting the world" ("Life Is War," 21).
48. Matthews, *Honoring the Ancestors*, 11.
49. Chireau, *Black Magic*, 4.

mostly in relation to the retention (or not) of distinctive African cultural forms, but these forms are seen as having "very little or nothing at all to contribute to the *interpretation* of black religious experience."[50] The debate over so-called African retentions in Black American religion,[51] employs disjunctive categories of Euro-Western thought, and thus inevitably sets African and Christian against one another as competing (either/or), rather than complementary (both/and) elements within Black American religion. The debate itself enshrines the dominance of Euro-Western Christianity, marginalizes African contributions to Black American religion, and forecloses the possibility of faith that is both African *and* Christian.

The disjunctive, dualistic approach to Black religion fails as a means of uncovering manifestations of the primal imagination within Black American Christianity, particularly given the historically perceived antithesis between Black or African religion, and Christianity. These are not the only methods available for the study of Black religion, however. Dialectical approaches, that seek to hold together form and meaning, provide an alternative framework for understanding Black religion, and align with the indigenous methodologies. Donald Matthews identifies two implications of applying a dialectical analysis in matters of theology that are helpful in revealing the primal nature of Black American Christianity:

> (1) The preponderance of African cultural forms in African American religion means that African religious meanings are also present, and (2) there is a free-flowing relationship between the form and themes that are generated by African American religion.[52]

What Matthews calls "African" may also be called primal, for it is the sixth, integrating feature of the primal worldview that insists on the connection between form and meaning within the context of a sacramental universe. Matthews explains further:

> Whether feeling is called a structure or a theme, for instance, depends on how the term is defined because in reality feeling operates as both a structure and a theme, as both form and meaning. One can observe the presence of emotion through the bodily movements and the intensity of the performance (form) of the spirituals, and one also can observe the presence of feeling through the use of particular lyrics that emphasize emotional attachments. . . .

50. Harvey, "Life Is War," 18; emphasis added.
51. Harvey, "Life Is War," 379; see also Baer and Singer, *African American Religion*, 1.
52. Matthews, *Honoring the Ancestors*, 15.

Feeling is intricately related in form and meaning, and it expresses African and African American spirituality.[53]

Consequently, the theological meaning attached to manifestations of the primal imagination need not be, and often is not expressed in the formal propositions typically demanded by Euro-Western thought. Such religion is not, as usually conceived in Euro-Western theology, a "system of ideas," but is instead a way of "living religiously as being in touch with the source and channels of power in the universe."[54] Indeed propositional categorizations are inherently reductionist, and static and so do not capture the *holistic* and *dynamic* nature of a primal epistemology that is born of "relational knowing, from both inner and outer space."[55] This study, however, privileges the experiential and intuitive sources of knowledge derived from the dynamic context of the Black spiritual/Pentecostal church tradition, a tradition which lays great emphasis on attentiveness to the Holy Spirit for insight and guidance in both spiritual and practical concerns. It also seeks to identify theological insights emerging from the structural elements of Black religious experience (e.g., sermons, worship services, etc.), as well as the meanings attached to those experiences by participants.

The obscuring of the primal features of the New Testament text that developed within Euro-Western Christian scholarship raises methodological challenges to any efforts to illumine such features. Similar problems have emerged from the use of a dualistic disjunctive approach to Black American religion. Despite this, scholars from indigenous societies that remain in vital connection with the primal dimension of their own traditions have developed and continue to develop methods that prove helpful in this task. African scholars like Kwame Bediako and Benhardt Quarshie have been engaged in similar efforts to ground theological interpretation in the person of Jesus Christ rather than in the Euro-Western formulation of Christian theology. To counter these difficulties, I have used an indigenous framework for assessing the primal features of the New Testament text while outlining some of the key considerations that emerge from these methods in their application in this study, as well as a dialectical approach to the study of Black American religion that delivers a more holistic analysis than is possible with the dualistic and disjunctive methods frequently applied to its study. By this I affirm as foundational a relational view of

---

53. Matthews, *Honoring the Ancestors*, 15.
54. K. Bediako, *Christianity in Africa*, 106.
55. Kovach, *Indigenous Methodologies*, 57.

knowledge that is consonant with a biblical view. As the study proceeds, these considerations provide a touchstone for reading and encountering the primal imagination.

Black Pentecostalism in Historical Context

The primal imagination that finds expression in the pneumatic sacramentalist tradition traces its root to the development of Black American Christianity in general. The importation of enslaved Africans into what became the United States brought them into contact with Euro-Western Christianity in its predominantly Protestant form. These enslaved Blacks were subject to varied attempts at Christianization, most notably in the Great Revival of the late eighteenth century. The primal vision that these enslaved Africans carried with them from their homeland, and that they shared with their white coreligionists, played a significant role in their conversion. This, alongside the persistence of varied traditions of conjure, laid the foundation for the later flourishing of the primal imagination within the pneumatic sacramentalist tradition.

The Churches

As mentioned above, the spiritual church movement is broad and diverse, with no single standard of belief to which all would agree or adhere. Some groups, such as the Universal Hagar's Spiritual Church, embrace beliefs and practices that place them definitively outside the Christian tradition.[56] Others, however, are much less heterodox in their views, and self-consciously identify themselves as Christian.[57] The study draws also on the example

---

56. Baer, *Black Spiritual Movement*, 98. For example, Father Hurley, the founder of Universal Hagar's Spiritual Church, is worshipped as God, and prayers are directed to him.

57. Previous research has tended to obscure these differences, subsuming substantial divergences in belief and practice under the single umbrella term "spiritual," without adequately interrogating the term or differentiating those groups that maintain an explicitly Christian identity and theology from others that do not. Perhaps this reflects the limitations of a purely anthropological approach to a religious subject that examines only phenomena, without attending to meaning. Harold Turner demonstrated a more integrated approach in his assessment of new religious movements that had arisen within primal religious societies that would likely be more helpful than a strictly anthropological one. See H. Turner, "New Religious Movements." While it is not the purpose of this study to explore these differences, it is important to note them.

of two churches, which, although representing divergent strands of the spiritual church movement, are both explicitly Christian in their belief and practice.

The first is the All Saints Holiness Church (ASHC) of Nashville, Tennessee, founded by Florida Walton (later Gilmore). It began its life as a spiritual church and later transitioned into a more mainstream Pentecostal congregation.[58] The second is the St Martins Spiritualist Church of St. Louis, Missouri (SMSC). This church has maintained its identity as a spiritual congregation for over one hundred years.[59] Both churches are of similar size, were founded by women, and serve a similar demographic. Neither church is affiliated with a larger denomination or association. Founded in 1964 and 1915 respectively, ASHC and SMSC represent a type—the small, "storefront"-type church born of the diversification in Black religion during and after the Great Migration.[60] It was in "storefront" churches like ASHC and SMSC that the practices most associated with "African worldviews and religious folk culture . . . with rural life or Slave Religion"[61] continued to flourish. Though there have been changes and adaptations, these churches provide a unique window into a continuity of religious expression across generations and still retain "those elements which were brought over from Africa and grafted onto Christianity."[62] They are well suited to demonstrate how the primal imagination manifests itself in aspects of Black American

---

58. This is my natal church in which I was reared and thus have extensive personal experience since my childhood days.

59. I spent an intensive ten-day period with the SMSC in January 2016 in which I attended all the services, including Sunday school, Sunday worship, and spiritual development class. I interviewed the pastor and had informal interaction with members. I took still photos of the church and its environs, and audio recordings of meetings I attended, which were later transcribed. In addition, I obtained video recordings for several services I could not attend, and later watched and transcribed sermons from the pastor as well as other ministers, which had been uploaded to YouTube. The sermon dates are Apr. 2, 9, and 23, 2017, and May 14, 2017. (I watched others as well but did not transcribe them.) In the case of SMSC, a previously published historical research on the founder of the church conducted in 2008 was consulted.

60. Baer and Singer, *African American Religion*, 47–49. *Great Migration* refers to the large-scale movement of Blacks from the rural, agrarian South to industrial centers in the North, Midwest, and urban South during the early to mid-twentieth century. This migration transformed Black Americans "from an agrarian peasantry into a diversified urban proletariat" (44).

61. Clemmons, *Bishop C. H. Mason*, locs. 584–86. See also Harrison, "Storefront Church," 244.

62. Hurston, *Sanctified Church*, 105.

Christianity, particularly in its pneumatic sacramentalist strands. I describe each church—its physical characteristics, demographics, and its history. This is followed by an exploration of how the primal imagination manifests within the practices and teaching of the church. These are set against the backdrop of previous studies, which help situate the case studies within a larger framework of the spiritual and Pentecostal movement.

Previous research conducted on both the spiritual church movement and a mainstream Black Pentecostal denomination, the Church of God in Christ provides additional information to support and undergird the insights emerging from the case studies. In the case of the former, the research provides information concerning the spiritual churches as they appeared in the mid- to late twentieth century. Unfortunately, much of that information is lost—particularly on the small independent congregations that are the central concern of this project—as many of the churches themselves have disappeared; it is mostly irrecoverable except via such published research as is now available. For the spiritual churches, I draw extensively on studies conducted by Hans Baer on spiritual churches in Nashville, Tennessee, and on Michael P. Smith's *Spirit World* photo journal of spiritual churches in New Orleans from 1968 to 1983. For Pentecostal churches, I draw on Craig Scandrett-Leatherman's study on the Church of God in Christ, the largest Black Pentecostal denomination in the United States.[63]

As mentioned in chapter 1, my own experience growing up in the spiritual church cum Pentecostal church movement forms part of the interpretative grid applied to this study. Though I have attended and served in a variety of churches—Baptist, Presbyterian, nondenominational charismatic—and have worked within the context of an interdenominational, broadly evangelical para-church ministry, I have always considered Pentecostalism to be my ecclesiastical and theological home. Some may question the validity of author as source since the information emerging from the source cannot always be independently verified. Since this is a true and valid concern, effort has been made to corroborate details of memory wherever possible. Yet the inclusion of this experience is a key part of my methodological approach, which understands knowledge to exist within the context of relationships.[64] It is out of my own multiform experiences over decades of involvement with my own natal church, as well as with

---

63. Scandrett-Leatherman's PhD dissertation is an ethnographic study of the Church of God in Christ, the largest Black Pentecostal denomination in the United States, conducted between 1994 and 2005.

64. Wilson, "Indigenous Research Methodology," 177.

various other Pentecostal congregations, that I gained access to the insider perspective. There is, therefore, an unavoidably autobiographical element present. Though cognizant of the limitations imposed by this familiarity, I also recognize the significant role the autobiographical form plays within the Black American literary tradition. This form has become classic within the Black literary form because it enables the writer to present him or herself as representative of the entire community out of which he or she emerges.[65] What is true in its literature is true also within the Black church where the personal testimony has long been a staple of Black Pentecostal piety. The testimony has been described as "the liminal core of Afro-Pentecostal worship."[66] I do not stand apart from, or outside of the pneumatic sacramentalist tradition, nor can I, but was formed both spiritually and theologically by it. My knowledge is limited, as is all such human knowledge (cf. 1 Cor 13:12), yet it is true knowledge to which I bear witness, and of which I testify.

The New Testament

I have already described how the historical-critical method of biblical studies, the cessationist assumptions of Euro-Western Protestant scholarship, and the naturalistic perspective on religious phenomena all contribute to obscuring the relationship of the gospel to the primal in the New Testament. This is important because while the Old Testament has been considered as reflective of a more primitive, less well-developed (and consequently sub-Christian) religious sense, the New Testament is the quintessentially Christian text, a thoroughly Christian composition that includes the primal as an essential feature. Manifestations of the primal imagination within the New Testament therefore cannot be so readily dismissed. Tellingly, it is in the African context, where New Testament exegesis occurs against the backdrop of an extant primal traditional culture, that these resonances are most apparent. Recent work by scholars such as Kwame Bediako and Benhardt Quarshie are indicative of this approach, but remain exceptions that prove the rule, even within Africa.[67] Thus, in the next chapter I explore how the primal imagination underlies and informs the New Testament itself, and how the primal imagination is manifest within it.

65. Morrison, "Rootedness," 57.
66. Scandrett-Leatherman, "Can't Nobody Do Me," 283.
67. See K. Bediako, "Christian Faith"; Quarshie, "Paul and the Primal Substructure."

5

The Primal Imagination in the New Testament

THUS FAR I HAVE primarily focused on historical and methodological concerns. The New Testament itself, the primary and essential basis for Christian self-understanding and theological reflection, now comes into focus. Notwithstanding the signal contribution of scholars such as Rudolph Otto and Kwame Bediako,[1] the New Testament has not received the kind of *sustained* consideration as a primal religious text as has the Old Testament. Yet the events recorded in the New Testament unfolded against the backdrop of a primal religious environment, and the Christian faith was articulated in light of the assumptions of the primal imagination.

Before proceeding, it is important to clarify how Harold Turner's six-feature analysis of the primal interacts with our reading of the New Testament. As a reminder, Turner's six features—kinship with nature, the finitude and dependency of man, belief in a nonphysical world of spirit powers more ultimate than man, the ability of mankind to enter into relationship with those powers, the expectation of continuation of life beyond death, and the presence of man within a sacramental universe[2]—taken together, comprise what Kwame Bediako terms *the primal imagination.*[3]

---

1. See Otto, *Idea of the Holy*, especially ch. 11; K. Bediako, *Jesus and the Gospel*, 22–33.
2. H. Turner, "Primal Religions," 30–31.
3. K. Bediako, *Christianity in Africa*, 92.

Turner's Six-Feature Analysis and the New Testament

Turner's six-feature analysis of religion provides the key hermeneutic for this study of the New Testament. The texts selected for examination are analyzed in terms of their coherence with those features identified by Turner. Furthermore, since the New Testament is a collection of confessional and didactic writings, written out of and into communities who expressed faith in the person of Jesus as God incarnate, Messiah, and Lord, what is required is a participatory approach to the text, a confessional approach wherein "God is not bracketed out in some desire to achieve an illusion of objectivity."[4] The aim is not epistemological certainty, as in the historical critical method, but instead a holistic appreciation of the author's communication, including his underlying worldview, and with what the text reveals about the nature of reality and consequently about theology. The worldview perspective of the authors is treated not simply as background, but as an essential part of their witness to Christ and a source of theological insight. As the Christian doctrine of inspiration has special bearing on the assumptions that underlie this study, it is necessary to briefly touch on it before proceeding.

Inspiration and the Biblical Text

Every Christian and all Christian theologies accept the Bible as inspired. That is, all would agree, at least in a provisional sense, with the assertion that "God's self-revelation has come to be expressed in the words of the Bible."[5] However, there are different understandings of inspiration as it relates to biblical texts, both in how it occurred and the implications for the authority and reliability of the actual text of Scripture itself. Thus, it is important for me to clarify what is meant by the term "inspiration" and more importantly, what is *not* meant by the term.[6]

---

4. LeMarquand, "New Testament Exegesis," 92.

5. Milne, *Know the Truth*, 47.

6. This clarification is necessitated in part by the narrowing and secularization of the English term "inspiration," which has, in popular usage, lost the full import of the original meaning of being in-spirited, that is, being breathed into and/or filled with spirit. Hence the KJV rendering of 2 Tim 3:16, "All scripture is given by inspiration of God." The debate over the meaning of inspiration is mostly a reaction to the Enlightenment and reflects Christian attempts to respond to the rise of the historical-critical method and retain biblical authority in the face of the critiques of that authority that rose from it.

On the one hand, belief in divine inspiration of the Bible does not necessarily warrant belief that the Bible, either in its original autographs or in translation, was dictated by God in any sort of automatic manner, with the concomitant implication that those who wrote were "simply the human keyboards or dictaphones through whom the Word of God passed on its way to eventual incorporation in the sacred canon."[7] Nor does the notion need to imply that God simply "accommodated himself to the limitation of the human authors,"[8] and thus the text is limited in its ability to accurately communicate the mind of God without taint. It is my assumption that "God . . . prepared the human vehicles of inspiration for their task, and caused them . . . to perform it through the normal exercise of the powers He had given them."[9] Consequently, it is unsurprising that the human element in the transmission and establishment of the New Testament is so evident. Indeed, the human element, more particularly the worldview of the authors, is an essential feature.

Due to the implicit recognition of divine—human collaboration in the salvific enterprise in the written and oral traditions of the faith, the synthesis whereby "holy men of God spoke" (2 Pet 1:21 NKJV) as they were led of the Spirit is maintained. Consequently, issues of textual variation, scribal editorializing, and even transmission errors are rendered less problematic than if Christians held that Scripture was somehow delivered whole-cloth and in final form to the collected church at a particular point in time. Indeed, if one accepts what Kenneth Bailey has said about "the inspiration of the Gospels as a *process* that took thirty to fifty-plus years to complete,"[10] then such matters emerge as an intrinsic part of the process of inspiration itself, rather than detractions from it. Acknowledging this does not render the text in any way less sacred or revelatory. Indeed, the highest revelation of God lies in the person of Jesus Christ, and is not delimited by the words of a book or books, yet it is within the canon of the New Testament that our experience of the person of Jesus is mediated and clarified. Thus, the inspiration of Scripture means, among other things, that the Scriptures disclose for the reader the revelation of God; that it has the "power of bringing again or re-presenting the disclosure of the primordial revelation [of

---

7. Milne, *Know the Truth*, 49–50.
8. Milne, *Know the Truth*, 50.
9. Packer, "Revelation and Inspiration," 17.
10. K. Bailey, *Jesus through Middle Eastern Eyes*, 19; emphasis original.

Jesus Christ] so that it speaks to us in our present experience."[11] This is all the more the case if, as Aloysius Pieris notes, "language is our experience of reality and religion its expression,"[12] because the experience of reality in whatever language the Bible is translated is connected with the reality and actuality of the Living God.[13] The boundary between text and experience is minimized and the word is encountered as living and active, sharper than a two-edged sword, in a fresh way—indeed, in a primal way. Ultimately, the assertion of the divine inspiration of the biblical texts is grounded in the mystery of faith in the character and sovereignty of God. It is on the basis of this belief that this exploration of the New Testament proceeds.

Cultural Background: The Primal World of the New Testament

In *Honor, Patronage, Kinship & Purity*, David deSilva asserts:

> The tendency still exists to turn a blind eye to the Greco-Roman environment (or to deny its influence on early Christianity), not as a result of careful investigation but rather as an ideological conviction that then shapes (and largely determines) the result of the investigation. Judaism is seen as the only vehicle for divine revelation and thus becomes the only permissible influence on the early church (because any influence from the Greco-Roman world would be "pagan" and "polluting").[14]

DeSilva reinforces what has already been demonstrated concerning the distancing of Christian faith from the primal within Euro-Western Christianity and in the Christian academy. Yet he also helpfully identifies that the world of the New Testament was a thoroughly primal one. The interpenetration of Greco-Roman and Christian thought[15] coupled with assumptions that equate primal with nonliterate has mostly hidden this reality.[16] Yet the Greco-Roman world was no less primal for being literary and culturally sophisticated. Harold Turner alerts us to the fact that the

---

11. Macquarrie, *Principles of Christian Theology*, 8.
12. Pieris, *Asian Theology of Liberation*, 70.
13. K. Bediako, "Why Has Summer Ended," 7.
14. DeSilva, *Honor, Patronage, Kinship & Purity*, 19n4.
15. See Walls, *Missionary Movement*, 18–19.
16. See Baylis, *Introduction to Primal Religions*, 3. Her five general statements about primal religion include the assertion that "there are no written records or scripture; instead, there are myths, handed down in oral tradition."

highly literate "popular religions of Greece, Rome and much of the ancient Near East [were] essentially the tribal religions of these areas, associated with sophisticated civilisations."[17] As is the case in primal societies across time and throughout history, the Greco-Roman world was one in which the transcendent was conceived as part of the fabric of daily life, and was not confined only to religious events, but infused the mundane with supernatural presence and possibility. This was the assumed structure of reality itself for the vast majority of the Greco-Roman world. This is important to keep in mind when it comes to understanding the New Testament.

The New Testament Canon and the Primal Imagination

The first area of investigation lies not in any particular New Testament text, but with the canon of the New Testament itself, or, more specifically, the canonization process. The relevance of the canon, and the canonization process in an investigation into the manifestation of the primal imagination *within* the text of the New Testament canon may seem questionable. It is, however, important to begin here because as the church came to accept or validate the inspiration and authority of various texts, she exercised a judicial and interpretive authority utilizing criteria that in part reflect the primal imagination.

The criteria used in the canonization process are well known in scholarly circles and thus there is no need of recounting them here.[18] However, the relevance of these criteria for inclusion in the canon to understanding how the primal imagination manifested in the early church necessitates a deeper look at two of the criteria for canonization, apostolicity and orthodoxy.[19]

---

17. H. Turner, "Primal Religions," 28. See also Walls, *Missionary Movement*, 68.

18. Broadly speaking, the acceptance of any text by the church for inclusion in the canon rested primarily on three criteria. First, the validity of a text's claim to inspiration was strengthened to the extent that its authorship could be reliably linked to the apostles who had first-hand knowledge of the revelation of God in Jesus Christ. This is termed apostolicity. Second, the widespread (or catholic) acceptance of a text across the broad and diverse spectrum of the church was evidence of its probable inspired nature. Finally, and perhaps most critically, the revelation of the eternal God in the person of Jesus Christ is the essential reference point for Christian faith and consequently for any assertion of inspiration, hence any book accepted as canon presented an orthodox view of the reality of Christ and his incarnation. See Patzia, *Making of New Testament*, 102–7.

19. Catholicity as a criterion for canonization does not merit attention in this investigation, because it does not present itself as primal in the sense in which this study

Apostolicity

The broad and rapid spread of the gospel beyond Judea, and its increasing acceptance by non-Jews meant that writings, or writings associated with the apostles were treasured as first-hand witnesses to the divine self-disclosure in Jesus Christ. These writings were presumed to carry the weight of divine authority since they were written by those commissioned by Christ himself and after their death, became even more important as a means to resolve doctrinal disputes or to settle controversial questions.[20] When examined through the lens of the primal, this usage of the apostolic writings suggests that the apostles were treated similarly to how ancestors are within some primal religious systems. For example, within the African primal setting, "ancestors, 'the living dead,' [who] remain united in affection and in mutual obligations with the 'living living,'"[21] are considered the righteous dead who have lived an exemplary life and function both as mediators between the human and divine realms and as guardians of morality within a society. Additionally, the African ancestor is also believed to "punish those who violate the traditionally sanctioned code, and reward those who keep it"; sickness and misfortune are often attributed to ancestors "because of some guilt or misconduct on the part of the sufferer,"[22] while "those who obey the laws and customs and fulfil their obligations receive the help and blessing of the ancestors."[23]

I am not suggesting that the early church regarded the apostles in exactly the same way as an African ancestor might be considered. They were not, for example, believed to have obtained, by virtue of their apostolic commissions and death, certain "enhanced powers associated with their new status . . . particularly as mediators between man and God."[24] Nor

---

approaches the question. This is not to suggest that this criterion was something seen as altogether devoid of spiritual or supernatural import. To the contrary, the widespread acceptance of a text spoke to the church of its likely inspired, that is, Spirit-breathed, nature, and was consequently a potential candidate for canonization. Yet this criterion seems on its own to be the weakest and least primal of the three, at least not in any way that differs substantially from the other two criteria. Thus, it is excluded from consideration here.

20. Achtemeier et al., *Introducing the New Testament*, 592. It should be noted here that our concern is not with questions of authorship, but with the notion of apostolicity as a whole.

21. H. Turner, "Primal Religions," 32.

22. Opoku, *West African Traditional Religion*, 155.

23. Opoku, *West African Traditional Religion*, 156.

24. E. Smith, *African Ideas of God*, 26.

were the apostles seen as personally responsible for inflicting punishment or reward for adherence to their teaching. However, the early church did perceive the apostles as more than especially close disciples of Jesus. They understood the apostles to have received a unique and divinely sanctioned spiritual authority. In the text of the New Testament itself, Paul emphatically states that the church is "built on the foundation of the apostles and prophets, Christ Jesus himself being the cornerstone" (Eph 2:19–20 ESV). Their teaching was accepted as universally binding, and eternally significant and their words were seen as carrying the weight of divine sanction or endorsement.[25] Rejection of the apostolic teaching rendered one subject to divine punishment. The parallels between the underlying thought patterns of the early Christian church in relation to the apostles and canonization, and African beliefs about ancestors and their role in society, is striking.

Orthodoxy

The second criterion for canonization that presents itself for investigation in relation to the primal imagination is orthodoxy, where orthodox means conformity to the apostolic teaching about Christ. Unlike other messiah figures who had emerged and been killed or faded away into obscurity, the testimony of Jesus's disciples was that though he had indeed been killed, he had been raised again to life by the power of God, and that they were eyewitnesses of this resurrection. These miraculous events recast for them their entire understanding of the Hebrew Scriptures, which they now saw to be perfected in Jesus Christ.[26] Through oral tradition, the message of the apostles was passed on to new converts in an increasingly gentile church, and constituted what might be considered a kind of proto-Scripture, that became the guidelines of faith for the new Christian community.[27] These traditions included sayings of Jesus, some of which are recorded in written form, others of which are not.[28] It was in the continued retelling of these doctrines that the guidance of the Holy Spirit was perceived by the church

---

25. Jesus's words in John 20:22–23 come to mind: "And when he had said this, he breathed on them and said to them, 'Receive the Holy Spirit. If you forgive the sins of any, they are forgiven them; if you withhold forgiveness from any, it is withheld'" (ESV).

26. Achtemeier et al., *Introducing the New Testament*, 591.

27. Paul refers in Acts 20:35 to the remembered words of Jesus, which are not found in any of the four Gospels, showcasing the importance of oral tradition in the early church.

28. Jas 4:12 and 1 Cor 11 are examples.

to be present as Jesus had promised to send another "helper" who would "guide [them] into all truth." (John 16:13 NKJV) and "bring [his teachings to their] remembrance" (John 14:26 NKJV).

One must not permit familiarity with Christian teaching to obscure the deeply primal nature of these claims. Indeed, it is here that the third and fourth of Turner's six-features—belief in a nonphysical world of spirit powers more ultimate than man, and the ability of man to enter relationship with those spirit powers—emerge as fundamental to Christianity. What was claimed by the early church, and what continues to be claimed by Christians everywhere, is that the New Testament writers wrote, consciously or unconsciously, under the direction of the Supreme Being, and had been granted that ability through their relationship to a man named Jesus who, according to their own testimony, had been killed and was subsequently raised to new life through supernatural agency. The authenticity of these claims is not my primary concern, but rather with the nature of the claims themselves. These claims in no way belong to the post-Enlightenment intellectual framework that has dominated Euro-Western thought for the past several hundred years; a framework that substantially denies either the existence or relevance of any supernatural reality to material concerns. Yet this claim to extraordinary supernatural intervention became and remains the touchstone of Christian orthodoxy. No text would be considered eligible for canonization that deviated from this belief; it was the key metric upon which canonization hinged.

The New Testament Primal

Having established the primal nature of the criteria used in the canonization process, the text itself comes into view. A comprehensive treatment of every manifestation of the primal imagination in the New Testament is beyond the scope of the present project and would require a different study altogether. Indeed, the primal imagination informs the background of the entire New Testament, and its assumptions pervade the entire text. This study must necessarily be limited in scope to a representative sample of texts.[29]

29. To avoid any undue difficulty, I have intentionally omitted the book of Revelation from consideration. As a prophetic text of apocalyptic genre, it introduces hermeneutical complexities that would detract from my focus here, and as a text, it does not feature prominently in the life of the churches investigated here. Of course, the very notion of apocalypse—unveiling—implies the unmasking of an unseen but extant super-sensible

The first area of investigation is the dynamism of the spirit realm and engagement with it. Here the question of engagement with the spirit realm—dreams, visions, and magic come into view. The infancy narratives—Matthew's account in particular—anchor this discussion. The second area is specifically concerned with beings that animate the spiritual realm—angels, demons, and the living dead—ancestors. Here, in addition to the infancy narratives, the transfiguration and some sections of Matthew and 1 Corinthians are also examined. The third area is exorcism, healing, and spiritual warfare. Here particular attention is paid to exorcism in the ministry of Jesus and healing as a key focus of his ministry as well as that of the apostles. As a corollary to this third area, I examine the New Testament approach to the use of objects and ritual. These three areas are bound together by a view of the universe "as a unified cosmic system [that is] essentially spiritual."[30]

Manifestations of the primal imagination presented here are not restricted to the texts under investigation but occur more widely. Multiple expressions of the primal may be observed within a single passage. Consequently, though for ease of analysis the passages have been grouped into categories, these are necessarily imprecise. Because of the overall focus of the study, I have chosen to engage the text as a nonexpert reader finds it and as the New Testament itself is organized: a broadly chronological ordering, with the life and ministry of Jesus preceding the post-resurrection ministry of the apostles in the life of the early church. Consequently, concerns about the dating of texts, questions of theological development in the life of the early church, detailed investigations into authorship and source documentation, and others that are of concern primarily to experts have largely been laid aside, entering in only when necessary to shed light on the meaning of a specific passage under consideration.

---

reality that interacts with and impinges upon the sensible realm, a thoroughly primal concept. Revelation is replete with primal imagery—dreams, symbols, assorted spiritual beings, and the like. Its exclusion should not be taken as indicative that it fails to meet the primal imagination test.

30. K. Bediako, *Christianity in Africa*, 96.

Engaging the Dynamic Spirit Realm: Dreams, Visions, and Magic

The spirit realm is presented in the New Testament as a pervasive and dynamic reality that underlies the natural world. Engagement with that reality figures prominently within its pages, and it is difficult to read far into the text without encountering "eruptions" from the numinous realm, into the material creation. This is evident from the beginning in the infancy narratives.

Infancy Narratives

The events surrounding the birth of Jesus are recorded in only two of the four Gospels, Matthew and Luke. The narratives open with a recitation[31] of Jesus's ancestry—Matthew's at the very beginning of the text, prior to any description of his birth, and Luke's after the description of his birth, early childhood, and baptism, and prior to the beginning of Jesus's public ministry. The Matthean genealogy (Matt 1:1–17), based on a trifold division of fourteen generations each, authenticates Jesus's status first as a descendant of Abraham, and thus a legitimate Jew; second as an heir of David, and thus a legitimate king; and finally as the Messiah anticipated in the Jewish prophetic tradition since the time of the Babylonian captivity. Thus, the Matthean genealogy focuses on the specificity of Jesus as the fulfilment of Jewish religious aspirations.[32] On the other hand, the Lukan genealogy (Luke 3:23–38) works backwards from Joseph, Jesus's presumed and legal father, to "the son of Enosh, the son of Seth, the son of Adam, the son of God" (3:38 NIV), and points towards the universality of Jesus as "the new Adam, who once again comes 'from God'—but in a more radical way than the first Adam, not merely breathed into being by God, but truly God's 'Son.'"[33] I shall, for now, pass over the import of these genealogies, returning

---

31. I speak of recitation or of the hearer/reader as a reminder that "the early Christians were part of a culture that passed on ideas orally more than by the written word." Thus, most people likely encountered the New Testament texts in oral rather than written form (Patzia, *Making of New Testament*, 40).

32. Despite the Jewish specificity of Matthew's genealogy, Joseph Ratzinger points us to the fact that the four named women in the genealogy share in common their gentile origin, thus, even within a Jewish paradigm, pointing us towards the universality of Jesus's mission (*Infancy Narratives*, loc. 140).

33. Ratzinger, *Infancy Narratives*, locs. 189–90.

to them later when discussing ancestors. After the genealogies come the annunciation and birth of Jesus. The accounts contain numerous elements that point to a primal orientation on the part of the writers. Dreams, angelic visitations, divination, and the transfiguration of natural phenomena in conjunction with events of spiritual significance, all feature within the first two chapters of Matthew and Luke.

Matthew's Account

Matthew's account, beginning in 1:18, opens with the simple, yet weighty claim that Mary, the mother of Jesus, was found to be "with child by the Holy Spirit" (NASB).[34] One is immediately struck by decidedly primal cast of mind evidenced by the prominence of dreams and other miraculous occurrences in Matthew's narrative. Joseph, Mary's betrothed husband, in an effort to spare her the public shame that would normally attend such a situation resolves to "send her away secretly" (v. 19 NASB) yet is dissuaded from this course of action through a dream in which an angel informs him that the unusual pregnancy is the result of the Holy Spirit and a fulfilment of prophecy. In obedience to the command, Joseph takes Mary as wife, and when the child is born gives him the divinely appointed name Jesus (vv. 20–25). This is followed by the visit of magi from the east who, having been led by a cosmic sign, have come to pay homage to Jesus. After meeting Herod, these mysterious visitors are further led by the star to Jesus's exact location, present him with gifts, and subsequently are warned in a dream not to return to Herod and therefore return to their home country by a different route (2:1–12). Again, by a dream, Joseph is instructed to flee with his family to Egypt to escape the coming persecution at the hands of Herod (2:13) where he remains with the Holy Family until, being directed by an angel in a later dream, he returns to Israel (2:20) and more specifically to Galilee (2:22).

Luke's Account

Luke's account of Jesus's nativity, like Matthew's, is replete with primal imagery. His narration introduces another manifestation of the primal having

---

34. Unlike Luke, Matthew provides no explanation of the circumstances attending the conception of the child, but merely asserts it as fact.

to do with the supernatural beings encountered in the aforementioned dreams—angels. Luke's version, which covers all of chapters 1 and 2, interweaves the story of the miraculous birth of John the Baptist with that of Jesus. In both cases, the birth announcement is made by the angel Gabriel to persons who have no reasonable expectation of bearing children, one because of advanced age and barrenness, and the other due to virginity (1:13, 18–19; 1:26). In both cases, the angel gives the name that the child should be called and indicates the key role the Holy Spirit will play in their birth and throughout each of their lives (1:13, 15–17; 1:32, 35). Finally, Jesus's birth is announced by a chorus of angels to a local group of shepherds in a cosmic display that leads them to worship the child (2:8–20).[35]

Dreams

The prominence of dreams in the Matthean account—a total of four recorded within two brief chapters—is significant from the perspective of the primal imagination. The cluster of dreams attending the infancy narratives of Christ are one of only three such clusters in the Bible—"the early patriarchal period, the life of Daniel, and the infancy narratives of Matthew's Gospel"—all of them instances "in which dreams functioned as vehicles for divine revelation."[36] Aside these, later in Matthew, the wife of Pontius Pilate mentions that she had "suffered a great deal today in a dream because of [Jesus]" (Matt 27:19 NIV). While the precise content of her dream is not noted, the import is the same. In biblical times, dreams were not treated only as a "sequence of thoughts and images occurring during sleep"[37] or, to use psychological terminology, as "eruption[s] into the upper levels of the sleeper's mind of some of the impulses and symbolic images of the subconscious." They were occasions of genuine engagement with the spiritual

---

35. It is important to note the role of prophecy in the text as well. Both Mary and Zechariah initially respond to the news of the impending pregnancies and births with a questioning hesitancy, but ultimately utter songs/prophecies of praise in response to the unfolding events (Luke 1:46–55, 68–75). Luke also narrates Jesus's presentation in the temple and notes the presence of two individuals, Simeon and Anna, the former described as "righteous and devout" (2:25 RSVCE) and the latter as "a prophetess" (2:36 RSVCE), both of whom in different ways herald the child as "the Lord's Christ" and "the redemption of Israel." Prophecy is itself a primal activity wherein the human person becomes a channel for divine or supernatural speech.

36. D. A. Black, "Dreams," in Green et al., *Dictionary of Jesus*, 199. See also Adeyemo, "Dreams."

37. D. A. Black, "Dreams," in Green et al., *Dictionary of Jesus*, 199.

world, "a real experience of one element of the self which goes forth to these encounters while other elements sleep on."[38] In contexts where the primal imagination continues to hold sway, dreams are commonly believed to be "a means of communication between this world and the spirit world of the ancestors, divinities, and the High God."[39] While it is not suggested that these dreams were occasions for the souls or spirits of either Joseph or the magi to travel outside of themselves to encounter spiritual beings, it is evident, however, that the dreams are assumed to be *actual* encounters with *real* beings that inform and direct actions taken during the waking lives of the dreamers, and not just thoughts or imaginings that arise from within. This expresses Turner's third and fourth features and demonstrates the primal imagination at work.

The Infancy Narratives: Magi

Perhaps more compelling than the prominence of dreams as an expression of the primal imagination is Matthew's inclusion of the story of the magi. The visit of these mysterious wise men from the East is recorded only in Matthew and their identity has been the subject of intense speculation through the Christian centuries. Nothing in Matthew's account supplies answers to the many complex questions that arise from the story's inclusion in the text, and as they have preoccupied Christian scholars for centuries, a conclusive answer cannot be hoped for here. However, the wise men are differentiated from the other characters in the narrative in that they are not Jews, have no direct access to the Scriptures, and receive no direct instructions from God until *after* their encounter with the Christ child, through a dream.

The overall point of the magi narrative is the honoring of Jesus by gentiles. Their visit served as "an exoneration of the Gentiles and as an indictment of the Jews since they foretold the coming faith of the Gentiles and condemned the present unbelief of the Jews."[40] The inclusion of this story strongly suggests a primal religious orientation of Matthew and his audience—an orientation that was "tolerant of the religions of other peoples and sometimes borrow[ed] certain elements from them"[41] with-

---

38. John V. Taylor, *Primal Vision*, 50.
39. Adeyemo, "Dreams."
40. "The Second Homily: On Matthew 2," in Kellerman, *Incomplete Commentary*, 31.
41. Baylis, *Introduction to Primal Religions*, 3.

out being fundamentally changed or challenged by the loan. This is not to suggest that astrology and divination of the kind associated with magi were considered acceptable practices in Judaism. Both were opposed and proscribed by Scripture (Deut 4:19, 18:9–13; Isa 47:13). Simon, the dubious convert and former practitioner of magical arts, is condemned for his proposal to purchase divine power (Acts 8:9–24) while Bar-Jesus, the μάγος (*mágos*) who opposed the ministry of Paul, was called by him "a child of the devil and an enemy of everything that is right" (Acts 13:10 NIV). Nevertheless, during the time of Christ, "many . . . whether or not they regarded astrology as sinful, accepted astrology's accuracy in prediction" and "most Jewish people seemed to have acquiesced to its pervasive influence in late antiquity."[42] Matthew shows no qualms about introducing μάγοι (*mágoi*) into his infancy narrative, even though their inclusion implies, if not an outright acceptance of their presumed practice of divination, at least an openness to the possibility of God's involvement and perhaps even guidance in it.[43]

There is within the text an inner connection to the Old Testament story of Balaam, who is described by Philo as a magician (μάγος/*mágos* in the original Greek) and who also hails from the east.[44] He is recorded as giving a prophecy in Num 24:17—"I see Him, but not now; I behold Him, but not nigh: a star shall come out of Jacob and a scepter shall rise out of Israel" (RSVCE). This prophetic utterance by a pagan seer "features prominently in the history of the exegesis of the Magi story"; it is a "'pagan oracle' [that] would have circulated outside Judaism in some shape or form and would have set people thinking."[45] This connection not only reflects the am-

---

42. Keener, *Gospel of Matthew*, 101. See also Kapolyo, "Matthew," 1110.

43. In his commentary on the text, Kapolyo de-emphasizes the efficacy of divination, stressing rather that the passage shows "that God will reveal himself wherever people are looking for him," and that "the Magi needed to have their revelations confirmed by the revealed word of God, which only the Jews had" ("Matthew," 1110). While I agree ultimately that the fullness of revelation of God is found only in the person of Jesus Christ, Kapolyo seems too eager to downplay the full implications of the way divination is portrayed in the text. Even after their visit in Jerusalem, the magi continue to be led by the star to Jesus. The Hebrew Scriptures play only a marginal role in the whole encounter. Moreover, it is Herod, not the wise men, who consults the chief priests and scribes to determine where the Christ was to be born (2:4). Despite the fact that he had the Scriptures, Herod was apparently unaware that he had been born at all (2:7), relying instead on the pagan magi for this information!

44. Philo, *De Vita Mosis* 1.276.

45. Ratzinger, *Infancy Narratives*, loc. 1072.

bivalence with which divination may have been regarded by Matthew and his audience, but also points to the shared sense of the primal that underlies the religious understanding of Jews and non-Jews alike during this period.

The μάγοι (*mágoi*) arrive, having been guided to Judea by means of a celestial body, which they interpret as a sign indicating the birth of the king of the Jews. This interpretation reflects a primal framework in which "all events are interpreted in terms of the working of *spiritual forces* which permeate the environment . . . a personalised universe, where there is a will behind everything that happens."[46] The personal aspect of the star is emphasized as the star, having led the μάγοι (*mágoi*) as far as Jerusalem, continues to guide them the short distance from Jerusalem to Bethlehem, until it comes to rest directly above the place Jesus lodges. This is an indication that it is no ordinary celestial body, or cosmic sign, but is animated and directed by a spiritual force. In Brent Landau's analysis of the *Revelation of the Magi*, the star is not only a cosmic sign of Christ, but is Christ himself. Landau summarizes the relevant sections:

> The star appears in the sky, descends from the heavens, and enters the cave [where the Magi have heretofore performed their monthly rituals in accordance to received prophecy], inviting the Magi to come inside (12:3–5). In the cave, the star takes the form of a small and humble human being and tells the Magi that such a form is necessary for the inhabitants of the world to see the Son of the Father—indicating that this star-child is none other than Christ himself (13:1–2). Christ tells the Magi that he has been sent from the Father for the salvation of all humanity, and instructs them to follow the star to Bethlehem to see his birth in human form (13:8–13).[47]

This demonstrates the primal sense of a personalized natural order which pervaded the culture of New Testament times and which would have informed Matthew's view of the magi and the star. This was a primal culture in which it was assumed that "the divine may break through and manifest itself in the visible profane world at any time."[48] Such breakthroughs were not confined to the boundaries of Judea nor even to the chosen people of Israel.

---

46. Baylis, *Introduction to Primal Religions*, 10; emphasis original.
47. Landau, "Sages and Star-Child," 8.
48. Baylis, *Introduction to Primal Religions*, 11.

Animating the Spiritual Realm: Angels, Demons, and the Living Dead

The dynamism of the spiritual realm brings with it another dimension that must be considered. Spirit beings—angels, demons, and ancestors, are given a substantial place within the New Testament. These not only contribute to the dynamism of the spiritual realm, but engage actively in the material creation as well. Luke's account introduces into the New Testament one of the most important of these: angels.

Angels

The prevalence of angelic imagery surrounding Christmas celebrations has largely obscured the primal, otherworldly reality they represent in the biblical text. This is perhaps due to the way the New Testament refers to them in matter-of-fact language, as simply part of the "structure of reality" in which the authors and their audiences lived.[49] Within the infancy narratives, angels serve as messengers of the divine will, conveying specific instructions. This is in keeping with the classical Greek usage of the term ἄγγελος (*ángelos*), which designated "the ambassador in human affairs, who speaks and acts in the place of the one who has sent him. He is under the protection of the gods and is inviolate."[50] The term had a supernatural connotation, and though the word was at times used for human messengers, in the New Testament its usage is overwhelmingly in reference to supernatural spirit beings.[51] The biblical text is notably devoid of speculation about the angels' appearance or form, though Luke indicates that it is Gabriel[52] (who with Michael is one of only two named angels mentioned in the Bible) who announces the births of both John the Baptist and Jesus. The recipients of the angelic message in these narratives are not cautioned against worshipping them, as in other cases wherein those who encounter angels "end up facedown, overwhelmed with awe."[53]

---

49. M. J. Davidson, "Angels," in Green et al., *Dictionary of Jesus*, 8.
50. H. Bietenhard, "ἄγγελος," *NIDNTT* 1:101.
51. M. J. Davidson, "Angels," in Green et al., *Dictionary of Jesus*, 8.
52. That Gabriel is the angel named recalls the apocalyptic book of Daniel where he makes his first appearance in conjunction with prophecies about the end times (Dan 12:9), thus indicating that the births of John and Jesus are a signal that "the end time moment is indeed near but not yet" (S. Noll, *Angels of Light*, 73).
53. S. Noll, *Angels of Light*, 45.

As divine messengers and representatives of heaven, the appearance of angels signals a breaking in of the supernatural world into this one.[54] It is an encounter with the holy (and wholly) "other"[55] that is an essential feature of the primal imagination. The appearance of "an angel of the Lord" to the shepherds gathered near Bethlehem and a "multitude of the heavenly hosts" is an eruption of the spiritual, numinous realm into the arena of human affairs—a sudden effacement of the boundary between sensible and super-sensible realms assumed in the primal imagination. The reaction of the shepherds is similar to that of Joseph and others who encounter angels—surprise, amazement, and awe, followed by obedience—but not disbelief or incredulity. While these angelic appearances are unusual and surprising occasions, they are not described in mythic language. They are straightforwardly described as historical events, and self-evidently possible. The ability of mankind to enter into relationship with spirit powers more ultimate than himself is assumed by both author and audience. An encounter with an angel might be unusual but was by no means unthinkable.

Angels in Pauline Discourse: 1 Corinthians

Here I must step outside the infancy narratives to two other passages in the New Testament that shed greater light on this particular manifestation of the primal: the Pauline discourses in 1 Cor 11:10 and 13:1. In these passages, Paul explicitly links human action to the angelic realm. In the first case, it is the veiling of women. He asserts that woman "ought to have a symbol of authority on her head, because of the angels" (NKJV). This passage has been variously interpreted through the centuries of Christian scholarship. Tertullian held that veiling was necessary "because on account of 'the daughters of men' angels revolted from God."[56] The Corinthian women would then be presumably protected from the "gaze of these fallen angels" identified with the "watchers" of Gen 6:1–2.[57] Others have posited

---

54. H. Bietenhard, "ἄγγελος," *NIDNTT* 1:102.

55. Rudolph Otto describes it so: "The truly 'mysterious' object is beyond our apprehension and comprehension, not only because our knowledge has certain irremovable limits, but because in it we come upon something inherently 'wholly other,' whose kind and character are incommensurable with our own, and before which we therefore recoil in a wonder that strikes us chill and numb" (*Idea of the Holy*, 28.)

56. Tertullian, "On Prayer," 688.

57. Thiselton, *First Corinthians*, 839.

that the Pauline admonition has to do with holy angels or guardian angels who are present in worship with the church.[58] This position is consonant with the "Jewish tradition that Christians worship the transcendent God of heaven in company with the heavenly host,"[59] thus whatever is done within the context of Christian worship, not only in relation to "spiritual" matters, but also those which might be considered more mundane (head coverings) has supernatural implications. Both views are deeply primal in that they assume that whatever transpires in the sensible realms of human existence affects, and is affected by, what transpires in the super-sensible realm. Veiling, therefore—whether as a defense against fallen angels or in deference to holy ones—is a sacramental action birthed out of the primal imagination.

In the opening of 1 Cor 13, Paul refers briefly to "tongues of angels"— a phrase that invites questions about the nature of that language and the use to which it may be put. As Noll phrases it, "Is the term tongues of angels hyperbole, or does Paul believe that at least some glossolalia is angelic speech?"[60] The phrase appears only in this particular instance and is clearly not the primary focus of the text. Any conclusion must necessarily be tentative. Paul's usage of the term seems to indicate his belief in such angelic language(s), that human beings could, through a special grace of the Holy Spirit, employ, but which would otherwise be unintelligible. This Pauline reference to angelic tongues resonates with the African primal sense that "gods do not communicate in human languages, but in 'primal tongues,' as a sign of the limitations of human language."[61] Though the Bible never considers angels as divinities or "gods," the overall sentiment is the same. Whatever else these languages may signify, Paul's reference to them demonstrates that he shares the primal understanding of the supernatural realm as one replete with supernatural agents who can and do communicate with human beings, and with whom human beings may also communicate.

The "Living Dead": Jesus's Ancestral Legacy

Returning briefly to the infancy narratives, the matter of Jesus's ancestors comes to the forefront. The recitation of Jesus's ancestors at the very beginning of the Gospel account points strongly to the importance of situating

---

58. S. Noll, *Angels of Light*, 188.
59. Thiselton, *First Corinthians*, 841.
60. S. Noll, *Angels of Light*, 187.
61. Asamoah-Gyadu, "Drinking from Our Own Wells," 57.

Jesus's birth within the context of his ancestral lineage. Jesus does not appear, as in the more abstract opening of John's Gospel, as the preexistent λόγος (*Logos*) upon whom creational reality depends, and who "became flesh and dwelt among us" (John 1:14 ESV), but rather as one who is himself dependent upon his ancestors. As the genealogy is recounted, the hearer/reader is reminded that these recalled ancestors are those who have played their role in the "transmission and safeguarding of life [that] the ancestors are in some ways our 'origins,' those from whom we emerge."[62] There is an organic link between the ancestors of Jesus and Jesus himself; he descends from them and is, in a real sense, dependent upon them for life itself. However, just as Paul would remind the Roman church in distinguishing the true Israel of faith from mere biological descent,[63] so too, an ancestor is not one whose life-giving function is only biological. The ancestor is one who "sows peace, joy, love" and is, therefore, "*allied* with life, is a 'giver' of life"[64] in an ethical and moral sense as well. Jesus depends on his ancestral lineage not only for his biological life, but also for the ethical instruction in the law passed down through them and that he would ultimately be understood to embody, making him both the true Israelite and the true Son of Man.[65] In the person of Jesus, it is not only that the God of his Jewish ancestors is made known, but they themselves are experienced as immanent.

Here is a parallel to the primal African sense of ancestors as the "living dead . . . a person who is physically dead but alive in the memory of those who knew him in his life as well as being alive in the world of spirits. So long as the living-dead is thus remembered, he is in the state of *personal immortality*."[66] They may therefore also be termed the *remembered dead*, or, as Rev. Anderson would term them, the *so-called dead*. This interpretation is not as far-fetched as it may at first appear, for Jesus implies as much in Luke 20:38: "Now he is not God of the dead, but of the living, for all live

---

62. Kabasélé, "Christ as Ancestor," 120.

63. "Not all are who are descended from Israel belong to Israel" (Rom 9:6 ESV; cf. Luke 13:28)

64. Kabasélé, "Christ as Ancestor," 120.

65. Seen in this light, the disciples' later response to Jesus's inquiry, "who do people say that I am" (Mark 8:28 ESV; cf. Matt 16:13–15, Luke 9:18–20), takes on additional significance, as their answers can be understood as references to Jesus's embodiment of the ancestors of Israel, including the recently executed John the Baptist. This also provides an additional dimension to Jesus's claim in John 8:56–58, that Abraham "rejoiced to see [his] day," and that "before Abraham was, I am" (NKJV).

66. Mbiti, *African Religions and Philosophy*, 25.

to him" (ESV; cf. Mark 12:27, Matt 22:32). This passage adds additional complexity to the issue, as it positively asserts that though the patriarchs/ancestors of Israel are clearly dead, "if God says that he is still in a relationship with them, then they must still in some sense be alive."[67] Thus, the listing of Jesus's genealogy recalls the recitation of the ancestors that takes place during the pouring of libation in traditional Akan religious practice. In that case, the recitation is not intended only to recount their names and evoke memory of their deeds, but is an invocation as well, inviting the participation of the ancestors in the event: *Begye nsa ncm* (Come and receive drinks) and *Gye nsa nom* (Receive drinks). In light of this, the recitation of the genealogies can be read not only as situating Jesus in his historical and lineal contexts, but also as an acknowledgment of the attendance of his ancestors upon his entry in the world.

The "Living Dead": The Transfiguration

Turning from the infancy narratives, one comes to another signal event in the life of Christ replete with primal overtones: the transfiguration. The transfiguration is recorded in Matt 17:1–9, Mark 9:2–10, and Luke 9:28–36, and is referred to in 2 Pet 1:16–18. The event occurs within the same narrative context in all the Synoptic Gospels—shortly after Peter's confession that Jesus is the Messiah and before his healing of a boy and a second prediction of the passion. The placement of the transfiguration in the same narrative context in all three accounts suggests the historicity of the event.

The transfiguration is described straightforwardly in the three Gospel accounts though differing in some minor details. Following Peter's confession of Jesus as Messiah, Peter, John, and James alone among the disciples are led by Jesus to a mountain. While there, Jesus's physical appearance changes and his clothes become gleamingly white. Elijah and Moses appear together, talking with Jesus (according to Luke) about his impending departure at Jerusalem (Luke 9:31). Peter then proposes the erection of three tabernacles—a proposal that is immediately followed by the envelopment of the group in a cloud[68] and a declaration of Jesus's sonship reminiscent of that heard at his baptism, coupled with an instruction to listen to him. The event ends as abruptly as it began, and the disciples are found alone

---

67. Isaak, "Luke," 1244.

68. It is unclear if the "them" in the text refers to Jesus, Elijah, and Moses alone, or to the entire group inclusive of the disciples.

with Jesus who commands them to remain silent about it until after the resurrection. The description of the event in 2 Peter differs little from what is found in the Gospel accounts.

Diverse interpretations of the meaning of the transfiguration have been offered and there is no space to detail them all here. Yet an examination of the event through the lens of the primal yields an additional perspective especially in relation to the status of the dead, which might otherwise be obscured. In particular, the connection between Peter's confession (Matt 16:13–20, Mark 8:27–33, Luke 9:18–20) and the transfiguration itself becomes clearer. His confession comes as a response to Jesus's question to the disciples about who people think he is and how the disciples themselves identify him. The opinion of the people is clear: Jesus is John the Baptist, or Elijah, or perhaps some other prophet returned from the dead. Peter's definitive answer, rendered on behalf of all the disciples, is that Jesus is none of these, but is, in fact, the anticipated Messiah. Although Jesus confirms the validity of Peter's confession, neither Peter's confession, nor Jesus's affirmation negate the implications of the responses of the people. The assumptions that underlie their responses are suggestive. The notion that Jesus somehow embodies one of the departed prophets of Israel, including the recently executed John the Baptist implies an underlying belief that the dead were *potentially* active agents in the affairs of the living even to the point of returning under certain circumstances. This belief is similar to those held among some groups in African and other primal contexts.[69]

Jesus's prophetic words following the Petrine confession heighten this ambiguity. Positioned between the statements that the people believe Jesus is a prophet returned from the dead, and the transfiguration, in which Jesus converses with long deceased figures from Israel's history, Jesus's prophecy becomes even more enigmatic. The framing of the prophecy makes clear that it is not a reference to resurrection, nor to the transfiguration event. Jesus's words imply that at least some of his hearers will not die at all until they have seen him in his glory. The prophecy reflects a continuity of thought on the relationship between the living and the dead from the Old Testament accounts of Enoch (Gen 5:24) and Elijah (2 Kgs 2:11), neither of whom "tasted death" (Luke 9:27 RSVCE) but were taken to be with God without dying first. Jesus's prophecy can then be taken to mean that

---

69. For example, the belief that "each baby is said to be a reincarnation of someone who died . . . is by no means rare in Africa," and is "also well known for South Asia and Native North Americans" (Gottlier, "Non-Western Approaches," 151).

a similar destiny awaited some of those present. Perplexing though Jesus's words may appear from the perspective of the post-Enlightenment West, the underlying sentiment is primal, for in the primal worldview, the boundary line between the realms of the living and the dead is not so firmly fixed.

Death was not considered a permanent or inviolable condition and the presumed state of the dead decidedly more ambiguous than a post-Enlightenment cosmology would admit. Paul's rather cryptic reference in 1 Cor 15:29 to baptism for/on behalf of the dead in his apologetic for bodily resurrection is notable here. Space does not permit a full exploration of this passage, which is, in any event, rather too vague to assert any conclusive reading of the text. "Scantiness of the evidence [of the practice] has given rise to scores of interpretations, some of which are fanciful and highly speculative";[70] there is no need to add to them here. It is sufficient to note that Paul's reference to the practice underscores the ambiguity of relationship between the living and the dead within the New Testament primal vision.

Finally, and most intriguingly, the transfiguration features Jesus in dialogue with Moses and Elijah, prominent ancestors of Israel. Various interpretations have been offered for why Moses and Elijah are the particular persons with whom Jesus communes, but that is a secondary concern. Whatever their specific presence may signify in relation to Jesus's ministry and mission, Moses and Elijah, ancestors of Israel, appear, fully alive, communing and conversing with Jesus. The three disciples are caught up into this communion as well. They too were enveloped in the cloud and "heard this very voice borne from heaven" (2 Pet 1:18 ESV). The transfiguration is not merely an observed phenomenon or a strictly spiritual, that is, non-physical, occurrence, but an experienced material event. Peter's desire to erect physical structures to shelter each person is evidence of this, for if Moses and Elijah were disembodied spirits, there would be no need for physical shelters. At the moment of transfiguration, they seem to "occupy

---

70. Brauch, *Hard Sayings of Paul*, 175. Intriguingly, the *Africa Bible Commentary* offers nothing of commentary except to note that the existence of the practice indicates that "if the living have so much concern for the dead as to be baptized for them, then the dead must have an existence beyond death" (Datiri, "1 Corinthians," 1396). While the fifth of Turner's six features, the primal belief in life beyond death, is affirmed by this comment, one would hope, given the prominent place of ancestors within African cosmology, that more would be said about this. One wonders if this could be a legacy of the enduring effect of Euro-Western scholarship in its reluctance to fully engage the primal even among African scholars.

the ontological state between God and men"⁷¹ as do ancestors in other primal contexts. Based on their discussion of Jesus's impending departure at Jerusalem—his passion, resurrection, and ascension—these living dead forefathers appear to have some degree of knowledge of future events. This, too, is primal, as it is believed that ancestors "in their spiritual state can see more and hear more" than others.⁷² In short, the whole scene resounds with primal echoes that are clear when read through the lens of the primal imagination.

The "Living Dead": The Resurrected Ones

The transfiguration recalls another signal, yet seldom remarked text related to the dead: Matt 27:52. "The tombs also were opened. And many bodies of the saints who had fallen asleep were raised, and coming out of the tombs after his resurrection they went into the holy city and appeared to many" (ESV). The episode is recorded only in Matthew and does not fully harmonize with Paul's declaration of Jesus as firstborn from the dead. A further complication is that the passage problematically implies that after the tombs of these departed saints were opened, they "sat around in their tombs for some days before emerging."⁷³ From the standpoint of the primal imagination, whether Matthew portrays these dead as having been raised at the time of Jesus's own death and resurrection, or whether he describes a "space-time collapse"⁷⁴ wherein the eschaton is brought forward in an apocalyptic prophecy, is largely immaterial. In the ancient primal Hebrew understanding, "texts that describe the future often do so in terms of the past, and thus view events as cyclical, or at least as recurring."⁷⁵ Matthew, as an inheritor of this tradition, would likewise have been less concerned about a strictly linear recounting of events. Indeed, the eschaton itself need not be necessarily considered the end of time.⁷⁶ In the primal understanding, "nothing can happen in the physical world that has not [already] been ordained in the spiritual world."⁷⁷ Consequently, *when* these events occur

71. Mbiti, *African Religions and Philosophy*, 27.
72. Baylis, *Introduction to Primal Religions*, 26.
73. Wenham, "When Were Saints Raised," 150.
74. Waters, "Matthew 27:52–53," 505.
75. Brettler, "Cyclical and Teleological Time," 123.
76. Brettler, "Cyclical and Teleological Time," 122.
77. Quarshie, "Paul and the Primal Substructure," 9.

is less important than *that* they occur. That said, I agree with those scholars who conclude that Matthew "understood that the events which allegedly occurred at Jesus's death, belonged to real history . . . to have actually occurred in time and space."[78] As in the transfiguration scene, the boundary line between living and dead is effaced and the saints—whether the Christian saints of the eschaton[79] or Israel's "saints of old"[80]—make their appearance, are seen by many, and apparently disappear again. The primal nature of this event is undeniable.

Exorcism, Healing, and Spiritual Warfare

Turning now to other important manifestations of the primal imagination in the New Testament, one finds two activities that, taken together, comprise a significant portion of the ministry of Jesus and the apostles: exorcism and healing. Indeed, if so-called nature miracles are set aside, it becomes evident that "the Gospels portray Jesus as spending a large proportion of his time . . . as a miracle worker"[81]—healing the sick and casting out demons. The ministry of Jesus and the apostles as recorded in the New Testament may be fairly characterized as a ministry of exorcism and healing. Given the number of healings and exorcisms recorded in the Gospels, not to speak of the larger New Testament canon, an exhaustive treatment is not possible. A more limited survey is sufficient, however, to demonstrate the primal imagination at work. Since demonic activity was believed to be behind some, though not all, physical illnesses (as in the case of the epileptic boy of Mark 9), and thus exorcism a specific type of healing, I begin with it.

Exorcism: Background and Cultural Context

Exorcism was not an unusual occurrence in Jesus's day. Belief in demonic possession was "widespread in the Greco-Roman world" and the consequent need for exorcism was commonly held.[82] The New Testament affirms that Jesus and his disciples were not unique in exorcising demons, the

78. D. Anderson, "Origin and Purpose," 275–76.
79. Waters, "Matthew 27:52–53," 511.
80. Wenham, "When Were Saints Raised," 152.
81. Twelftree, *Jesus the Miracle Worker*, 19.
82. S. Noll, *Angels of Light*, 131.

unknown exorcist of Luke 9:49 (cf. Mark 9:38–39) and the sons of Sceva in Acts 19:11–20 being examples. Exorcism was so important to Jesus's work that Matt 12:28//Luke 11:20 portray his "dealings with the demon possessed" as being "of central significance in understanding Jesus and his ministry," while four of the thirteen stories of healing recorded in Mark are exorcisms.[83] According to Peter Bolt, in the Greco-Roman world, *daimons* were frequently linked with the dead, and were, at the level of popular culture—the culture of the early readers of the Gospels—"persistently identified with ghosts."[84] That the Gerasene demoniac of Mark 5:1–20 had his dwelling among the tombs further supports this association. Bolt's analysis underscores the effacement of the line between the living and the dead that is so much a feature of the primal background of the New Testament. These dead are not, however, in the same category as the ancestors of African primal thought, nor of the saints in other portions of the New Testament. The *daimons* of the Greco-Roman world were believed to be "the ghosts of the wicked, bent on human destruction"[85] and thus inimical to the fulfilment of a good life. Driving them out was therefore a means by which the destruction of human life could be averted.

Exorcism in the Ministry of Jesus

Only four detailed narratives of exorcism are found in the Gospels: the demoniac with the unclean spirit (Mark 1:21–28, cf. Luke 4:31–37), the Gerasene demoniac (Mark 5:1–20), the demonized daughter of the Syrophoenician woman (Mark 7:24–20), and finally, the epileptic boy whose

83. Twelftree, *Jesus the Miracle Worker*, 282.
84. Bolt, "Jesus, Daimons and Dead," 96.
85. Bolt, "Jesus, Daimons and Dead," 96. Incidentally, that *daimons* are the "ghosts of the wicked set on destruction" challenges the facile association some African Christians make between ancestors and demonic forces. James Nkansah-Obrempong's article "Angels, Demons and Powers" in the *Africa Bible Commentary*, where he asserts "many such incidents [of people receiving messages from their deceased relatives] actually involve impersonation by demons" (1454), is one such example. Though Nkansah-Obrempong carefully avoids the assertion that any communion with the ancestral realm is automatically fellowship with demons, that he makes the association at all illustrates my point, especially since there is no clear biblical warrant for this association. An ancestor is, by definition, one of the righteous dead of a society who has contributed in a life-affirming way to the good of society, and since, as Kwame Bediako affirms, "African ancestors . . . do not become after death what they were not before death," associating the ancestral realm with the demonic may be problematic (*Christianity in Africa*, 218).

demon the disciples were unable to cast out (Mark 9 14–29). No definitive pattern is discernible in Jesus's approach to the demonized, but the stories contain elements that have parallels in other ancient literature on exorcism that help elucidate the primal orientation of the background culture.

Contestation of Power

One key feature in all these is the contestation of authority. In the New Testament world, exorcism "was seen as local access to power for the routine treatment of certain ailments" and thus an encounter with the demonic was invariably construed as a power encounter.[86] It is in light of this understanding that the members of the synagogue in Luke 4:36 comment on the authority and power with which Jesus commanded unclean spirits. This was the lens through which Jesus's actions were interpreted in Matt 12:24 (cf. 9:34, Mark 3:22, Luke 11:15), when he was accused of casting out demons by Beelzebub, the prince of demons. In this view, Jesus was simply an exorcist who had aligned himself with the greatest demonic power available. Jesus does not dispute the belief that he is engaged in a power encounter but asserts that the source of his power is the "finger of God" (Luke 11:20 NKJV), a phrase that links his activity with the signal deliverance of Israel from Egyptian bondage in Exod 8:19, and thus with the eschatological hope of the Jewish people. Jesus's exorcisms are binding the strong man and spoiling his goods. Again the power contest is seen in the case of the Gerasene demoniac where in response to Jesus's attempt to cast out the demon (Mark 5:8), the demon attempts to bind Jesus (v. 7) using a formulaic term, ὁρκίζω (horkizō), that was commonly used by exorcists.[87] Jesus then requests the demon's name (v. 9) as an alternative means by which to disarm and demonstrate mastery over the demon, a technique that coheres with that found in magical texts.[88] The primal sense of the spirit world as a realm of power relations emerges clearly in these episodes—a reality later echoed in the well-known Pauline admonition of Eph 6:11–12.

---

86. S. Noll, *Angels of Light*, 131–32.

87. Bolt, "Jesus, Daimons and Dead," 98; cf. Acts. 19:13.

88. Graham H. Twelftree, "Demon, Devil, Satan," in Green et al., *Dictionary of Jesus*, 167. Cf. *PGM* IV. 3080: The would-be exorcist is instructed to demand of the demon his identity and what sort of demon he is so that, "every spirit and daimon, whatever sort it may be, will be subject to [him]."

The Importance of Names

What emerges also is the importance of names within the primal framework of the New Testament. As has already been mentioned, Jesus's demand for the name of the demon was a well-known means of subduing the spirit. Names signify the reputation or authority of the person; "to know a person's or a deity's name is to know something fundamental about him or her."[89] Likewise, to "call upon" a name is to invoke the authority and ownership value associated with that name, though this could apparently be attempted illegitimately. It is in this light that one must read of the sons of Sceva's attempted exorcisms using the name of Jesus (Acts 19). A similar dynamic appears to be at play in Mark 9:38–41 when the disciples complain that Jesus's name is used to perform exorcisms by someone who is not part of the community of disciples. Though the outcomes associated with the invocation of Jesus's name differ in each of these cases of attempted exorcism, what emerges from both is the use of the name as a means of invoking power in a spiritual encounter.[90] However, the power of a name goes beyond the realm of spirit—the arena in which demonic deliverance presumably occurs—to the sensible realm as well as in the case of physical healing.

Healing

The Acts 3 account of Peter and John healing the lame beggar in the temple is perhaps the quintessential text linking physical healing with the name of Jesus. Upon healing the man, Peter explains to the crowd that "his [Jesus's] name—by faith in his name—has made this man strong whom you see and know, and the faith that is through Jesus has given the man this perfect health in the presence of you all" (v. 16 ESV). This passage extends the ministry of Jesus as a healer into the lives of the apostles and of the church.

---

89. B. Eastman, "Name," in Martin and Davids, *Dictionary*, 785.

90. The difference between the two seems to be the lack of an inward relationship to the "name" being invoked. In the case of Mark 9, Jesus's response indicates that though the exorcist using his name is unknown to the disciples, he is operating "for" Jesus and not against him. The exorcist may be unknown to the disciples but not, apparently, to Jesus's cause or to the demons that oppose him. This is contrasted with the case of the sons of Sceva where the demons indicate they do *not* know the would-be exorcists who are adjudged to not be acting *for* Jesus but rather contrary to his purposes. See also the earlier discussion of how "calling on the name of the Lord" is actualized within the ritual practice of some Pentecostal congregations.

Jesus's ministry, and that of the apostolic community, may be fairly described as a ministry of healing. Indeed, Jesus summarizes his ministry as one where "the blind receive their sight, the lame walk, lepers are cleansed, and the deaf hear, the dead are raised up, the poor have good news preached to them" (Luke 7:22 ESV). Not only that, but during his lifetime Jesus sent out the twelve disciples to exorcise demons, proclaim the kingdom of God, and heal the sick (Luke 9:1–2), an instruction that is repeated in his sending of the seventy-two (Luke 10:9). "Gifts of healing" (ESV) is among those spiritual gifts listed by Paul in 1 Cor 12, and elders are admonished in Jas 5 to anoint the sick with oil "in the name of the Lord" (ESV) so that they might receive healing. Though each healing recorded in the New Testament can be considered extraordinary, two—the healing of the bleeding woman (Mark 5:25–34, Matt 9:20–22, Luke 8:43–48) and the healings associated with Paul's handkerchiefs and aprons (Acts 19:11–12)—emerge as exceptional in their expression of the primal nature of Christian faith.

Sacramental Use of Objects in Healing

The primal nature of these cases of healing emerges from their sacramental use of objects to convey physical health to those who encounter them. While this is also indicated in the James passage in relation to the use of oil, James is careful to note that it is "the prayer offered in faith" along with the confession of sin that brings healing (Jas 5:15–16 NIV); the oil appears to be incidental. In the other cases, however, including a brief comment in Matt 14:36, and the episode involving Peter's shadow in Acts 5:15, these objects—Paul's handkerchiefs and aprons, the fringe of Jesus's garment—behave very much in line with Kwame Bediako's description of the sacramental perspective of the primal: "The 'physical' acts as sacrament for 'spiritual' power."[91] Jesus affirms this view when he notes, "Someone touched me, for I perceive that power has gone out from me" (Luke 8:46 ESV). While Jesus acknowledges the role the woman's faith plays in her healing (v. 48), his recognition that a cure has been effected by means of his garment is in line with the primal mind that expects "that the powers, the presence, or the personality of God, or some other spirit or spirit being can be . . . mediated by a mere object or symbol."[92] There is no indication that

91. K. Bediako, *Christianity in Africa*, 101.
92. Maggay, "Persistence of Old Gods," 28. The terms "cure" and "healing" are used intentionally since, while the former term connotes only a biomedical intervention, the

Jesus rejects or refutes the validity of this perspective; indeed his response to the request of the sick in Matt 14:36 to touch the fringe of his garment, as well as his use of spit/clay to heal the blind man in Mark 8:23–25 (cf. John 9:6–7) rather indicates that he operated within the same framework. In addition to this, Jesus's use of the word "power" in reference to the healing of the bleeding woman is significant for it is an additional affirmation of the spiritual realm as a realm of power relations.

Laying On of Hands

The use of objects in a sacramental way leads to the consideration of another ritual act in the New Testament that expresses the primal imagination, one not directly related to healing, but often used in concert with it—laying on of hands.[93] The pastoral instruction in Jas 5 concerning the laying on of hands on sick persons by elders of the church has already been mentioned. Additionally, Jesus is mentioned as laying on hands to heal (Matt 8:1–4, 8:14–15, 20:32–34; Mark 1:40–44, 6:5, 7:32, 8:22–25; Luke 4:40, 5:12–14, 13:13, 22:50–51), and laying on of hands is performed in conjunction with healing in Acts 9:17 and 28:8, as well as being mentioned as one of the "signs following" in the extended ending of Mark 16:9–20. Laying on of hands is mentioned in connection with ordination or commissioning (Acts 6:6, 13:3; 1 Tim 4:14, 5:22; 2 Tim 1:6), with blessing (Mark 10:16, cf. Matt 19:15), and with the reception of the Holy Spirit (Acts 8:17–18,

---

latter is a more holistic concept involving social relations as well. See Eve, *Healer from Nazareth*, 52–53. Those relations need not be considered as restricted to the arena of human relations, but may also extend to the supernatural sphere.

93. Baptism is another such act, but given the abundance of scholarship on the sacramental nature of baptism, and the prominence of laying on of hands in the Pentecostal tradition especially, it is that which commands attention here. As for baptism, it is necessary simply to note that in the New Testament it does not function only or simply as an initiatory rite. It is rather presented as a sacramental ritual, the enactment of which changes the spiritual status of the recipient by symbolically burying him—where the sign and the thing signified are one and the same—placing him into Christ, and raising him into a new, different reality where death "no longer has dominion over him" (see Rom 6:1–10 ESV). It is the act, and not only the idea, of baptism that matters. Ongoing disagreement about the form, meaning, and formula for baptism confirm that the Christian church continues to recognize intuitively, if not always consciously, the primal nature of the act. Indeed, a major divide within Pentecostalism is premised on a dispute over whether baptism is to be administered in the name of Jesus only, or in the name of the Father, Son, and Holy Spirit. The very efficacy of the rite itself, and thus the salvation of the baptismal candidate, may be questioned if the improper formula is used.

19:5–6). It is also mentioned as one of the elemental teachings of Christ in Heb 6:1–2. In each of the cases cited, the laying on of hands functions in keeping with the primal understanding of reality—as vehicles for the conveyance of spiritual power. The transfer of power is clearly indicated in Acts 8:17–18 where Simon offers to purchase the divine power evidenced in Peter and John, as well as in 1 Tim 4:14 and 2 Tim 1:16 where Timothy's gifts have come through the laying on of hands. Yet, this spiritual transfer is not unidirectional.

The instruction "do not be hasty in the laying on of hands" (1 Tim 5:22 NIV) is followed by "do not share in the sins of others," implying that laying on hands could facilitate the spread of a spiritual contagion via contact with the sinful person. A straightforward reading of the passage is that a hasty or ill-considered ordination leads to complicity in whatever wrong may later be committed by the ordinand, yet the additional admonition to "keep yourself pure," especially when read in light of the primal concern for purity,[94] evinces a deeper concern about spiritual contamination resulting from the laying on of hands. The sacramental act of laying on hands becomes in this case a vector for the spread of spiritual corruption—the physical again acting as a vehicle for the spiritual—except, in this case, in a negative manner. Avoidance of laying on hands thus functions as a defensive strategy against possible spiritual contagion or even spiritual attack, a concern that points towards one of the most significantly primal texts in the New Testament, Eph 6:10–20.

Spiritual Warfare: Ephesians 6:10–20

The book of Ephesians reflects a period in the life of early Christianity when "the church began to emerge as a social and intellectual force in the Greco-Roman world," and felt an increasing need to proclaim the sovereignty and universality of Jesus.[95] While both the authorship and the audience of Ephesians are disputed in the scholarship, what is undisputed is the primal worldview of the recipients of the letter. The context was one in which a multitude of spiritual powers were perceived to exercise authority over various spheres of human life and were associated with "regimes

---

94. See DeSilva, *Honor, Patronage, Kinship & Purity*, chs. 7–8.
95. Achtemeier et al., *Introducing the New Testament*, 377. Similar themes emerge in Gal 1:4 and Col 1:15–20.

of human political life"[96]—standing behind both natural phenomena and human systems of governance. The letter is written with an eye to these concerns, ones that would be especially relevant if the traditional ascription to Ephesus—a city known "as a center of magical practice and of the worship of the Ephesian Artemis"[97]—is accurate.

The language and imagery in the first part of the letter, ending at 3:20, is warlike, its tone militant. It contains a series of affirmations related to spiritual power—the power God has given to the believer through the risen Christ (1:17–23), the victory they have over the "prince of the power of the air" (2:2, 6 ESV), the church as the "dwelling place" of God's Spirit (2:19–22) and witness and evidence to the cosmic powers of God's wisdom and rule (3:10). The Akan proverb ɔbra yɛ ku (life is war) is one to which the New Testament bears strong witness. Walter Wink's exploration of Eph 3:10 helpfully underscores the warlike undertones of Ephesians, as he describes the heavenly realm as "a dimension of reality . . . in which unredeemed Powers still exercise dominion and must be fought with, preached to, and made to know the manifold wisdom of God."[98] Despite all that has been accomplished for the community of believers, "supernatural enemies who exercise their rule in the world of darkness outside the Christian community"[99] continue to oppose them. Importantly, the image is not "of a heavily armed God appearing on the scene to battle injustice but of God's people putting on the armor that God supplies and defending themselves."[100] It is not God, but believers who fight against various "principalities and powers."[101] This reflects a primal view of mankind existing in "close relationship with a world inhabited by an infinite variety of spiritual beings"[102] many of whom are hostile. The weapons to be employed in this warfare are not, as 2 Cor 10:4 asserts, the weapons of the world, but rather the "armor of God."

---

96. S. Noll, *Angels of Light*, 138.

97. Thielman, *Ephesians*, 20.

98. Wink, *Naming the Powers*, 89.

99. Achtemeier et al., *Introducing the New Testament*, 388.

100. Thielman, *Ephesians*, 418.

101. The term is used here as a shorthand reference for those "powers that were created by God but in some way are hostile to Christ and his church," not only in Ephesians but throughout the Pauline corpus. See Reid, "Principalities and Powers," in Hawthorne et al., *Dictionary of Paul*, 746.

102. Baylis, *Introduction to Primal Religions*, 11.

Conclusion

In this chapter I explored the New Testament through the lens of the primal imagination. Both the compilation of the New Testament canon and the Christian doctrine of inspiration were reflect, in part, the primal orientation of the early Christian community and of orthodox Christian theology. This was followed by a discussion of how the primal expresses itself in the New Testament anchored in a representative sampling of texts around key thematic areas that have emerged within the larger body of research. These texts open a vista into the historic and cultural world of the authors and audience, and demonstrate various ways in which the primal imagination manifests itself in the concerns and communication of the New Testament. What emerges from this limited survey is a clear picture of a deeply primal worldview.

The New Testament world is one in which the supernatural does not exist in a conceptual or ideological way, but in which it, and the multitude of spiritual beings and powers emanating from it, impinge on day-to-day life through dreams, cosmic signs, angelic visitations, as well as in other ways. The veil between the living and the dead appears thin and permeable under the right conditions, with the deceased representing potent presences either as revered ancestors or feared demons. Persons, ritual actions, and physical objects are all potential conduits for spiritual power and for the transference of that power from one person to another. In short, the New Testament, and the Christianity reflected in it, is a thoroughly primal text with primal assumptions. It is not difficult then to see how Black American Pentecostals and spiritual people have fully appropriated this text as one that resonated with and reinforced their own primal imagination, and how indeed the broader Christian community remains reliant, if even unconsciously, upon a primal vision, to sustain its own sense of spirituality. It is to the concrete experiences and practices of these churches that I now turn.

6

Black Pentecostal Churches in Historical Context

THE COMPLETE STORY OF Black American Christianity in general, and the Black holiness Pentecostal/spiritual churches in particular, is as complex and multifaceted as the history of Black Americans themselves and is quite beyond the scope of this book. There are a number of historical studies of Black religion refracted through the lens of Euro-Western tradition which is hostile to primal religion generally and African religion specifically. Because Black religion primarily has been framed as a religious response to racism in American society[1] in a manner that forecloses meaningful engagement with Black religion in expressly religious or theological terms, the specific traditions under consideration need to be set within a broader historical context. My emphasis is primarily on the *theological* rather than the sociological or anthropological aspects of these churches—theology expressed primarily through religious practice. This chapter gives an overview of Black American Christianity with special emphasis on the emergence of holiness Pentecostal/spiritual churches, and some of their distinctive features and beliefs.

---

1. Baer and Singer's work *African American Religion* is representative in this regard.

Churches of the Spirit

Before proceeding, I want to further explain why I have captured holiness Pentecostal and spiritual churches under the same umbrella within this study, despite their apparent differences. Pentecostals have been averse to comparisons between the two groups and are careful to draw clear lines between themselves and spiritual people. However, both traditions, along with the newer charismatic churches, fall within the "churches of the Spirit" that Kwabena Asamoah-Gyadu describes in reference to both African independent/indigenous churches (AICs) and to more explicitly Pentecostal congregations "in which the Spirit existed as experience and not merely as doctrine."[2] His assertions are pertinent not only to the Ghanaian African context from which he hails, but to the broader fabric of global Pentecostalism. Harvey Cox, for example, writes of Pentecostals' "stress on the immediate experience of the Spirit of God" and of their theology "imbedded in testimonies, ecstatic speech, and bodily movement,"[3] which transcends both national and ethnic boundaries as defining features of the movement. Anticipating Asamoah-Gyadu, Cox includes AICs under the rubric of Pentecostalism, affirming that these groups are both phenomenologically Pentecostal and have historic ties to the American Pentecostal movement.[4] While the latter assumption is debatable, the former rests on firmer foundations.

In the same vein, I consider these churches to be exemplars of a unique strand of Black American Christianity. Though they share many features in common with the broader Black church, their emphasis on "ceremonial spirituality"[5] marks them as a distinct tradition. I term this tradition *pneumatic sacramentalism*. They are pneumatic due to the orientation they share with all such "churches of the Spirit" where experiences of and with the spiritual realm are prioritized and can even be considered a defining feature. They are sacramental because of the ways in which the physical is understood to be a conduit for the manifestation of spiritual realities or spiritual power. I shall now consider the broader religious and historical development of Black American Christianity.

---

2. Asamoah-Gyadu, *African Charismatics*, 22.

3. Cox, *Fire from Heaven*, locs. 332, 335. *Fire from Heaven* was first published in 1995, ten years prior to Asamoah-Gyadu's work.

4. Cox, *Fire from Heaven*, loc. 3991.

5. Murphy, *Working the Spirit*, 6.

Alternative Religious Subtexts and Contexts: Conjure and Christianity

Before examining the mainstream historical development of Black American Christianity, an alternative and primal spiritual tradition running beneath, and alongside orthodox forms of Christianity must first be explored. That tradition is *conjure*, "a magical tradition in which spiritual power is invoked for various purposes, such as healing, protection, and self-defense,"[6] and it has had a dynamic and complex relationship with orthodox Christian belief in the formation of Black American Christianity—at times competing with it for adherents or coming in for periodic condemnation from church officials, but more often complementing and even informing its ritual practices. Conjure has been described as a "magical means of transforming reality," as a form of "ritual speech and action intended to perform what it expresses."[7] This description suggests a primal orientation in the minds of its practitioners where form and substance are mutually dependent and reinforcing. Conjure is frequently reduced to occult practice, which obscures its broader features and makes it appear to be inherently irreconcilable with Christian faith, and thus "syncretic" when it appears in Christian contexts. However, conjure has often operated as a "strange but potentially suitable bedfellow"[8] to more orthodox practices within Black American Christianity. Within the academic study of religion, conjure has often been categorized as magic, and set in opposition to Christianity.[9] Yet this says more about the typological categories of the interpreters than about the phenomena itself. Indeed, the term is broad enough to encompass both pharmacopeic (healing/harming) intent and the employment of biblical figures in the configuration of cultural experience.[10] The more dichotomized interpretation derives from a truncated view of conjure that sees it only through the lens of sorcery or witchcraft while omitting its "medicinal and quasi-medicinal purposes . . . [its] *pharmacopeic tradition* of practices."[11] It is this healing function that features most prominently in Black American religious experience, without excluding other elements; "conjure in its full ethnographic and phenomenal reality requires that we

---

6. Chireau, *Black Magic*, 12.
7. T. Smith, *Conjuring Culture*, 4.
8. Chireau, *Black Magic*, 13.
9. Chireau, *Black Magic*, 12.
10. T. Smith, *Conjuring Culture*, 5–6.
11. T. Smith, *Conjuring Culture*, 5; emphasis original.

hold in concert both its therapeutic or benign referents and its occult and malign attributes."[12]

Preaching and Conjuring

During and after the antebellum era, the authority of the Christian preacher in Black American communities was matched only by that of the conjurer who "was the preacher's chief rival for authority of a supernatural kind."[13] Conjurer and preacher alike dealt with the supernatural, and both invoked spiritual power to avert, alleviate, or remove things that were inimical to a good life. In either case, the spiritual means employed were participatory rather than abstract—ritual forms superintended by ritual specialists—the conjurer or the preacher, both of whom were seen as being "empowered to manifest the spirit . . . for the benefit of the community."[14] Whereas preaching in the Euro-Western Protestant tradition is not generally considered a participatory ritual act, but an address intended to convey information to listeners who are more or less passive recipients, in the Black American tradition, preaching is as much concerned with its stylistic elements as with its content. Just as takes place within conjure, style and content are mutually reinforcing elements, and audience participation is a vital element in the ritual of preaching. Such preaching evinces a "preference for ceremonial precision over systematic thought" not found in Euro-Western Protestantism, and is "indicat[ive of] an alternate spirituality,"[15] one that includes the audience as an active participant in the ritual performance. Within the Black religious context, "the dynamic pattern of call and response between preacher and people was vital to the progression of the sermon, and unless the spirit roused the congregation to move and shout, the sermon was essentially unsuccessful."[16] The call-and-response pattern characteristic of Black preaching is a "custom from their African heritage [that] provides the audience an opportunity to participate and feedback favorably to the message of the sermon" and that in many cases "audience participation

12. T. Smith, *Conjuring Culture*, 6.
13. Raboteau, *Slave Religion*, 237–38.
14. Murphy, *Working the Spirit*, 185. It should be noted that in the case of the conjurer, the spiritual benefit derived was more often a specific and individualistic protection from or infliction of harm rather than something that accrued to the community as a whole.
15. Murphy, *Working the Spirit*, 183.
16. Raboteau, *Slave Religion*, 237.

precedes the words of the speaker."[17] Preaching within the tradition is dialogical and may thus be considered a fully participatory ritual act within Black American Christianity, with roots in the African primal imagination. In this sense then, the conjurer and the preacher both performed invocatory spiritual acts that were intended to bring blessings to the participants.

The Shared Primal Underpinnings of Conjure and Black American Christianity

The relationship between conjure and Black American Christianity is based on a shared primal understanding of the nature of reality and a consequent concern for spiritual power. For both the enslaved Africans who became the progenitors of Black American Christianity, and for those who became practitioners of conjure, there existed but a single "spiritual reality [that] governed human life, within belief systems that were not elaborated as philosophical or speculative knowledge but rather enfolded ways of being and living."[18] In other words, belief was encoded in practice and in ritual performance rather than being articulated in formalized creeds. This is consistent with a primal epistemology that is holistic, dynamic and integrative of physical and spiritual reality. The inscribing of belief in ritual reflects a "ceremonial spirituality" in which "the spirit is recognized as present by means of the actions of the community in ritual time and space."[19] Theologically this means "living religiously as being in touch with the source and channels of power in the universe," as opposed to theology that operates primarily as a "system of ideas."[20]

The emphasis on supernatural power—power to resist oppression, to defend oneself and one's community from harm, and to overcome evil—is key to understanding the relationship between conjure and Black American Christianity, and indeed to understanding Black religion generally.

17. Niles, "Rhetorical Characteristics," 51.
18. Chireau, *Black Magic*, 38.
19. Murphy, *Working the Spirit*, 6. Murphy's use of the term "spirit" does not necessarily connote the orthodox Christian theological meaning of Holy Spirit. He instead hearkens to a more foundational sense of transcendence and divinity shared between and across various primal diasporan communities: "'The spirit' can, at once, refer to God in the person of invisible power, to one power among other powers that emanate from God, and to the spirit of the diasporan people, the *geist* that characterizes and inspires them" (*Working the Spirit*, 8).
20. K. Bediako, *Christianity in Africa*, 106.

Therefore, though conjure was, in principle at least, "in conflict with Christian beliefs about the providence of God," in practice. Blacks refused to "dichotomize power into good and evil."[21] This refusal to dichotomize perhaps reflects the lingering legacy of the "fundamental anthropocentricity of African traditional religion wherein "spirits are 'good' or 'evil' insofar as they help or afflict human beings,"[22] an assessment based on their behavior and not their ontology. Christianity and conjure were complementary rather than in opposition to one another. Thus from the very beginnings of the formation of Black American Christianity, although elements of orthodox White Protestant Evangelicalism were present, Black Americans combined a primal and African sensibility[23] "about the essentially spiritual nature of historical experience with a radical secularity related both to religious sensibility and to the experience of slavery and oppression"[24] and therefore developed a Christian faith more invocatory, performative, pharmacopeic, and potentially transformative of both natural and supernatural realities than that contemplated by their White coreligionists.

The influence of this pharmacopeic tradition within Black American Christianity is seen within both spiritual and Pentecostal traditions, where physical healing assumes such a prominent place. The predominantly Black Church of God in Christ, the largest Pentecostal denomination in the United States, maintains divine healing to be a core tenet of the faith.[25] In its ritual practices as well, "the Church of God in Christ concentrates on it: healing, techniques of healing, and on the use of material in healing."[26] Within the Black spiritual churches, healing and prophecy are prominent features and, "regularly scheduled worship often includes a healing ritual

---

21. Raboteau, *Slave Religion*, 286–87.

22. Ferdinando, "Screwtape Revisited," 113. Kwame Bediako has noted that African scholars Alexis Kagame and Vincent Mulago have likewise identified the fundamentally anthropocentric nature of African religion. He says that for Kagame, "at the centre of Bantu religious thought is the belief that man is himself at the centre of God's universe, and so at the heart of religion; but not man as individual, but rather as humanity," and quotes Mulago (from *La religion traditionelle des Bantu et leur vision du monde*): "African religion revolves around two truths/beliefs as around two vital centres: God and man" (K. Bediako, *Theology and Identity*, 380–81).

23. Primal and African are related, but not interchangeable: the primal being a larger and more fundamental category than the African primal. The European primal was a contributor to Black American religious development as well.

24. Wilmore, *Black Religion*, 24.

25. Church of God in Christ, "What We Believe."

26. Scandrett-Leatherman, "Can't Nobody Do Me," 205.

that is similar to what occurs in Pentecostal or charismatic groups."[27] Black Pentecostals and spiritual people both[28] embrace a common concern for ritual healing that points to a common theological orientation and belief set—one shared with conjurers and rooted firmly in the primal imagination. "Practitioners of all three traditions held similar assumptions about the body and embraced analogous visions of misfortune, conceptions of disease, and the uses of spiritual power for extraordinary cures."[29] Physical suffering and personal affliction, whether due to enslavement or disease, were not attributable to chance, but "were seen as the outcome of malicious human actions or destructive powers,"[30] and thus occasioned spiritual intervention of some kind.

The relationship between conjure and Christianity persisted from colonial days, through the antebellum period of American history and well into the twentieth century when the Pentecostal and spiritual church movements began. This primal tradition is particularly evident in Pentecostalism, a movement that, despite scholarly neglect of Black agency in its origins,[31] owes a great deal to Africa and whose seminal event, the 1906 Azusa Street Revival, was led by a Black man—William Seymour (1870–1922). This, however, is anticipation, and so I turn to explore the historical context of Black American Christianity.

Historical Context: Beyond Slavery

It is impossible to pinpoint with any degree of certainty the precise starting point of Black American Christianity. Though it is possible "that a few enslaved Africans may have had some contact with Christianity in their

---

27. Jacobs and Kaslow, *Spiritual Churches*, 154.

28. Hans Baer observes that "members of Spiritual churches generally reject the term 'Spiritualist' in referring to themselves or their religion," a term that is frequently used to describe White groups, because of the term's association with "communication with [deceased] loved ones, séances, and fortune-telling." Baer quotes pseudonymously a Bishop Gilmore, pastor of the similarly pseudonymous All Souls Christian Church No. 2—which I recognize as my paternal grandmother and natal church respectively—as stating, "Spiritualist is a word that we have fought so hard" (*Black Spiritual Movement*, 115). I can affirm Baer's observation from personal experience.

29. Chireau, *Black Magic*, 93.

30. Chireau, *Black Magic*, 101.

31. Alexander and Yong, "Introduction," 1.

homeland"[32] and been converted prior to their transit to the Americas, the larger story of Black American Christianity can reliably be said to have begun on the shores of North America itself in the context of enslavement within the emerging global mercantile capitalism of the early modern era.[33] Black American Christianity is inextricably bound together with the socio-economic realities of chattel slavery in which it was largely formulated and the ideological architecture of Eurocentric White supremacy with which it was forced to contend long after the formal abolition of slavery. Christianity was conscripted to support this ideology as divinely ordained and scripturally valid. Eurocentric White supremacy is the stage upon which the story of Black American Christianity unfolds, and consequently exerts a powerful influence on the interpretation of Black religion in scholarship, particularly in respect to whether Black religion was liberationist or accommodationist in relation to the social situation of Black Americans.

Nonetheless, Black religion defined exclusively in relation to Eurocentric White supremacy is not the whole story, nor even the most significant part of the story. To suggest otherwise is to annex Black American Christianity as a subplot to the story of Black resistance to White supremacist claims, thus degrading its epistemological and theology value. If Black American Christianity is nothing more than "a religious expression of a pragmatic and democratically pious response to a racialized and enslaving modernity,"[34] then race itself becomes a transcendent and totalizing reality thus ironically reinforcing the racist assumptions of Eurocentric White supremacy. On this basis therefore, Black theology, may be rightly critiqued for its reduction of Black American Christianity to "a divinely-sanctioned Christological struggle against the violence of white supremacist oppression."[35] Among other things, this reductionism fails to take into account the primal and African features of Black religion as essential contributors to the epistemology and theology of Christianity itself.[36] Euro-Western racialist ideology

32. Raboteau, *Slave Religion*, 6.
33. Baer and Singer, *African American Religion*, 3.
34. Carter, *Race*, 127.
35. Harvey, "Life is War," 3.
36. Frederick L. Ware has identified three schools of thought within the academic study of Black religion, and while what he termed the Black hermeneutical school, whose content is defined by liberation derived from Christian and biblical categories, has been the "most prolific and popular of the three schools of academic Black theology," it must be acknowledged that other schools of thought have emerged that do not posit liberation, understood in a socio-political sense, as their central theme, nor are reliant solely

was but one of several elements out of which Black American Christianity may be said to have been "conjured" into being.

Early Efforts at Slave Conversion

During the late seventeenth and early eighteenth centuries, Africans enslaved on the farms and plantations of what was to become the United States of America were, for the most part, not seen as candidates for conversion by the planter class whose wealth depended upon a quiescent labor force and who were concerned that baptism would lead to emancipation; "would-be missionaries to the slaves complained that slaveholders refused them permission to catechize their slaves because baptism made it necessary to free them ... the Christian commission to preach the gospel ... ran directly counter to the economic interest of the Christian slave owner."[37] These concerns were partially calmed by legislation that denied the possibility that Christian baptism would lead to emancipation while religious leaders sought ways to alleviate planters' worries.[38] For example, Anglican cleric Francis Le Jau sought to allay such fears by extracting from his enslaved converts a sacred oath:

> You declare in the Presence of God and before this Congregation that you do not ask for the holy baptism out of any design to free yourself from the Duty and Obedience you owe to your Master while you live, but merely for the good of Your Soul and to partake of the Graces and Blessings promised to the Members of the Church of Jesus Christ.[39]

The Christianity proclaimed among enslaved Africans was one that not only severed the relationship between the social and spiritual status of the enslaved but sanctioned the severance by an oath administered by an official of the state church. Regardless of the spiritual benefits the enslaved could be expected to reap from conversion, Blacks could not be permitted to entertain the notion that the gospel of Christ had anything to do with their social status.

---

on biblical or Christian categories. Nevertheless, the theme of liberation in opposition to Eurocentric White supremacy remains for many, a defining feature of Black theology (Ware, "Methodologies," 131). See also Ware, *Methodologies of Black Theology*.

37. Raboteau, *Slave Religion*, 98.
38. Baer and Singer, *African American Religion*, 4.
39. Le Jau, "Slave Conversion," 25.

Despite these assurances, conversion of the enslaved populace continued to be a problematic proposition for planters. First of all, the time-consuming nature of religious instruction made it uneconomical from the planter's point of view.[40] Time spent in religious instruction was time spent not working. Protestant emphasis on biblical knowledge posed other, more significant, problems, however. Slave literacy threatened White interpretive control of the biblical text. Independence of thought was not a characteristic to be encouraged among the enslaved who demonstrated that their capacity to think for themselves readily lent itself to interpretations of Christianity inimical to quiescent servitude. This concern prompted Le Jau to "fear that those Men have not judgment enough to make good use of their Learning"—and consequently "not to urge too far that Indians and Negroes shou'd be indifferently admitted to learn to read."[41] Furthermore, it was widely believed that Christianity made them "proud and Undutiful"[42] and "infuse[d] them with thoughts of freedom."[43] This latter concern was not without foundation, as the enslaved, once converted, could and did plausibly lay claim to fellowship with their masters on an equal basis, "a claim that threatened the security of the master-slave hierarchy,"[44] and which would, in fact, be frequently asserted. Indeed, a threatened slave rebellion in 1731 was based in part on the conclusion drawn by enslaved Blacks in Virginia "that Christianity and bondage were incompatible and that if freedom continued to be denied them, they had every right to resort to force in order to secure their liberation."[45] Slave owner and enslaved alike recognized the implicit egalitarianism of Christianity posed a challenge to the slave system and to the Eurocentric White supremacy that legitimized it. Thus, it is quite early in the history that the link between Christianity and sociopolitical freedom emerges as one of the most enduring features of Black American religion.

Notwithstanding the missionary efforts of the Anglican Church in the late seventeenth and early eighteenth centuries, very few slaves were willing to convert. It is easy to ascribe this reluctance to convert to the slave

40. Baer and Singer, *African American Religion*, 4.
41. Le Jau, "Slave Conversion," 27.
42. Le Jau, "Slave Conversion," 29.
43. James Blair to Bishop Gibson, Williamsburg, Virginia, July 20, 1730, quoted in Frey and Wood, *Come Shouting to Zion*, 65.
44. Raboteau, *Slave Religion*, 101.
45. Frey and Wood, *Come Shouting to Zion*, 70.

owners, but to do so largely overlooks the agency of the enslaved Africans themselves and shows an unwillingness to examine paternalistic assumptions. Though the intransigence of planters undoubtedly played a role, "the vast majority of bondspeople . . . were offered no convincing, or compelling, reasons to abandon their traditional beliefs and rituals in favour of those espoused by colonial clergy."[46] By and large, Blacks continued to adhere to the primal beliefs and practices brought with them from West and Central Africa and passed down to their American born descendants. Ironically, the primal worldview and practices to which they were so ardently attached, were to prove fertile ground for the religious fervor that accompanied the eighteenth-century Great Awakenings.

Awakening and Revival

The decades preceding the American War of Independence saw evangelical missionaries, John and Charles Wesley and George Whitefield among them, making special efforts to reach out to enslaved Blacks, by "addressing black men and women as spiritual equals and by encouraging the formation of informal Methodist societies on plantations."[47] Many of these early missionaries held distinctly anti-slavery attitudes, and even though Whitefield is a notable example of evangelical backsliding on this issue—he eventually "repented" of his anti-slavery outlook, became an advocate for slaveholding and a slave owner himself[48]—the ethos of the First Awakening was far more egalitarian than any previous effort at converting the enslaved. However, the Second Awakening was far more momentous than the first in terms of Black American Christianity. Beginning in the 1780s, the Great Revival, as it is sometimes termed, swept large numbers of previously indifferent enslaved Blacks into Christianity, "becoming by 1815 a dominant religious influence among Afro-Atlantic peoples."[49] The comparatively egalitarian approach employed by evangelical preachers surely played some role in the willingness of the enslaved population to respond to the gospel message. Yet perhaps more importantly, the evangelical emphasis on experience—"the claim to extraordinary communication and of witness of the

---

46. Frey and Wood, *Come Shouting to Zion*, 75.
47. M. Noll, *Rise of Evangelicalism*, 175.
48. Frey and Wood, *Come Shouting to Zion*, 93.
49. Frey and Wood, *Come Shouting to Zion*, 118.

spirit"—resonated deeply with African antecedents,[50] and cannot be overlooked or underestimated as a contributory factor. The enthusiastic tenor of the Great Awakenings connected deeply with them, and their participation also gave shape to American evangelical revivalism itself:

> For African Americans, if not for all white evangelicals, conversion was often a ritual of collective catharsis and collective commitment that was performed collaboratively. . . . Through a relatively brief period of sustained contact, the sort of possession behavior exhibited by black evangelicals may have carried over to white evangelicals.[51]

Cultural Commingling

The evangelical religion to which Black converts were exposed during the Awakening was both experiential and pragmatic—much like the traditional religions they had known in Africa—and took for granted "the existence of a Supreme Being, the reality of the spirit world, and the revelatory significance of symbols and myths."[52] It was, in a word, essentially primal in its core assumptions. Yet the primal religious expressions of these Black converts were not exclusive to them, nor entirely attributable to their recent African origins. The emotive primal religiosity of the Awakenings was *shared* and *shaped* by both African and European spirituality. The distinctive behaviors seen in American frontier revivals was:

> Reminiscent of the patterned behavior exhibited during the Methodist revivals of 1758 at Cambuslang and Kilsyth in Scotland, and Everton and Bristol in England. . . . The conversion ritual was characterized by the same eccentric repertory of motor behaviors seen in the Scottish and English revivals: violent contortions of the body and spasmodic jerkings, rolling and spinning, running and leaping.[53]

The occurrence of such phenomena among Whites as well as Blacks indicates that such modes of religious behavior were not peculiarly nor exclusively African. Descriptions of White Methodist revivalist John McGee's

---

50. Frey and Wood, *Come Shouting to Zion*, 101.
51. Frey and Wood, *Come Shouting to Zion*, 123–24.
52. Wilmore, *Black Religion*, 32.
53. Frey and Woods, *Come Shouting to Zion*, 143.

preaching during the Logan County, Kentucky, revival sound more like what would be expected among contemporary charismatics: "[McGee] went through the housing shouting, and exhorting with all possible ecstasy and energy, and the floor was soon covered with the slain."[54] John Thompson, a White Presbyterian, "danced around the preaching stand for over an hour chanting in a low voice, 'this is the Holy Ghost—Glory!'"[55] These similarities occurred because the expected pattern of conversion in which "the seeker was in a dejected state, was called by name, was shown the depths of hell, and was saved and shown God in all the glory of paradise"[56] was shared between Black and White Evangelicals alike. It was primal.

The evangelical conversion of the slaves produced a Christianity that was "something more than a dispassionate system of theology and a code of behavior," but that instead welded the "spirited, evangelical interpretation of the Baptist and Methodist preachers"[57] onto existing African maps of reality. These maps admitted no rigid demarcation between the natural and supernatural realms of existence,[58] but saw all of life as infused with various powers and forces at work for the good or ill of man; "the individual and the community were continuously involved in the spirit world in the practical affairs of daily life."[59] The maps employed by enslaved Blacks were not so different than those used by Whites. Both saw "the universe as a territory inhabited by a hierarchy of forces and spirits [and] developed rituals to allow them to interact with benevolent forces and defend themselves against the malevolent forces that existed within that universe."[60] The Enlightenment project had not yet succeeded in entirely closing the Euro-Western universe to supernaturalism, and there was no need as yet for Christian theology to reach an accommodation with its claims. Thus, orthodox Protestantism continued to "read unusual events as evidence of the divine presence in everyday life" and to consider "disruptions of the ordinary [as] demonstrations that foretold God's will or signaled his displeasure."[61]

---

54. John McGee to Rev. Thomas L. Douglass, June 23, 1820, quoted in Frey and Wood, *Come Shouting to Zion*, 141.

55. Frey and Wood, *Come Shouting to Zion*, 141.

56. Cornelius, *Slave Missions*, 20.

57. Wilmore, *Black Religion*, 29.

58. See Walls, "Christian Scholarship in Africa."

59. Wilmore, *Black Religion*, 37.

60. Chireau, *Black Magic*, 43.

61. Chireau, *Black Magic*, 44.

Although the requisite intellectual and cultural preconditions were present, the ideology of Euro-centric White supremacy was still in its naissance, and thus many practices that would eventually be excluded from proper "civilized" White behavior were initially shared between Blacks and Whites without much controversy. Over time however, such phenomena were increasingly and exclusively associated with Black people, characterized as "noisy, crude, impious . . . dissolute,"[62] and derided as marks of cultural and religious inferiority. As the ideology of race and assumptions of Euro-Western cultural superiority grew more prominent, "White Christians rejected rituals that had an apparent African style or feeling and were associated with supposed racial inferiority."[63] The rejection of such phenomena can be understood not only as the entrenchment of White supremacy as a racialist ideology, but also as an increasing discomfort and distancing of Europeans from their own primal religious heritage. Initially, however, each cultural group borrowed freely from the other spiritual traditions and practices, some of which (i.e., witchcraft and the like) came in for periodic condemnation from ecclesiastical authorities, but which nonetheless continued to hold sway among large swathes of the population.

The commingling of cultures that took place during the Great Awakening, and indeed throughout the antebellum period, makes it difficult to parse what elements of Black American Christianity in early America derived from specifically *African* antecedents and which are attributable to a more generally shared *primal* orientation common to both Blacks and Whites in this period. Both Black and White Christian evangelical spirituality was experimental, pragmatic, and expressive. What is clear, however, is that despite the similarities in worldview shared between Black and White in early America, Black American Christianity developed in ways that ritually and theologically preserved a primal orientation as an essential feature. This preservation of the primal is attributable partially to the close and dynamic engagement of orthodox Christian belief with the aforementioned "conjure" traditions that persisted throughout the antebellum era and well into the twentieth century—traditions that ultimately contributed to the emergence of spiritual churches.

---

62. Frey and Wood, *Come Shouting to Zion*, 147.
63. Frey and Wood, *Come Shouting to Zion*, 147–48.

Antebellum Christianity: Slave Religion

The seeds of Christianization that were sown in the Great Awakening were nourished throughout the antebellum era by plantation missions organized by the various Christian denominations, though such efforts were complicated by the admittedly mixed and contradictory motives that impelled them:

> The desire to evangelize the poor, the desire to make slaves docile, the desire to create a model plantation, and the desire to defend slavery against abolitionist attacks were all reasons for supporting plantation missions.... Not only was Christianization of the slaves a rationale for slavery, but it was, as it had been from the beginning, a balm for the occasional eruptions of Christian conscience disturbed by the notion that maybe slavery was wrong.[64]

The response of enslaved Blacks to these missions varied, but "by the eve of the Civil War, Christianity had pervaded the slave community" with most having become, if not adherents of Christian faith, at least roughly familiar with the outlines of its "doctrines, symbols, and vision of life."[65]

There was a persistent duality in the Christian religious life of the enslaved which developed as a result of the slave system which discouraged independence of thought or action on the part of the enslaved. Consequently, the visible, institutional forms of Christianity were but one element of religious life in the slave community. The slave owners saw only what the enslaved wanted them to see; "in the secrecy of the quarters or the seclusion of the brush arbors ('hush harbors') the slaves made Christianity truly their own."[66] They often risked horrible punishment, including death, in order to worship God as they saw fit.[67] Thus large portions of the religious lives of the enslaved were pushed into the shadows, beyond the prying eyes of slave masters who, no matter how pious "did not countenance prayers for his slaves' freedom in this world."[68] In clandestine meetings, Blacks

---

64. Raboteau, *Slave Religion*, 174.

65. Raboteau, *Slave Religion*, 212.

66. Raboteau, *Slave Religion*, 212. Although there were established and growing independent Black churches in the North (notably the AME and AME Zion), the vast majority of Blacks in this period were enslaved within the plantation economy of the American South and thus the religious life of these people may be considered as broadly representative.

67. Raboteau, *Slave Religion*, 215.

68. Raboteau, *Slave Religion*, 219.

preached, prayed, and worshipped God in ways that suited their own primal sensibilities and oppressive circumstances while employing various techniques to avoid detection. It was in these meetings also that the distinctly African forms of religion—"hand-clapping, foot-tapping, rhythmic preaching, hyperventilation, antiphonal (call and response) singing, and dancing"[69]—continued to be expressed and were passed on to subsequent generations. Dance especially remained a crucial part of worship for both the enslaved and formerly enslaved and continues to feature prominently within Black Pentecostalism as an embodied aesthetic healing ritual.[70]

Postbellum Christianity: The Emergence of the Independent Black Church

Following the abolition of slavery at the close of the Civil War, the religious life of Black Americans emerged from the shadows to shape what, over time, became the most prominent social institution in Black America. Though there were Black churches and denominations that had been long established, notably the African Methodist Episcopal Church (AME) and African Methodist Episcopal Zion Church (AME Zion), as well as several Baptist churches in both the north and south, prior to the Civil War most Blacks had been held in chattel bondage and thus worshipped in churches controlled by Whites. Their religious life was circumscribed by the exigencies of that peculiar institution. After the war, the formerly enslaved took advantage of their newfound liberty to form independent religious bodies free from White dominance and control. Many of the former adherents of the Methodist Episcopal Church, South, for example, exercised their new found freedom by leaving the church of their erstwhile slave owners and streaming into the AME.[71] Partially to stem this tide, in 1870, the Colored (now Christian) Methodist Episcopal Church was carved out of the Methodist Episcopal Church, South, in recognition of the change in the "ancient relation of master and servant" and the understanding that "social religious equality, as well as any other kind of social equality, was utterly impracticable and undesirable."[72] Many thousands of independent Baptist churches sprang up across the Southern landscape as well. However,

69. Raboteau, *Slave Religion*, 65.
70. Scandrett-Leatherman, "Can't Nobody Do Me," 329.
71. Holsey, "Colored Methodist Episcopal Church," 235.
72. Holsey, "Colored Methodist Episcopal Church," 235–36.

whether Baptist or Methodist (for scarcely any other kind were present among the Black population of the South), expressive forms of religiosity continued to prevail, often to the chagrin and disappointment of observers who viewed such religion with disdain. Boston-based Black author William Wells Brown (c. 1814–84) observed with evident displeasure:

> It will be difficult to erase from the mind of the negro of the South, the prevailing idea that outward demonstrations, such as, shouting, the loud "amen," and the most boisterous noise in prayer, are not necessary adjuncts to piety.[73]

He believed the solution to what he perceived as deficiencies in religious practice lay in the provision of an educated clergy, though he was doubtful that "the uneducated, superstitious masses" could be induced to support them.[74] His views were consonant with those of AME Bishop Daniel Payne (1811–93) who described such exertions as "a heathenish way to worship and disgraceful to themselves, the race, and the Christian name."[75] Sentiments such as these were common, and particularly acute since Christianity and civilization, i.e., White Euro-Western norms of conduct and behavior, were so closely aligned. Any behavior that potentially marked Blacks out as primitive, backwards, or uncivilized drew special censure from educated Blacks who sought to combat prevailing negative views of Black people. Christianity was seen as a tool for civilization (really Europeanization or whitewashing) and advancement by both Blacks and Whites alike.

William Wells Brown's advocacy for an educated clergy is indicative of a larger passion for education in the emerging independent Black church during the postbellum years and was likewise seen as a tool for civilization. Black church leaders were as enthusiastic in building schools as they were in building churches. For example, Black ministers in Savannah, Georgia, over the course of two years, established a network of 120 Black schools staffed with Black teachers.[76] Black churches also provided seed money for colleges and universities, and in some cases housed them in their facilities in the early stages.[77] These colleges and universities would in turn eventual-

---

73. Brown, "Black Religion," 241.

74. Brown, "Black Religion," 243.

75. Daniel Alexander Payne, *Recollections of Seventy Years*, quoted in Anyabwile, *Decline*, 224.

76. Cornelius, *Slave Missions*, 203.

77. Cornelius, *Slave Missions*, 203.

ly supply the bulk of the educated Black clergy as well as lay the foundation for the Black middle class. The middle-class congregations that would emerge as a result of these educational advances generally "saw adherence to African worldviews and religious folk culture [as] associated with rural life or Slave Religion, which reflected a low cultural standing" and therefore "[sought] assimilation in the majority white culture [and] preferred European worldviews shaped by the Enlightenment."[78] Gradually, a religious class divide began to emerge as congregations of urban-educated Blacks increasingly shunned inherited patterns of Black religious culture and rather sought to navigate the complexities of a White supremacist society by aping White cultural forms and religious practices, while simultaneously functioning as centers of political and social activism. Many, if not most Blacks, however, continued to worship in congregations led by untrained clergy in much the same ways they had for generations, albeit with decidedly more freedom than they had in the antebellum period. The vision of Christianity as a tool for assimilating Blacks into White norms of religious expression would be rejected by pioneering Black Pentecostals like Charles Harrison Mason (1866–1961), who "insisted upon the centrality of personal inner transformation without shedding distinctive African cultural expressions,"[79] a stance that led to an intentional perpetuation of the primal imagination within Black Pentecostalism generally, and the Church of God in Christ in particular.

By the turn of the twentieth century, thirty-five years after the end of the Civil War, and despite ongoing and indeed intensifying racial oppression, the independent Black church was an established and thriving institution—"the one institution where black people were able to act as a community, especially in the South."[80] Almost all of those who professed Christian faith were Protestant, and of those, nearly all were either Baptist of Methodist.[81] It was within these ecclesial communities that Black ministers and congregants sought to carve out a meaningful existence against the backdrop of a hostile White supremacist society in which vigilante violence coupled with state sanctioned legal and economic restrictions made life extremely difficult for Black people. The eruption of the Pentecostal movement would radically disrupt the dominance of these denominations

78. Clemmons, *Bishop C. H. Mason*, locs. 584–86.
79. Clemmons, *Bishop C. H. Mason*, locs. 583–84.
80. Baer and Singer, *African American Religion*, 14.
81. Daniels, "Navigating the Territory," 43.

and permanently alter the fabric of Black American religious life and global Christianity as well.

The Emergence of Pentecostalism

Pentecostalism emerged in the first decade of the twentieth-century during the apex of the Edwardian Age in which it was truly said that the sun never set on the British Empire. All of Africa, with the exceptions of the ancient Christian kingdom of Ethiopia, and the quasi-free American colony of Liberia, had been divided among the various European imperial powers. Much of Asia too lay prostrate at Europe's feet. The horrors, disenchantment, and ensuing cultural crisis of the First World War lay in the future. At the 1910 World Missionary Conference in Edinburgh, the capstone of a missionary movement now recognized as the final flourish of Christendom,[82] religion of the kind breaking forth at Azusa Street in Los Angeles, California would be dismissed simply as animism, E. B. Tylor's "theory of the origin of religion" that "assumed that tribal societies represented the 'primitive' mode of thought out of which 'civilized' religion had evolved."[83] The phenomenon of speaking in tongues associated with Pentecostals would be characterized as a "recrudescence of psychic phenomena of a low stage of culture,"[84] nothing more than a hold-over of primitivism and therefore deemed "unworthy of serious theological consideration."[85] It was seen to have no place in the modern civilized world, and certainly not in the United States, the ultimate exemplar of White Euro-Western civilized culture, or in Los Angeles, a city celebrated as "the future world capital of Aryan supremacy, a 'new Rome' whose virile sons and daughters would one day lead the world."[86] Nevertheless, within a few decades, the Pentecostal movement had spawned dozens of new denominations and, within a century, would become one of the leading expressions of Christianity in the world.

---

82. Walls, *Missionary Movement*, 237.
83. Friesen, *Missionary Responses*, 137.
84. Henke, "Gift of Tongues," 206.
85. K. Bediako, "Understanding African Theology," 15.
86. Cox, *Fire from Heaven*, locs. 928–29.

Background to the Azusa Street Revival

The 1906 Azusa Street Revival, frequently cited as the seminal event of the worldwide Pentecostal movement, presents us with a dramatic reassertion of primal religious phenomena in the modern era. William Joseph Seymour, the leader of the revival, was a Black holiness preacher born of Catholic ex-slave parents in southern Louisiana, in a context where a primal imagination held sway over most of the population. Many former slaves, while officially adherents of the Roman Catholic Church, were practitioners of hoodoo, a conjure tradition closely related to voodoo. It was an environment in which

> symbols, spells, incantations, sympathetic magic, and root work were a regular part of life. . . . They believed in a Divine spirit, in the supernatural including the empowerment of individuals, signs and wonders, miracles and healings, invisible spirits, trances and spirit possession, visions and dreams as a means of Divine communication, as well as other phenomena described in the Bible. They sang, clapped, trembled, shouted, danced, played drums, and developed a "call and response" preaching style.[87]

The African-influenced primal religious environment of southern Louisiana undoubtedly shaped the leader of Azusa Street Revival throughout his formative years.[88] As an adult, Seymour moved to Indianapolis, where he had a conversion experience in the Methodist Episcopal Church, but underwent some further experience of conversion or "sanctification" among the Evening Light Saints (now known as the Church of God Anderson, Indiana).[89] His primal sensibilities received additional affirmation through his participation in Martin Wells Knapp's God's Bible School. It was here that Seymour's existing sense of the ways in which the spiritual realm worked was reinforced, and he was provided guidance about how to discern the validity of such phenomena that would serve him well during the Azusa Street Revival.[90]

Here again, a lively tradition within Black religious culture, with which Seymour would have been familiar, emerges into view. "The claim

---

87. Robeck, *Azusa Street Mission*, 23.

88. As shall later be shown it was within this environment that the spiritual church movement likewise finds its roots.

89. Robeck, *Azusa Street Mission*, 29.

90. Robeck, *Azusa Street Mission*, 33–34.

to extraordinary communication and of witness of the spirit" so much emphasized in Early American Evangelicalism resonated deeply with Black people during the Great Revival has already been mentioned.[91] This is seen also in the stories of conversion and calling among Blacks both during and after slavery. Guidance through dreams, visions, and other supernatural means were commonly accepted in the Black community as means by which God communicated to mankind. So common were these experiences that Zora Neale Hurston could still assert well into the twentieth century that "[the vision] almost always accompanies conversion. It almost always accompanies the call to preach."[92] Her observations are borne out not only by her own observations as an anthropologist, but also by the many slave narratives that "featured vision- and voice-based revelations, with the recipient recording very little surprise or disbelief at the prospect of hearing or seeing God through dreams or visions."[93] The category of "special revelation" was more expansive within the Black religious tradition from which Seymour and other early Pentecostals (and spiritual people) emerged, than what obtained in most Protestant theology of the day.

William J. Seymour was not the first to speak in tongues, even in the modern era. However, his leadership of the Azusa Street Revival was far more important to the emergence of Pentecostalism as a global religious force than that of Charles Fox Parham, the White Ku Klux Klan sympathizer "who is credited with laying [Pentecostalism's] foundations by formulating its central doctrine of the baptism of the Holy Spirit being accompanied with the initial evidence of speaking in tongues."[94] The revival, and the movement it sparked was marked in its early stages by a radically countercultural inter-racialism that placed Black and African modes of primal religious expression—the "visions, signs, wonders, and healings—that were edited out during the Protestant Reformation"[95]—at the center rather than the periphery of Christian experience. This was a direct result of Seymour's roots in the Black religious tradition which had maintained a keen sense of the primal imagination. The Azusa Street Revival and subsequent emergence of Pentecostalism reaffirmed the normative and vital nature of such occurrences within Christian spirituality.

91. Frey and Wood, *Come Shouting to Zion*, 101.
92. Hurston, *Sanctified Church*, 85.
93. Anyabwile, *Decline*, 33.
94. Alexander and Yong, "Introduction," 1.
95. Cox, *Fire from Heaven*, locs. 903–4.

Pentecostalism and its Detractors

As the Azusa Street Revival gained momentum, the revival was alternately scoffed at and condemned by observers. Yet in many ways, the Azusa mission operated much like any other Christian congregation.[96] Given the seemingly mundane nature of the stated program, the celebrated spontaneity of the mission is an inadequate explanation for the condemnation continuously heaped upon the revival at Azusa Street and on Pentecostals generally in the ensuing years. The revival camp meeting atmosphere and the emotional expressiveness of the meetings were not unique to Azusa Street mission nor to newly emergent Pentecostal groups. These could be found elsewhere in the American religious landscape.[97] Seymour's leadership, and the attendant embrace and even celebration of primal religiosity stemming from the Black religious tradition points towards a plausible answer.

Newspaper reports of the revival described it in sensational and exotic terms. The *Los Angeles Daily Times* christened the revival "a new sect of fanatics . . . breaking loose" led by "an old colored exhorter" wherein "the bounds of reason are passed by those who are 'filled with the spirit,' whatever that may be"[98] Charles Parham, when invited by his one-time mentee William Seymour to visit the revival, found little to commend. He rather lamented what he called the "darky camp meeting" atmosphere that prevailed, though it is probable that he was less concerned about the religious fervor he witnessed than with the breaches of racial decorum that were an inherent rejection of White supremacist norms.

> "Men and women," he wrote, "whites and blacks knelt together or fell across one another; frequently a white woman, perhaps of wealth and culture, could be seen thrown back into the arms of a 'buck nigger,' and held tightly thus as she shivered and shook in freak imitation of Pentecost. Horrible, awful shame!"[99]

Parham's palpable disgust was undoubtedly founded on his rejection of race mixing as inimical to God's created order and which figured in his theology as the proximate cause of the Noahic flood.[100] His virulent dis-

---

96. Robeck, *Azusa Street Mission*, 136.
97. Robeck, *Azusa Street Mission*, 138.
98. "Weird Babel of Tongues," *Los Angeles Daily Times* (Apr. 18, 1906), 1.
99. Cox, *Fire from Heaven*, locs. 1061–63.
100. A. Anderson, "Dubious Legacy," 53.

dain for what he saw at Azusa Street is unsurprising given the prevailing ethos of Eurocentric White supremacy that dominated American culture and governed the interpretation of Black peoples and religious expression. However close Seymour and Parham might have been in their interpretation of Scripture concerning the Holy Spirit baptism, Seymour's vision of interracial social equality, was a bridge too far for Parham to accept. The same racially tinged sensationalism that attended the reporting of Azusa Street was evident also in the coverage of C. H. Mason's 1907 Memphis revival. For detractors, Mason's meetings "show[ed] what has been contended for years, that the Negro's religion is sound instead of sense."[101] This was to be expected from people in a "low stage of culture . . . largely controlled by their feelings."[102]

Later interpreters of Pentecostalism were equally harsh, even if less overtly racist. Pentecostals, especially Black Pentecostals, were frequently the object of derisive commentary from those who considered themselves the arbiters of good taste and the guardians of Euro-Western White Christian civilization, including many in the Black religious and scholarly establishment. Joseph Washington roundly condemned them as cults:

> [They] are without theology, though they use Biblically-interpreted terminology; without a style of worship, though they are demonstrative; without ethical emphasis, though they conform to an expected code of morality; and they are highly individualistic in their organizational structures.[103]

These harsh words from a Black scholar typify the pervasive derision heaped upon Pentecostal groups—a derision derived in part at least from an implicit assumption of Christianity as civilized, that is, conformable to the norms of Euro-Western mores. For Washington and others like him, such groups were at best enclaves of escapism, where enterprising "religious pimps" exploited the pain and poverty of the ignorant in ways that distracted them from what they saw as the more central task of socioeconomic uplift and/or assimilation into mainstream White American life.[104] At worst, they represented embarrassing reversions to primitive African barbarism,

---

101. "Fanatical Worship of Negroes Going on at Sanctified Church," *Commercial Appeal* (May 22, 1907), quoted in Sanders, *Saints in Exile*, 31.
102. Henke, "Gift of Tongues," 199.
103. Washington, *Black Religion*, 120.
104. Washington, *Black Religion*, 120.

a blight on Black America's quest for respectability, and a hindrance to the assimilationist aspirations of the upwardly mobile Black middle classes:

> Mainline black churches saw adherence to African worldviews and religious folk culture associated with rural life or Slave Religion, which reflected a low cultural standing. Rising middle-class educated blacks seeking assimilation in the majority white culture preferred European worldviews shaped by the Enlightenment.[105]

Other criticisms were more veiled. For example, the "accentuated rhythm" that characterized Black Pentecostal worship came under criticism for being "secular and offensive rather than African,"[106] yet given the centuries long association of Black people with dissolute behavior and exoticism, this was a distinction without difference.

What observers and interpreters of Azusa Street and early Pentecostalism held in common was their palpable disdain for what appeared to them to be an eruption of African "barbarity" masquerading as religion. Given the prevalent racism and settled assumptions of Christianity as Euro-Western "civilized" religion, it is not difficult to see that an interracial religious mission, "led by an African American pastor, dominated by an African American membership, and heavily influenced by African American worship patterns"[107] would merit particular harsh censure because it was not only exceptional, but represented a unique threat to the prevailing assumptions of Christianity as an artifact of Euro-Western civilization.

The Spiritual Movement

The spiritual church movement has not received the same attention as Pentecostalism, perhaps due to the explosive growth of the Pentecostal movement over the past hundred years, its institutionalization, and its continuing influence on broad segments of the global church. However, despite the neglect in scholarship, the spiritual church movement was one of the most significant elements in the Black religious experience during the twentieth century. It emerged in the same milieu as Pentecostalism, and played on the same themes—dissatisfaction with what was on offer from mainstream religious alternatives, and a hunger for solutions in an

---

105. Clemmons, *Bishop C. H. Mason*, locs. 584–87.
106. Reed, "Shared Possessions," 12.
107. Robeck, *Azusa Street Mission*, 138.

increasingly complex world—and with these, a desire to reassert a primal vision for life that implicitly, if not explicitly, rejected the claims of both liberal Protestantism and dry fundamentalism that both excised the supernatural from daily life. Both movements drew inspiration from the traditions of the "invisible institution" of Black religion and reconfigured them for a new environment. Unlike the Pentecostal movement however, which can be plausibly linked to the eclectic and dynamic Azusa Street Revival, the precise origins of the spiritual church movement are diffuse and thus far more difficult to identify.

Chicago was an important early center of the Black spiritualist church movement, with several congregations organized by 1920, including the Eternal Life Christian Spiritualist Church led by Mother Leafy Anderson, founded in 1913.[108] Mother Anderson would go on to establish a spiritual congregation in New Orleans and become a significant figure in the development of the Black spiritual movement in that city, while New Orleans itself became a vital center of the movement. Given the diverse religious environment of southern Louisiana and New Orleans in particular, it is unsurprising that both the spiritual movement and Pentecostal forerunner William Seymour can trace their roots there. The large role played by New Orleans in the movement invites a closer look at the religious dynamics of that southern Louisianan city.

New Orleans: Voodoo, Hoodoo, and the Origins of the Spiritual Movement

The religious climate of southern Louisiana was complicated and diverse.[109] Unlike other areas of the United States, southern Louisiana's unique colonial and cultural history made for a more eclectic religious scene than could be found elsewhere. Practitioners of voodoo, hoodoo, Roman Catholicism, spiritualists, and various Black Protestant groups lived and worked side by side in New Orleans. The lines delineating the various groups were neither hard nor fast. The area's history as first a Spanish, then a French colony meant that Catholicism exercised much more influence there than in other parts of the United States. However, much of the Catholicism practiced by Whites and Blacks alike was of the folk variety, with magico-religious use of Catholic sacramentals frequently predominating over more orthodox

108. Baer, *Black Spiritual Movement*, 18.
109. Robeck, *Azusa Street Mission*, 23.

forms of faith.[110] In the post–Civil War period, numerous Black Protestant churches with distinctly Black forms of Christianity also sprang up, providing an alternative to the nominally integrated Catholicism that had dominated religious life in the antebellum period.[111] The periodic influx of Blacks directly from Africa or from the Caribbean islands added the element of voodoo practice to the mix.[112] In the United States, the Afro-Catholic religion of voodoo was transformed into hoodoo, a more generalized conjure tradition involving "the practice of spells and other forms of magical manipulation"[113] to secure the practitioner's well-being, protect from harm, or inflict harm on others. The three Marie Laveaus—mother, daughter, and granddaughter—were celebrated as great conjurers, exercised tremendous influence in New Orleans throughout the nineteenth century, and were held in awe by Whites and Blacks alike.[114] Many of the practices used by hoodoo doctors in the early twentieth century, were attributable to the Laveaus, and many practitioners counted themselves among their spiritual, and sometimes even biological, descendants.[115]

American spiritualism, broadly defined as "talking with the dead," had gained "thousands and perhaps millions" of adherents during the mid- to late nineteenth century, primarily in the New England states.[116] Exported to southern Louisiana in the postbellum period, it too became part of the dynamism of the New Orleans religious scene. The liberal and egalitarian nature of spiritualism afforded women in particular opportunities to express leadership at a time when few American women were permitted to speak in public.[117] Spiritualism was generally opposed in the South due to its association with the abolition of slavery.[118] Nevertheless, spiritualist circles were formed, which included ex-Catholic free people of color as members, who maintained registers documenting their meetings and recording messages received from the dead.[119] The liberal outlook of spiritualism, coupled with

110. Jacobs and Kaslow, *Spiritual Churches*, 24.
111. Jacobs and Kaslow, *Spiritual Churches*, 28–29.
112. Jacobs and Kaslow, *Spiritual Churches*, 24.
113. Chireau, *Black Magic*, 77.
114. Jacobs and Kaslow, *Spiritual Churches*, 26.
115. Hurston, "Hoodoo in America," 327.
116. Nartonis, "19th-Century American Spiritualism," 361.
117. Nartonis, "19th-Century American Spiritualism," 363.
118. Nartonis, "19th-Century American Spiritualism," 371.
119. Jacobs and Kaslow, *Spiritual Churches*, 28.

its compatibility with African religions, meant that "[it] found adherents among the Black population," especially in New Orleans.[120]

It was within this multiethnic, multireligious context that the Black spiritual church movement was born; New Orleans can rightly be considered "the Mecca of the Spiritual movement."[121] Mother Anderson's Eternal Life Spiritualist Church in the Crescent City, established around 1918,[122] became the mother church of several other congregations in New Orleans and other cities, while "she trained several other women, who established congregations of their own."[123] In 1922, Mother Catherine Seals established the Temple of the Innocent Blood which likewise gave birth to other spiritual churches. Rev. Thomas Watson became a key figure in the spiritual movement not only by organizing several churches into the Divine Spiritualist Churches of the Southwest (DSCS) but also because his articulation of a creed for the church with explicit references to a Christocentric theology thitherto unnamed.[124] This represents a self-conscious effort on the part of spiritual people to position themselves more explicitly within the Christian tradition and to gain a degree of legitimacy with other Christian congregations. By the 1970s, direct references to the person of Jesus as Son of God and Savior were both explicit and common—a clear departure from the earliest days when in Leafy Anderson's group the "congregation was not allowed to call his name [since] as a man . . . Jesus was not important."[125] Watson would go on to play a key role in the formation of what is perhaps the largest Black spiritual association, the Metropolitan Spiritual Churches of Christ (MSCC), headquartered in Kansas City.[126] Watson's connection with MSCC reflects the reality that though the spiritual movement received much of its early impetus from New Orleans, it spread rapidly across urban areas in the North and South, experiencing something of a heyday during the 1920s and 1930s. Chicago became a center of the movement, with reports of up to 10 percent of congregations in the Black Bronzeville neighborhood being associated with the movement.[127]

120. Baer, *Black Spiritual Movement*, 19.
121. Baer, *Black Spiritual Movement*, 22.
122. Hurston, "Hoodoo in America," 319.
123. Baer, *Black Spiritual Movement*, 19.
124. Jacobs and Kaslow, *Spiritual Churches*, 44.
125. Jacobs and Kaslow, *Spiritual Churches*, 52.
126. Baer, "Metropolitan Spiritual Churches," 143.
127. St. Clair Drake and Horace R. Clayton, *Black Metropolis*, cited in Baer, *Black Spiritual Movement*, 23.

Belief Systems

Unlike Pentecostals, whose core beliefs are well known and often explicitly articulated, those of the spiritual church are less known, hence the need to provide a preliminary sketch of those beliefs here. Identifying the core beliefs of the spiritual church movement is difficult, because "there is a pattern of great flexibility in beliefs and practices in the movement as a whole, even among those groups that publish manuals and formal creeds in an attempt to make their doctrines fairly explicit."[128] Perhaps the best summary description of the eclectic nature of the churches is found here:

> Their clergy blend Roman Catholic iconography and material culture (altars, statuary, priestly vestments, etc.) with energetic Pentecostal preaching style and scriptural exegesis. Prophecy, spirit communion, "laying on of hands," and other ecstatic forms of worship are employed by some of the most gifted ministers and bishops. To this blend is added a proliferation of tools and techniques for physical and spiritual healing drawn from several corners of the African diaspora, or (to a lesser degree) from European mystical systems. A rich pharmacopeia of herbs, sacred oils, incenses and other *materia sacra* are incorporated into both the communal and private rites of the Spiritual Church.[129]

This eclecticism has led to the frequent characterization of spiritual people as "syncretic" by scholars of religion, implying a modification and accommodation of essentially different beliefs and practices into a new system.[130]

Parenthetically, while the term "syncretism" may be defensible and understandable from an anthropological perspective, the term is problematic insofar as it presupposes the normative and norming status of Euro-Western cultural and theological categories. The theological divisions that arose in consequence of the unique historical and cultural circumstances of Euro-Western Christianity are often assumed to be definitive and binding, and thus borrowing or combining from one or another tradition is deemed syncretic. This is even more the case when such traditions are combined with primal religious practices as are found in conjure. The question that presents itself forcefully when syncretism is alleged is this: If the gospel is essentially located in the person of Jesus Christ, why is it that non-White

---

128. Baer, *Black Spiritual Movement*, 110.
129. Wehmeyer, "Indians at the Door," 17–18.
130. Hesselgrave, *Communicating Christ Cross-Culturally*, 281.

and non-Western peoples who encounter Jesus and appropriate the gospel on their own terms and in their own way are often called syncretic, especially when such labels are infrequently or never applied to the conversion and Christianization of Europe, or to Euro-Western theology in general? The question forces one to confront the strong association of Euro-Western cultural norms with Christian faith forged through Christianity's centuries long sojourn in Europe, and the ideas of forcible cultural and religious conversation that are an intrinsic part of that legacy. Considering this history, allegations of syncretism may represent a kind of ideological and even linguistic violence. We need not tarry here, however, and so return to the central theme.

Charges of syncretism should not be permitted to obscure recognition of the theological and religious impulses that underlie the movement. Beneath the diversity and flexibility of the spiritual church, one may clearly discern the various influences that have informed the movement. The first, and most prominent of these influences is the Christian tradition itself, specifically the Roman Catholic and Black Protestant. Spiritual people have seen themselves foremost as Christians practicing a spiritual way of life, and not as a separate religious group. This can be observed both from their creedal statements, and from their religious practices. For example, the doctrinal statement of the DSCS formulated by Thomas Watson borrowed extensively from those of other established Christian bodies, specifically the 1920 Methodist Episcopal Church's *Doctrines and Discipline*, the 1921 Roman Catholic *Catechism of Christian Doctrine*, and the *Confession of Faith* of the Church of God in Christ, a Black Pentecostal group.[131] Another example of this type of intentional creedal identification with Christianity is found in the 2016 informational brochure of St Martins Spiritualist Church (SMSC) of St. Louis, Missouri. The brochure emphasizes "maintain[ing] a spiritual relationship with God the Father, the Son, and the Holy Spirit," with the goal of "spread[ing] the gospel of JESUS CHRIST." Their website too is careful to note the connection between their beliefs and practice and those of the Bible: "Here at SMSC we do not go against the teachings of the BIBLE. WE acknowledge the fact that the spirit world exists. We believe in Jesus and that the message of salvation is the main message." Christian has been a part of the name of the SMSC since its founding in 1915, reflecting the founder's intention to place the congregation firmly within the ambit of Christianity even from earliest times. These two examples, nearly a century

---

131. Jacobs and Kaslow, *Spiritual Churches*, 53.

apart, reveal a self-consciousness about placing themselves within the confines of historic Christianity, and not some other faith.

In terms of religious practice, the extensive use of Catholic paraphernalia by some churches—statuary, holy water, crucifixes, and the like—and rituals—genuflection, recitation of the Hail Mary, the burning of incense and candles, among others—all testify to the influence of Catholicism on the spiritual movement. It has been plausibly suggested that the prominence of Catholic practice and belief within the spiritual church movement came indirectly through voodoo.[132] It is, however, more likely that the dominance of Catholicism in southern Louisiana, combined with its sacramental orientation, simply made it a more compelling source from which to draw inspiration for the early spiritual pioneers. For some, the association with Catholicism is a self-conscious act. Rev Anderson, current pastor of the SMSC, notes that it was from their fathers (i.e., the founders of the church) that they learned to be "like unto the Catholics" in their religious services.[133]

The influence of Black Protestantism on the spiritual church is likewise extensive and is particularly evident outside the Catholic dominated regions of southern Louisiana.[134] This influence is seen in the patterns of religious observance and worship services. These services have been described as

> closely resembl[ing] Black Holiness and Pentecostal sects in the style of their services. This is demonstrated by their emphasis on spirit possession, divine healing, prophecy, shouting, hand clapping, foot stomping, and tambourine playing. Many Spiritual people also refer to glossolalia, or speaking in tongues, as one of the "nine gifts of the Holy Spirit."[135]

I can from personal experience attest to the accuracy of these descriptions. The similarity between spiritual people and Pentecostals in their worship style led some to describe themselves as "sanctified Catholics" since both groups "emphasize unstructured opportunities for the Holy Spirit to operate."[136] Perhaps equally important is the emphasis placed on "accept-

---

132. Baer, *Black Spiritual Movement*, 131.
133. Rev. Harold Anderson, sermon, Jan. 3, 2016.
134. Baer, *Black Spiritual Movement*, 136.
135. Baer, *Black Spiritual Movement*, 135.
136. Jacobs and Kaslow, *Spiritual Churches*, 73.

ing Jesus as a personal Saviour,"[137] a feature not particularly prominent in Catholicism.

Voodoo or hoodoo is considered by some to exercise a prominent influence on the spiritual church movement. There are those who contend that voodoo was "the earliest form of the Spiritual religion in Louisiana,"[138] a claim that accords with Hurston's description of the "strong aroma of hoodoo [that] clings about"[139] the spiritual churches she encountered. The connection between them is, however, vehemently denied by spiritual people. Contrary to their intentional embrace of the broader Christian tradition, spiritual people self-consciously reject any association between their own faith and practice and voodoo or hoodoo. Mother Leafy Anderson, the undisputed founder of the first spiritual (or spiritualist) church in New Orleans, allegedly "detested" voodoo,[140] and many spiritual people have historically denied any link whatsoever with either hoodoo or voodoo. In the photo journal *Spirit World* by Michael P. Smith, Smith's various interlocutors all expressly deny any connection between their own practices and voodoo or hoodoo, pointing instead to the Bible and the Holy Spirit as inspiration.[141] These leaders do, however, suggest that though they themselves disdain such practices, they suspect others in the spiritual church movement of "being involved in 'hoodoo' or 'witchcraft,' and of having prophets who are charlatans and confidence people" and are thus "careful to distinguish their organizations or congregations from other spiritual groups, often regarding some of the latter in a disparaging manner."[142] The tendency to distance themselves from voodoo stems from an acceptance by spiritual people of the negative stereotypes associated with it.[143] This assertion fails to account for the quite different theologies associated with each faith community, and even for the broad differences within the spiritual church movement itself. The similarities between voodoo and the spiritual church movement may instead be the result of their shared primal

---

137. Jacobs and Kaslow, *Spiritual Churches*, 53.
138. Jacobs and Kaslow, *Spiritual Churches*, 30.
139. Hurston, "Hoodoo in America," 319.
140. Baer, *Black Spiritual Movement*, 19.
141. M. Smith, *Spirit World*, 45-46, 57. Interestingly, Archbishop Johnson claims to have been a disciple of Leafy Anderson.
142. Baer, "Anthropological View," 55.
143. Baer, *Black Spiritual Movement*, 127.

orientation and origin, particularly the conjure tradition, without one having borrowed from the other.

Finally, the connections between the Black spiritual church and the broader movement of American spiritualism appears clear to some observers, though Black spiritual people themselves mostly disdain any such connection.[144] The most obvious connection between the two lies in their shared rejection of a supernatural realm distinct from the natural, though this belief is primal and not necessarily confined to any particular religious group. More specifically, both groups generally hold that communication from and with the spirit world, including communication with the "so-called dead," is possible.[145] Rev Anderson affirmed this idea in a sermon in which he referred to the transfiguration as such an occurrence, for if they were dead, he asked, how could they talk to Jesus?[146] Nonetheless, the Black spiritual movement should "not be merely viewed as a minority counterpart of white Spiritualism."[147] Indeed negative connotations of the term "spiritualist" may have led many Black spiritual groups to begin referring to themselves as "spiritual."[148]

From the earliest days of Anglican efforts at conversion, through the Great Awakening and Great Revival, to plantation missions, and the rise of the independent Black church, Black religion has always demonstrated a close affinity with and remained in close dialogue with primal forms of religious observance, most notably the conjure tradition. This close association continued and found fresh expression in the emergence of Pentecostalism at the turn of the twentieth century and also in the dynamic and eclectic Black spiritual movement, which is its close kin. One is reminded throughout that the development of Black Christianity and even its primal orientation occurred within a context of first slavery and then institutionalized racial oppression undergirded by assumptions of Euro-Western cultural supremacy and White racial hegemony that was frequently justified on a biblical basis. It becomes clear that neither the experience of Black Christianity nor the way in which it has historically been assessed can be effectively separated from this history, though it cannot delimit it absolutely.

144. Jacobs and Kaslow, *Spiritual Churches*, 73.

145. Baer, *Black Spiritual Movement*, 117. Baer quotes here from a manual of the pseudonymous St. Cecilia's Divine Healing Churches, "We affirm that communication with the so-called dead is a fact scientifically proven by the phenomenon of spiritualism."

146. Rev. Harold Anderson, sermon, Jan. 3, 2016.

147. Baer, "Metropolitan Spiritual Churches," 141.

148. Baer, *Black Spiritual Movement*, 7.

7

The Primal in the Pentecostal
A Case Study of the All Saints Holiness Church

All Saints Holiness Church

Physical Description

SITUATED AT A QUIET corner in a rapidly gentrifying neighborhood in a major city in the southern United States, the All Saints Holiness Church (ASHC) blends unobtrusively into the predominantly white, upper middle-class neighborhood surrounding the church. The building itself was acquired in 2005 from another Pentecostal congregation. Originally housing a White Methodist congregation, the sturdy brick structure is an upgrade from the wood-frame building that had been the church's longtime home in a poorer, blacker area of town.

Inside the sanctuary, one finds the simplicity typical of many Protestant congregations. There is little adornment here: a single large bronze-colored cross hangs behind the podium on the elevated platform. Beneath the cross, on a slightly raised platform, sits the communion table, except on communion Sundays when it is moved to the main floor directly in front of the podium. It is likewise devoid of any adornment, though at communion services, one would observe the elements covered in a draped white cloth. On the podium stands a bottle of consecrated oil, used to anoint those who come for prayer. To the left of the podium, an organ and the drum set, which is located on the main floor, just to the right of the organ. Seats for the choir are set further back on the platform, to the left of the organist who sits with his right side to the congregation; to the right, a large chair where the pastor sits. Seats for the other ministers are placed to his right, mirroring the arrangement of the choir. Hidden from view at the rear of the platform is another entrance, originally the main entry of the church, with stairs that lead to the basement. To the left at the top of the stairs, one finds a small study and washroom for the pastor or visiting ministers, and to the right another room in which a large metal tub has been set up as the baptismal pool the original Methodist owners saw no need for.

The congregational seating is made up of approximately twenty long pews, ten on each side, which face the platform. The auditorium can comfortably seat around 150 people, though a typical Sunday would see closer to 40 in attendance. At the rear of the sanctuary, one finds glass doors leading to a wide but short vestibule, which has a few chairs and a clothes closet. A picture of the current pastor hangs here, while another of the founding pastor hangs at the foot of the stairs at the entrance of the building. The contrast between the pictures is striking and mirrors the transition the church has undergone over the years. The photo of the current pastor shows him dressed as any contemporary Black Pentecostal pastor would be—in a suit, his electric smile beaming out over a simple clerical collar. The portrait of the founder, his mother, reflects a different aesthetic, and a different religious sense. She wears a long, white robe, suggestive of those worn by Catholic priests, with a purple stole and cap. Her expression, pleasant yet enigmatic, is evocative of someone who is comfortable with the things of the Spirit. Above the vestibule is a rather claustrophobic sound room. In the basement, a fellowship hall and three or four classrooms, decorated in the same minimal way as the rest of the building. Nothing of the building's furnishings or interior décor suggests the church's roots in the spiritual church movement. It was not always so.

Entirely missing are the religious paraphernalia that adorned the church in earlier days—burning candles on the altar standing alongside bowls of water and incense censers; an iridescent picture of a bearded, white Jesus carrying a lamb on his shoulders; a white, cloth-covered kneeler encircling the altar table and two small chairs that flanked each side of the table, where one sat or knelt when in need of special prayer. While never as elaborately decorated as some spiritual churches, "the elaborate altars embellished with images of the saints, the use of votive candles, incense, holy oils, holy water, and the elaborate vestments worn by the clergy"[1] found in other spiritual churches could likewise have been applied to the All Saints Holiness Church. Now, however, all of these are gone.

The membership of ASHC has never been large, and has always been anchored by a few families, most of whom are connected by deep and long-standing ties of family or friendship to the founder of the church. Although the membership still draws largely from the same lower-income and middle-class demographic as at the beginning, most of the long-standing families in the church have gradually moved up the economic ladder and can boast of spacious homes in the suburbs, far from the inner-city. Others though, continue to struggle. As a mostly family church, the congregation reflects the dynamics of multigenerational families—seniors and older married couples along with their adult children, mostly unmarried, grandchildren, assorted in-laws, and other relations comprise the core of the membership. Aside the regular attendees, others attend on special occasions, considering it their home church, even if they have not attended regularly for many years.

The congregants' dress is not especially noteworthy, and though one would not observe any dramatic difference in dress between now and the early years, some changes are evident. The religious regalia—"elaborate vestments similar to those worn by a Catholic priest while saying mass . . . long robes of a wide variety of colors, accompanied by elaborate turbans or other types of headdress"[2]—has entirely disappeared. Unlike in its earliest days, none of the members wear robes, except the pastor and other ministers, and that only occasionally. Gone are the white doily-type head coverings, lace scarves, and simple napkins that would have adorned the heads of many of the women. Yet the congregation still dresses conservatively—"as becoming saints, in decent and modest apparel"—suit and tie for the older men and male ministers, slacks and buttoned shirts for the others. For the women, the same conservative suits and dresses that one finds in other urban Black Pentecostal churches are worn; "on Sunday the black saints came to church 'as humble as we know how,' but dressed in honor, respect and glory."[3] Younger members dress in a decidedly more casual fashion.

---

1. Jacobs and Kaslow, *Spiritual Churches*, 65.

2. Baer, *Black Spiritual Movement*, 125. Though vestments such as these were uncommon among the ministers of my own church during my youth, they were worn occasionally. They were much more commonly worn by visiting clergy.

3. Scandrett-Leatherman, "Can't Nobody Do Me," 261.

While the restrictive dress code of earlier years has been relaxed, modest, conservative dress still predominates even among the youth. Some of the older women, church mothers, as well as missionaries and deaconesses, wear hats or other hair coverings, as required for women serving in official ministry roles though only loosely enforced.

Currently, the pastorate of the church is held by Bishop Joseph Allen, the eldest son of the founder, the late Bishop Fannie Rockson (1928–2014). He has been a part of the church since its founding and served as assistant pastor for many years. He assumed the office in July 2001 when Bishop Rockson retired from active service. He is assisted by two other associate ministers, several deacons, and a church steward, who are jointly responsible for managing the business affairs of the church. The church missionaries, who are "anointed and licensed after meeting spiritual qualifications," and mothers—senior women with recognized moral authority—form the last segment of the leadership structure.

History in Brief

The founder of All Saints Holiness Church, Fannie Gilmore, was born July 3, 1928, in Holly Springs, Mississippi, the only child of Addie Johnson and James Gilmore. Reared by her maternal aunt, Rose Cowell, Fannie began her faith journey as a child in the United Primitive Baptist Church and in her youth experienced a sense of call to spiritual leadership. However, like many women who encountered barriers to leadership within mainstream denominations, she found the spiritual church a more conducive environment for her spiritual development.[4] In the late 1950s, Gilmore left the Primitive Baptist Church, and began attending St. Paul's Spiritual Church, pastored by Dawson Trigg, where she met a woman named Mother Waterford.[5] At St. Paul's, "she served faithfully for many years as a missionary

---

4. See Baer, "Limited Empowerment of Women," 71–72.

5. There is some discrepancy between Baer's account of these events and that of Bishop Allen. Baer indicates that Dawson Trigg founded St. Paul's Spiritual Church in 1947 (*Black Spiritual Movement*, 34), while Bishop Allen indicates that Mother Waterford was the founder, though Trigg pastored the church. Since Baer's claim that Trigg had been "ordained as a Spiritual minister in St. Louis" (34) accords with Allen's description of Mother Waterford as having established a church in St. Louis and being linked with an association there, it is probable that Trigg either established the Nashville congregation while remaining under Waterford's leadership, or that Waterford established the group and handed it over to Trigg to pastor while retaining some measure of authority over him.

and deaconess"[6] before her connection with Mother Waterford led her to a meeting in St. Louis, where she encountered the Universal Unity Union, a spiritual association with churches in several cities scattered across the eastern United States. Through this association, she met and befriended Elder Sallie Swift—a friendship that would change the trajectory of Gilmore's life and ministry forever.

Elder Sallie M. Swift, a pastor who had set up her own Indianapolis-based organization in the 1940s, prophesied to Fannie Gilmore that if she would straighten up her life, God would bless her and her children, and that she would become a powerful woman of God. Encouraged by this prophecy, Gilmore became friends with Swift and affiliated herself with the Universal Unity Union, traveling with them to conventions in various cities across the eastern United States. It was during this period in the late 1950s, she began to experience a growing sense of calling from God to preach. Her experience of calling to ministry would later provide the material of her annual "I Have a Dream" demonstration service, where she likened her experience to that of the biblical Joseph.[7] Like Joseph, she too had a prophetic dream in which she experienced rejection, after which she was accepted, blessed, and commissioned for greater service. During a convention, when presented for ordination, Gilmore was initially rejected by the ordination council. Elder Swift and one Bishop Ashwood, under whom she had studied, spoke up for her, assuring the council that she was indeed ready, leading the council to reverse their decision. The following night, Monday, August 5, 1963, she was ordained to the ministry of "Preaching, Prophecing [sic], healing, Divine Mediumship & Divine Miracles in the Spirit of God."

Thus empowered, newly ordained Evangelist Gilmore returned to her hometown, and while still attending St. Paul's, used her existing connections to begin a prayer band with a small group of women. These women traveled from house to house conducting prayer meetings. This prayer band became the genesis of the All Saints Caribbean Mission established in 1964 with the help of Bishop Cecil Bishop, a native of the Caribbean (hence the name). The name would later be changed to All Saints Spiritual Church

6. Interview with Bishop Joseph Allen, Jan. 14, 2016.

7. Baer defines a demonstration as a special service whose "principal goal is to obtain a blessing [that] . . . involves some idiosyncratic ritual which has been developed by a prominent member of the congregation (*Black Spiritual Movement*, 73–74). Gilmore's "I Have a Dream" demonstration was conducted annually for many years, the last time being in the early 2000s.

No. 2, and finally, to the All Saints Holiness Church. It was in 1966 that Gilmore attached her congregation to Sallie Swift's existing organization, which, though formally established in 1947, held their first convention in 1967 in Indianapolis.

The earliest years of the church were marked by fragility and instability. The failure of the mission to develop led to the departure of the cofounder, Bishop Cecil Bishop, back to his native country, which left the group in the hands of Evangelist Gilmore and members of her prayer band. The future of the group seemed doubtful in these early days. Between its founding in 1964 and 1971, the church met in four different locations, including the home of a member, an empty warehouse, and two different storefronts. Despite the instability, however, under Gilmore's leadership the congregation grew and in 1973 the church was able to purchase the building that was to be its home for the next thirty-two years. That building was superior to the rented warehouses and storefronts that were typical for many spiritual congregations and gave the church a degree of stability that many of its counterpart spiritual churches lacked.

Fairly early in its history the word "spiritual" was dropped from the name of the church. The negative associations of the name—in the words of Gilmore, the term "spiritual" had become "dirty"[8]—were what led to the change, though other factors were at play as well. ASHC was led away from identification with the movement at least partially by a sense that "other churches were looking down on them . . . because of all the bad publicity that the spiritual church had gotten in the past." The change in name was not superficial, however. It marked a shift in identity, as the group began to align itself intentionally more with the holiness Pentecostal movement than with the spiritual movement out of which it had emerged, especially since there was a widespread belief that these churches embraced "hoodoo." In keeping with this change, unlike some spiritual churches, ASHC began to emphasize a strict moral code. Members are admonished to, among other things, live holy lives by separating themselves from the world, abstaining from the use of tobacco products, keeping their mind and body clean, shunning gambling and bribery and, dressing "as becoming saints in decent in modest apparel" and "abstain[ing] from heavy make-up, excessive, and/or flashy jewelry."[9] These principles are regularly reinforced in teaching

---

8. Baer, *Black Spiritual Movement*, 37.
9. *I'll Go* (self-published organizational manual, n.d.), 8.

and sermons, and by example as when one member of the congregation testified, "[God], you've taken me out of everything!"

Despite this shift in theological emphasis, at the level of practice, the church retained "many of the basic elements of the Spiritual movement"[10] and continued to maintain connections with other spiritual congregations in the city for many years, including demonstration services, bless services, and even the funeral of Dawson Trigg, pastor of St. Paul's Spiritual Church, when he died in 1985, a funeral I attended as a child.

Change and Continuity in the All Saints Holiness Church

Throughout the more than fifty-year history of the church, there have been many changes, and much continuity. Yet upon examination, it becomes clear that while most of the changes may be regarded as superficial, the continuity of primal imagination that animates the worship rituals of the church remains.

Ritual Use of Candles and Incense

Many things that formerly characterized the worship services of the ASHC have ceased. Most of those are ritual practices that the current pastor and son of the founder describe as reminiscent of Catholic piety:

> They would do the Hail Mary's, and they would . . . light the candles, and they would burn the incense. . . . Now I realize where that structure came from, not realizing it at the time. I just thought it was kind of something weird because, you know, I'd never been in a church that lit candles and burnt incense and sprinkled water . . . holy water everywhere. . . . I didn't understand it at the time, but now that I realize that . . . the basic structure that they got all this from was from the Catholic Church. So, whoever really started the spiritual church movement was reared in . . . the Catholic Church and that's where they got the basic principles of how the spiritual churches operated.

These rituals were used to invoke the presence of the Spirit of God; burning incense was seen as prayers ascending to God; different candles were lit for different purposes and on different occasions. Green candles, for example, were for prosperity, while white was burned for the purpose

---

10. Baer, *Black Spiritual Movement*, 37.

of purification. "Redemption" services were held wherein the Spirit of God was invoked to, in the words of the current pastor, "come in and righten some wrong" that had been committed. Against a background of belief in curses, hexes, voodoo, and hoodoo, church members were careful to guard themselves against things that could expose them to harm, including one's physical posture. The pastor recalls an incident when he was praying at the altar in church with his arms crossed only to be confronted angrily by another member, "Stop crossing folks up!," his folded arms having been interpreted as a hostile gesture.

Ecstatic Behavior, Healing and Prophecy

Whereas certain paraphernalia and rituals have disappeared from the ASHC, others have remained or become amplified. For example, healing and prophecy, considered by some to be the key "distinguishing features" of the spiritual church, with leaders who claim to be healers, prophets, or both,[11] are not alien to the church. The bishop recalls:

> I remember Mother Waterford, she was a prophetess, and she would prophesy to the people, and she would also lay hands on people . . . she had the gift of healing, which my mother had the gift of healing too at the time . . . somebody would get up and maybe they'll have a testimony, and someone would shout, or someone would start speaking in tongues.

Like other Pentecostal groups, ASHC considers healing a key ministry of the church, and prayer for healing takes place regularly. A request for special prayer for healing was made during my visit to the church in January 2016. She informed the congregation that she was to have made the request the previous week (ostensibly under the direction of the Spirit) but did not, after which she exclaimed, "God said there needs to be healing in the land." Her remark reflected a concern for healing that extended beyond those present, and beyond only physical needs. Ecstatic phenomena like shouting and tongues speaking also remain. The sight of someone overwhelmed with crying while speaking in tongues, or dancing in the aisles while being attended to by an usher, is not unusual. Though perhaps not emphasized quite as strongly as in earlier days, prophecy too remains a common feature of worship at the ASHC.

---

11. Jacobs and Kaslow, *Spiritual Churches*, 149.

Altar Prayer

At the midpoint of the Sunday worship service there is an "altar prayer" (though the physical table that served as an altar has long disappeared) during which a designated person, usually a minister, missionary, or deacon, prays for and with the congregation who gather in a semicircle around the front area of the church—a space that, though lacking in visual interest or religious paraphernalia—is treated as sacred, at least while prayer is being conducted. For many years, this was a time when a "silver offering," i.e., coins, was collected. Congregants would bring their offerings, which would be placed in a water-filled bowl that had been placed on the altar, dipping their hands into the water in the process, after which they would make the sign of the cross and join the circle surrounding the altar. Some, after placing their coins in the bowl, would elevate their right hand and say a brief, silent prayer.[12] The altar prayer is preceded each Sunday by a reading of Jas 5:12–20, which calls for anointing with oil and prayer in response to conditions of sickness within the community, as well as emphasizing the importance of faith. It is during this time that prayers for healing of the sick or for others may be offered.

Altar Call

Another prayer time, the altar call, follows immediately after the sermon. This session is a fixed part of the service, originally and primarily intended as a time when "the doors of the church are opened," i.e., an opportunity for people to offer themselves for membership in the church or as candidates for baptism. It has evolved, however, into a time of general response to the sermon and the worship service. During this time of prayer, as opposed to the altar prayer, it is only those who offer themselves for anointing and prayers who come forward. Just as during the altar prayer, this is also a period in the service during which manifestations of the Spirit—speaking in tongues, prophecy and the like—are more likely to occur. Unlike the general altar prayer, however, the altar call time tends to be more intense. Laying on of hands almost always occurs during this session and the prayers themselves are more specifically targeted to the direct request of the responders. It is a liminal period—a moment of transition and ambiguity wherein the Spirit takes over the gathering, temporarily restructuring it into a "communion of

---

12. Baer describes a similar occurrence (*Black Spiritual Church*, 6).

equal individuals who submit together to the general authority of the ritual elders,"[13] in this case, the person(s) leading the prayer. Anyone may shout, speak in tongues, or exhibit other manifestations of the Spirit's work without regard to their formal status or position within the church. It is, to borrow from the primal Celts, a thin time, when the supernatural "imping[es] on and interact[s] with the present life."[14] The sacrality of the altar prayer and the altar call exists both temporally and spatially as people are strongly discouraged from entering or exiting the sanctuary during this time.

Testimony Service

Another such period in the worship service is the testimony service, the "liminal core of Afro-Pentecostal worship."[15] It is a core part of the worship at ASHC, though it is not held every Sunday as in the case of some other Pentecostal congregations.[16] This description, derived from the context of the Church of God in Christ, applies to ASHC as well.

> Different people testify, play organ, sing, stomp, shout, pray, drum, speak in tongues, run, and dance. And the modes of expression circulate not only within the community but in the testimony of a single person, which may include a song, greetings, scripture, story, shout, a bodily expression, and interpretation of the physical expression, a prayer request.[17]

The testimony service is simultaneously an individual and corporate expression. Each person speaks of his or her own experience with God, sharing joys or struggles, sometimes in intensely personal ways, yet in a ritual context where they are borne along in their sharing by the entire community. The whole of the gathered community participates with them as each person comes "in their own way." It is democratizing and empowering in ways similar to that of the altar prayer, though perhaps more so, in that once someone stands to give testimony, it is unlikely that they will be restricted in any way; "the only qualification for speaking to the whole body

13. V. Turner, *Ritual Process*, 96.
14. Joyce, *Celtic Christianity*, 10.
15. Scandrett-Leatherman, "Can't Nobody Do Me," 284.
16. Anecdotally, in my experience in a variety of Pentecostal congregations and services, it appears that the testimony service features less and less frequently as part of Sunday morning worship.
17. Scandrett-Leatherman, "Can't Nobody Do Me," 287.

is the ability to rise to be seen by one of the leaders."[18] Michael Smith shared his own experience of "testifying" when he was called upon to explain to the congregation the nature of his work. After a false start, where he tried to explain himself in cognitive terms, he changed his approach:

> When I talked from my head, they had no way of relating to what I said, were even intimidated and alienated. But when I spoke from my heart they understood and responded openly . . . our beings had gradually intermingled in a strange, interactive dance of consciousness toward understanding. My expression became more clear and flowing. It was an atmosphere which allowed me to transcend language and cultural barriers and to communicate my deepest feelings. As far as they were concerned, there had been a "visitation of the Spirit."[19]

His description provides a window into how testimony services illuminate "that sense of cosmic oneness which is an essential feature of primal religion"[20] by eroding, within a ritual context, the clean distinctions between the self, the other, and the divine. This is a key way in which the primal imagination is manifest within the church.

Continuities in Belief: Primal Foundations

The various elements of the worship service testify to a continuity of belief. For example, the foundational beliefs of the church—the problem of sin, the need to be born again, the importance of baptism and belief in the Godhead: Father, Son, and Holy Spirit—remain unchanged. Beyond these, however, ASHC retains belief in the availability, and indeed necessity, of spiritual power to help overcome life's challenges and to become better people. This belief has remained a constant throughout the history of the church, and is consistent with the second, third, and fourth features of Turner's schema, but more especially the fourth—the belief that humans may "share in [the] powers and blessings [of the spirit realm] and receive protection from evil forces."[21] I discuss this in greater detail below.

What has changed over time is the way this power is accessed or otherwise invoked. According to the bishop, when the church was aligned with

---

18. Scandrett-Leatherman, "Can't Nobody Do Me," 286.
19. M. Smith, *Spirit World*, 31.
20. John V. Taylor, *Primal Vision*, 64.
21. H. Turner, "Primal Religions," 31.

the spiritual movement, it was through one's ritual actions—lighting of candles, burning of incense, recitation of particular prayers or the performance of certain rituals—that this power was invoked in a nearly automatic fashion: "With the spiritual church, *you* do something to invoke the power, rather than your faith ... they were putting their beliefs on a material thing, whereas in the Pentecostal church or the holiness church, there's a faith thing." What mattered was the performance of the ritual, not one's faith nor the quality of one's spiritual life or relationship with God. The emphasis was the pursuit of "spiritual elevation regardless of how your life was." Seen in this light, the rituals performed when ASHC was more closely aligned with the spiritual movement could appear as essentially magical in nature— "efficacious, with its spells. curses, incantations, and formulae ... used for specific, personal ends ... operat[ing] mechanically—as opposed to prayer, which is communal, devotional and noncoercive."[22] This assertion would accord with Hans Baer's categorization of the spiritual churches as thaumaturgical sects wherein "success and economic prosperity ... may be obtained through the performance of special rituals and positive thinking."[23]

It is unclear, however, the extent to which this characterization of the activities of the spiritual church is an accurate reflection of their true beliefs. Since Baer's chief concern was "to understand collective religious response to the exclusion Black Americans have experienced from mainstream roles and opportunities,"[24] the question of the interior faith disposition of the practitioners was largely set aside in Baer's research. The interiority of faith is inaccessible in any case. Though the current pastor was involved with the church when it was aligned with the spiritual movement, he evidently regards that association with some ambivalence, which may contribute to his interpretation of their practices. As the church has become increasingly aligned with mainstream Pentecostalism, it is evident that the bishop too has adopted a similar view of the rituals of the spiritual church as being essentially magical in nature.

Magic vs. Faith?

Despite the pastor's views, the contrast between what occurred when ASHC was a spiritual church, or what happens in other spiritual churches,

22. Chireau, *Black Magic*, 3
23. Baer and Singer, *African American Religion*, 183.
24. Baer and Singer, "Typology of Black Sectarianism," 3.

and what transpires within the church now is perhaps less distinct than he would have it. According to him, the church now emphasizes the importance of prayers made in faith and trust in God for access to spiritual power rather than the performance of certain rites or rituals. On this reading, the rituals of the spiritual church were magical in nature. Yet this need not be the case and may not be an accurate interpretation. In their study into the spiritual churches in New Orleans, Jacobs and Kaslow discovered that among at least some ministers in spiritual churches, "the paraphernalia they use (e.g., candles, incense, and oils) and the rituals they perform or prescribe (e.g., spiritual baths, novenas, and anointings) . . . [are seen to] have no intrinsic power but only help to establish belief or faith in the 'minds' of clients and members of their congregations."[25] Thus such objects and activities may more properly be regarded as aids to faith, rather than objects of faith—a view in keeping with the sacramental and symbolic perspective that perhaps reflects the influence of Catholicism on the spiritual movement, or more broadly, of a primal perspective. In this, they would agree with the Roman Catholic view that Christ, who during his earthly ministry "conferred his blessings not only by word but also by gestures and other symbolic actions" and who "continues to speak through the proclaimed word," can be expected to "continue to act through sacramental rites."[26] The ritual practices of the spiritual church "take on a new character" when it is understood that religious ritual is not magical manipulation, but instead "a deliberately created 'sacred time and action'"[27] wherein the Spirit can work. This is a key insight, which shall be taken up shortly.

The Primal Imagination in the Practice and Beliefs of the ASHC

Perhaps the most fundamental presupposition in my analysis is that the history, beliefs, and practices of the ASHC are not unrelated to an epistemology and consequently a theology that implicitly reflects the primal imagination. The history, stated beliefs, and ritual practices of the All Saints Holiness Church constitute a way of knowing and of being in relation to God and to the supernatural that is consonant with the primal imagination as refracted through the lens of Black/African culture. Specifically, this manifests within the ASHC in three ways—belief in sacred times and

---

25. Jacobs and Kaslow, *Spiritual Churches*, 162.
26. Dulles, "Church, Ministry, and Sacraments," 111.
27. Jacobs and Kaslow, *Spiritual Churches*, 169, quoting Paden, *Religious Worlds*.

spaces; the mediation of power through physical means, including ritual; and finally a holistic perception of salvation in which healing, spiritual warfare, and spiritual gifts all play a role.

Sacred Times and Holy Places

The first of these, the belief in sacred times and spaces, may seem at first to be an untenable notion and indeed counter to the desacralizing impulse of low-church Protestantism. As indicated above, the church itself is not decorated in any way that would indicate its sacrality. Although services are held in the "sanctuary," this is as much a convention of speech as anything else. It is important here to clarify what is meant by the term "sacred" and "sacrality." In ordinary speech, it means something connected with God or a divinity/spirit, or considered to be holy. While this definition is implicit in my usage, the sacredness here referenced goes beyond that to include the idea of mediation—a *sacred space or time* is one that serves as the medium of encounter with the holy (and wholly) "Other."[28] It emerges therefore that the setting aside of physical and temporal space wherein the Spirit can work is a means by which that space becomes sacralized. The creation of this "space" is the integrating idea of worship in the ASHC, both when it was a part of the spiritual movement and today. This is, it seems to me, the theological hinge of Black Pentecostal/spiritual church piety. Worship and the Christian life are about creating opportunities for encounter with the Holy Other.

The Altar

Within the sanctuary there are areas that are considered more sacred, most notably the area designated as the altar. This area, really the front of the auditorium directly in front of the elevated platform and podium from which the pastor preaches, formerly did contain an actual altar table on which could be found candles, a bowl of water, and other ritual objects, including an incense censer. Presently, the altar prayer is usually conducted by a minister who stands at the pulpit, facing outward towards the congregation,

---

28. Otto, *Idea of the Holy*, 26. Here Otto describes the "Other" as "that which is quite beyond the sphere of the usual, the intelligible, and the familiar, which therefore falls quite outside the limits of the 'canny,' and is contrasted with it, filling the mind with blank wonder and astonishment."

praying over the people as it were, who gather in a semicircle around the altar area. Formerly, however, the designated pray-er stood or knelt facing the altar itself, along with the people, in a posture suggestive of a petitioner or intercessor alongside the people. Chairs placed on either side of the altar table, otherwise occupied by the deacons or missionaries who conducted the service, were vacated, and made available for those who needed "special prayer." Maintenance of the altar table, table linens, and other paraphernalia was the especial responsibility of the missionaries, who are appointed only after meeting spiritual qualifications before being permitted to serve in this way, highlighting the sacredness associated with them. These linens, and the official uniform of the missionaries who attend to them, were always white, white being a color often associated with purity or holiness. In addition to their symbolic value, the burning candles, incense, and blessed water provided sensory stimuli evoking an aura of holy "other-ness." These visual markers demarcated the space as sacred and were themselves treated as special objects.

It is not only the physical paraphernalia, however, that demarcates the sacrality of the altar area. The altar table has, after all, disappeared, and yet the space where it previously stood is still called the altar, and the call to response is still termed the altar call.[29] The most important marker of the sacrality of the space is the ritual action that occurs within the space. It is at the altar that the most significant rituals of the church occur and here where the expectation of encounter with the Spirit of God is most keenly felt. These ritual actions—the lighting of candles, burning of incense, dipping of hands in water, intercessory prayer, shouting, anointing with oil, etc.—are means by which the Spirit of God was and is not only evoked, but *in*voked by the community for the sake of the community, thus sacralizing the space in which these rituals occur. While the former implies only the remembrance of something or someone not present, the latter suggests presence. Joseph Murphy's concept of working the spirit is relevant here:

> The reciprocity between community and spirit is expressed in physical work as the community works through word, music, and movement to make the spirit present. The spirit in turn works through the physical work of the congregation, filling human actions with its power. Diasporan ceremonies [including Black American Christianity] are thus services *for* the spirit,

---

29. The altar call is, of course, closely linked to the revivalist traditions of Anglo-American Evangelicalism.

actions of sacrifice and praise to please the spirit. And they are services *of* the spirit, actions undertaken by the spirit to inspire the congregation.³⁰

Murphy uses the term "spirit" here broadly, concerned as he is with the spirituality of the broad African diaspora and not simply Christian spirituality. Yet the import is the same. The ritual work of the congregation on and around the altar renders the space a sacred site for the operation of the Spirit.

This sacrality is not only rendered in spatial terms, but temporal terms as well. As noted above, the altar prayer, Scripture reading, and altar call are designated "the most sacred parts of the service" at ASHC. This indicates the priority given to those experiential elements of worship that offer unmediated access to the divine—the reading of Scripture, and prayers. The emphasis is on creating a sacred space and time wherein the supernatural is easily accessed or may break through bringing healing, salvation, deliverance, etc. The high point of any service therefore is the "invoking" of the Spirit of God that occurs within that liminal space and what God does therein. It is a primal or "ceremonial spirituality" in which "the spirit is recognized as present by means of the actions of the community in ritual time and space."³¹ These rituals are indispensable elements of the Sunday worship service and are scarcely ever omitted.

The Sermon

Interestingly, the sermon was not designated as a sacred part of worship. This is not to say that the sermon is unimportant. Indeed, as a Black congregation, ASHC shares in the preaching tradition of the Black church, wherein "the preacher and the preached word [takes] the central position in worship, providing important information on and critiques of major spiritual and material concerns."³² Preaching itself is a participatory ritual—the audience together with the preacher through the call-and-response pattern characteristic of Black preaching craft the sermon in dialogue to a "point at which the audience *feels* the strength of the point of the sermon, embraces

---

30. Murphy, *Working the Spirit*, 7; emphasis original.
31. Murphy, *Working the Spirit*, 6.
32. Pinn, *Black Church*, 59.

it, and celebrates it corporately."³³ The role of the preacher is to conjure the "manifest[ation of] the spirit . . . for the benefit of the community."³⁴ Given this, preaching too can be understood as another means by which sacred space and time is created as well as an exposition that "surrounds the exuberant core of liminality to inform and interpret it."³⁵ This notwithstanding, there are occasions when the sermon is dispensed with altogether, especially when the service is "high." The willingness to dispense with the sermon perhaps arises from the fact that the sermon is one element of the service wherein encounter with God is less direct, but is mediated by the preacher through the scriptural text.

Tarrying Service

Though not described above, there are other special events in the life of the church which evince its primal orientation. One of the most important of these is the tarrying service.

The name "tarrying service" derives from the King James rendering of Luke 24:19, "And behold, I send the promise of My Father upon you: but tarry ye in the city of Jerusalem, until ye be endued with power from on high." This verse is linked to the Pentecostal belief in the baptism of the Holy Ghost as a gift of God distinct from and subsequent to regeneration. If the testimony service is the "liminal core of Afro-Pentecostal worship" then tarrying services are the apex. The service can perhaps be said to represent one of the most sacred "spaces" in the life of the church, just as it is also the most primal since it is organized with the explicit purpose of facilitating what is considered the ultimate transformative encounter with God. Tarrying is an initiatory ritual in which only those who have yet to be "filled with the Holy Ghost" participate as active seekers. Those who have already been so filled are present, but only as facilitators, aiding those who are in transition from one stage to another. Teresa Reed's description of a tarrying service can scarcely be improved upon and so is quoted here at length:

> The tarrying service would begin when a song leader initiated a repetitive, call-and-response, congregational song, usually to the accompaniment of hand-claps, foot-stomps, tambourines, drums, and keyboard instruments. To the sound of this music,

33. Niles, "Rhetorical Characteristics," 49.
34. Murphy, *Working the Spirit*, 185.
35. Scandrett-Leatherman, "Can't Nobody Do Me," 327.

> the "seekers" would be encircled and encouraged by helpers who assisted with prayer and praise until the achievement of infilling became evident. Often, the text of the opening song would give way to the rhythmic, continual repetition of the phrase "Thank you Jesus." After continuous repetition of the phrase, the evidence of the candidate's infilling (or possession) by the Holy Ghost was in whether or not he or she spoke in tongues. At the conclusion of tarrying service (which usually lasted for hours), candidates were asked to give their testimonies, and the leader judged at that point which cases of infilling were genuine and which were not.[36]

Tarrying services are not unique to ASHC but appear across the broad spectrum of Black American Pentecostalism and reflect a common pattern of religious experience within Black American Christianity.

Zora Neale Hurston (1871–1960) terms this a pattern of conversion characterized by seeking a transformative encounter with God and inducing it through ritual "coming through religion."[37] Bishop Allen notes that in the Primitive Baptist Church of his youth, "they believe[d] in putting people on the mourner's bench. And they would sit there, and they would pray for those people, and they would pray and they would pray and they would pray . . . until [as] they said, 'Pray until something happens.'" Yet at ASHC it is insufficient to pray "until something happens." The expected "something" is a definitive experience, the infilling or baptism with the Holy Ghost. As in most Pentecostal groups, it is believed that "when God baptizes with his Spirit, this same Spirit [Holy Ghost] shall testify or speak in new or other tongues."[38] This is the necessary, but not sufficient, sign that one has been filled or baptized in the Holy Ghost. The tarrying service is designed specifically to facilitate this process.

The hoped-for manifestation of the Spirit during the tarrying service—speaking in tongues—is usually accompanied by a strong emotional response and ecstatic behavior from those who are filled with the Holy Ghost—crying, shouting, dancing, and the like. This is not, however, the goal of the ritual. As in other diaspora rituals of the spirit, tarrying "affirms that the first occasion of an individual's ceremonial manifestation of the spirit transforms the inner nature of the individual."[39] Describing a discus-

---

36. Reed, "Shared Possessions," 15.
37. Hurston, *Sanctified Church*, 87.
38. Interview with Bishop Joseph Allen, Jan. 14, 2016.
39. Murphy, *Working the Spirit*, 185.

sion with his wife on the matter, Bishop Allen highlights the primary goal of this ritual manifestation:

> I have had this discussion with my wife on several occasions. She would say, you know, "All they need is the Holy Ghost." And my response to that is this, yeah you need the Holy Ghost, or you should have the Holy Spirit in your life. *However, you should allow the Holy Spirit to perfect you in areas of your imperfection.* We have faults, we have failures, we have things that goes on in our life. . . . Yeah, well, people have the Holy Ghost. They speak in tongues. They run, jump and shout in the aisle . . . but they don't allow the Holy Spirit to perfect them. They don't allow the Spirit of God to help them to overcome issues and problems of that nature or things like that. So just saying that you need the Holy Ghost is not the answer to all your problems.[40]

These remarks keenly reflect the deeply primal sense that,"man is finite, weak and impure or sinful and stands in need of a power not his own" in order to meet and overcome these. Perfection and the power to "overcome issues and problems" is the sought for goal. Equally important, however, is the recognition that "the true life of man . . . that can come only from the gods,"[41] or God is not something apprehended solely, or even primarily at the cognitive level. The tarrying service places the whole body as the locus of this apprehension. It is not the mind that appropriates the Holy Ghost, but the whole person is seized by divine power and therefore ecstatic behavior and emotional response, while not of primary importance, are nevertheless important adjuncts to this experience. They are the manifestation of a soul that has "caught on fire, burning with the Holy Ghost;" arms wave, legs pump up and down, tears flow, "the bodily expression is a bodily participation in the Spirit."[42] The believer, having successfully completed this ritual, becomes a new person—"saved, sanctified, and filled with the precious Holy Ghost"—his body now a sacrament through which God manifests his presence.

The expectation that spiritual transformation is manifested bodily is deeply embedded in Black American Christianity. As discussed earlier, nineteenth-century AME Bishop Daniel Alexander Payne encountered this belief when he rebuked church leaders for permitting the "praying and

---

40. Interview with Bishop Joseph Allen, Jan. 14, 2016.
41. H. Turner, "Primal Religions," 31.
42. Scandrett-Leatherman, "Can't Nobody Do Me," 236.

singing bands" that were popular among the people. In response to this rebuke, "He [the church leader] said: 'Sinners won't get converted unless there is a ring.... The Spirit of God works upon people in different ways. At camp-meeting there must be a ring here, a ring there, a ring over yonder or sinners will not get converted.'"[43] According to Payne, this was a widely held belief among Black Christians of his day. William Wells Brown likewise testifies to the prevalence of this view:

> It will be difficult to erase from the mind of the Negro of the South, the prevailing idea that outward demonstrations, such as, shouting, the loud "amen," and the most boisterous noise in prayer, are not necessary adjuncts to piety.
>
> A young lady of good education and refinement, residing in East Tennessee, told me that she had joined the church about a year previous, and not until she had one shouting spell, did most of her Sisters believe that she had "the Witness."
>
> "And did you really shout?" I inquired.
>
> "Yes. I did it to stop their mouths, for at nearly every meeting, one or more of them would say, 'Sister Smith, I hope to live to see you show that you've got the Witness, for *where the grace of God is, there will be shouting*, and the sooner you comes to that point the better it will be for you in the world to come.'"[44]

What obtained in their time is still current in the ASHC. What emerges here is the primal "this-worldliness" of Black American Christianity that "encompasses God and man in an abiding relationship"[45] expressed in concrete, physical terms, and not in the abstraction of ideas divorced from the material realm. Conversion and Spirit baptism are not concepts grasped cognitively and then applied systematically but are the inception of an ongoing experience of participation in and with the transcendent.[46]

It is important to note that tarrying is also a ritual of incorporation in which the person becomes fully inducted into the community by virtue of his participation in the Spirit. He now *is* a saint because he *participates* in the things of the Spirit. John V. Taylor's comment is instructive: "The child is not incorporated into this human organism by birth, just as a Jew does not enter the covenant by birth. He is made a member by a series of

---

43. Daniel Alexander Payne, *Recollections of Seventy Years*, quoted in Anyabwile, *Decline*, 224.

44. Brown, "Black Religion," 241; emphasis added.

45. K. Bediako, *Christianity in Africa*, 101.

46. K. Bediako, *Christianity in Africa*, 103.

mystically creative acts, each like a doorway."[47] In the same way, a Pentecostal (and any Christian for that matter) is not born, but made through rites of participation and incorporation, tarrying being one of them.

The ritual of tarrying is designed to endow the believer with spiritual power for ongoing participation in the transcendent, leading to transformation. This points to the next way in which the primal imagination is manifested in the ASHC: power from the realm of the transcendent is mediated through the physical, including ritual.

The Mediation of Power

Power is a key concept that animates the ritual practices of the ASHC, and indeed has always been a significant feature of the church's life even when it was more closely aligned with the spiritual movement. The use of rituals and physical objects to mediate or to "invoke power to help [members] overcome or to be better people," was important.

Tarrying: Calling on the Name of the Lord

In the tarrying services of my youth in the ASHC, the primary song used was the up-tempo, rhythmic, and repetitive call-and-response worship song "Power Lord."[48] Each phrase of the song would be repeated at least twice, at a gradually increasing tempo, before moving to the next phrase, culminating in the final phrase being repeated over and over again as long as the song leader chose. Other songs were sung at the tarrying service, almost all of which were about the power of the Holy Spirit, but "Power Lord" was always the last one sung before transitioning to the rhythmic, continual repetition of the phrase "Thank you Jesus"[49] or "Jesus, Jesus."

Another call-and-response song was "Ain't No Harm Done Calling on Jesus," in which the response to various lyrics of testimony was "Calling on Jesus." Romans 10:13 KJV reads, "For whosoever shall call upon the name of the Lord shall be saved." In the ritual of tarrying, this verse is applied concretely. Calling Jesus in this manner reflects an understanding of the "universe conceived as a unified cosmic system . . . in which the

---

47. John V. Taylor, *Primal Vision*, 92.

48. The full title of the song is "We Need Power," recorded in 1959 by the Davis Sisters, a Black gospel group.

49. Reed, "Shared Possessions," 15.

'physical'"—in this case the physical act of calling Jesus's name—"acts as sacrament for 'spiritual' power."[50] Yet it also reflects a continuation of the African primal sense of the withdrawal of God from the realm of human existence because "mankind (usually represented by a woman) has spoiled his work by committing some reprehensible deed."[51] If this is the case, then "calling on Jesus" is an expression of the deep sense that "it is man, not God, whose voice calls through the desolate garden, Where art thou?"[52] The rhythmic singing coupled with the repetitious calling on the name of Jesus intends to "call down" the saving presence of Jesus from the supernatural to the natural realm, and with him, power—power: to walk right, to talk right, power to overcome and live a transformed existence. While a person might initially receive the baptism of the Holy Ghost in another time or place, the ritual setting of the tarrying service was the ritual setting intentioned for it and calling on Jesus the expected means by which this infilling is accomplished.

Blessed Hands, Blessed Oil, and Blessed Water

Another way in which power from the spirit realm is mediated is by tangible objects—hands laid on, consecrated oil, holy water. Though these often go together, they are not synonymous; one may be done without the other. Because "the apostles often laid hands on the sick and anointed them with oil to prayer for their recovery," so too ASHC "follow[s] their example and James' exhortation" (Jas 5:14).[53] Though I do not recall ever hearing any extensive teaching on it, nor any specific manner in which the otherwise ordinary oil olive was consecrated,[54] "blessed" oil figures prominently in the prayer rituals of the ASHC. Oil is always used during ordination services, and almost always when prayer is said for the sick. It is both "symbol and material of healing connections and sacred set-apartness"[55]—just as it is in

---

50. K. Bediako, *Christianity in Africa*, 101.
51. O'Connell, "Withdrawal of High God," 68.
52. John V. Taylor, *Primal Vision*, 76.
53. *I'll Go* (self-published organizational manual, n.d.), 12.
54. Scandrett-Leatherman describes the consecration of oil that took place in one Church of God in Christ congregation, but notes, "I didn't see anyone specifically pray over the oil to bless it. It was blessed by being with the people who were consecrating themselves" ("Can't Nobody Do Me," 218).
55. Scandrett-Leatherman, "Can't Nobody Do Me," 208.

other Pentecostal churches and is used regularly during altar prayer and altar call, as well as at other times. On occasions when it is administered without being accompanied by extensive prayer or laying on of hands, the minister uses a small amount of oil to make a cross on the forehead of the congregant, after which the person simply returns to his or her seat. Some members have bottles of the oil in their home for use.

Laying on of hands with or without oil is a symbol of spiritual empowerment. Yet laying on of hands in the ASHC is more than a symbol. Laying on of hands does not only "*symbolize* spiritual blessing flowing from one person to another," it is intended to "*invoke* divine blessing."[56] Through this sacramental act, power is mediated through the hands of the one conducting the ritual, through the oil, or sometimes water, used for anointing. Consequently, it is unsurprising to see manifestations of the Spirit occur when hands are laid on. Through the media of touch and of oil, people experience the supernatural presence of God.

In earlier times, when ASHC was still more strongly influenced by the spiritual church movement, holy water or "blessed water" too was also one of the mediating substances used in the church. Blessed water would be used at times instead of blessed oil to pray for those who requested prayer during the altar prayer. As mentioned earlier, on the altar table would be placed a bowl of blessed water into which members would place their "silver offering" during the altar prayer. Some would also, having dipped their hands into the water, use it to anoint and cross themselves before moving away from the altar. Some, however, were more dramatic in their use of it. On one occasion, while visiting another spiritual church, one member splashed a copious amount of the water on herself. Interestingly, this did not take place during an ordinary prayer time, but at a random moment during the service. While this was unexpected, and not something I ever recall observing at ASHC, it was, nevertheless, not so unusual as to draw any commentary from anyone.

This water was, in all respects, quite ordinary. It was filled from the tap before service and disposed of afterwards. The sacred quality of the water derived from its placement on the altar table, and its use. There was other "holy water" however. This water, which was also ordinary tap water, was consecrated once a year during Holy Week. On Palm Sunday, members would bring containers of water—mostly plastic milk jugs and glass bottles—which would be placed around and beneath the altar table where

---

56. *I'll Go* (self-published organizational manual, n.d.), 12; emphasis added.

they would remain, undisturbed, throughout Holy Week, until the close of Easter morning service when each family would take their own water home. Its proximity to the altar was presumably enough to consecrate it for sacred use. This water was not generally used for anointing the body but was to be drunk as a remedy for physical ailments or other problems.[57]

Holistic Salvation

In the manual of the All Saints Holiness Church, the words of the founder are recorded, expressing her hopes for the organization, as well as its mission. The primary mission of the organization is said to be "to win souls for Christ" yet this is described in terms of reaching out "to those who are lost and have no hope . . . who are sick, not only physically, but spiritually as well," as well as "aid[ing] in the relief of the poor, and spread[ing] the gospel through all nations."[58] Among the "great things in Christ Jesus" emphasized as part of the organization's founding ethos is not only "sav[ing] souls"—a narrow focus on the spiritual state to the exclusion of other concerns—but also "heal[ing] minds, and elevat[ion] . . . according to His will."[59]

When Missionary Skinner declared during a church service, "God said there needs to be healing in the land,"[60] her words were laden with more significance than perhaps she was, or could have been, aware. Aside the immediate and apparent concern for the bodily health of those present in the congregation, or those immediately associated with them, healing has a broader meaning in the life of ASHC, as indeed it has historically had within Black American Christianity generally and Black Pentecostalism specifically.

> Within Afro-Pentecostal worship, healing is a central theme of testimony service *and a purpose of the church* . . . they testify about relationships that have been healed. Their distresses and diseases have many causes: social discord with society, work, family or church; physical discord with violence, poor health card, social discord internalized; spiritual discord from with a focus on self, problems or devil.[61]

---

57. Cf. Jacobs and Kaslow, *Spiritual Churches*, 154–55, 206.
58. *I'll Go* (self-published organizational manual, n.d.), 3.
59. *I'll Go* (self-published organizational manual, n.d.), 1.
60. Author's visit to ASHC, Jan. 10, 2016.
61. Scandrett-Leatherman, "Can't Nobody Do Me," 331–32. emphasis added.

Healing, in this reading, is the raison d'être of the church and yet health and healing are not to be understood only in relation to physical illness, but extend to familial, social, work, environmental, mental, and spiritual concerns as well. Healing encompasses the total well-being of the person. In terms of soteriology, the focus is broader than a singular emphasis on forgiveness of sins. Sin is one of the hindrances to salvation—the chief hindrance—but not necessarily the only one. Salvation, and thus healing, is seen in a holistic way. Rituals of healing are therefore conducted within the context of the "practical concern with securing *eudaimonia*, what the Greeks defined as 'the good life.'"[62]

The spiritual healing envisioned by Sallie Swift includes the necessity of dealing with spiritual entities that hinder salvation. Just as the spirit realm is the source of Holy Ghost power, so too it is the source of spiritual difficulty. Bishop Allen expresses the church's perspective thus: "The enemy of God is the enemy of Man, especially those that take up the name of Christian . . . the devil is real, and I believe that he has demons that are *set out to destroy people*."[63] His use of the phrase "to destroy people" is instructive, for it suggests a negation of life and of its value. This is even more potent given the background of Euro-Western White supremacy that has consistently sought to destroy the integrity of Black American lives (disintegration) and validity of their religious practice. There is in this a palpable awareness of harm that can come to a person via the spirit realm. Though Allen now sees the concern that his folded arms might be "crossing people up" as misplaced, the underlying fear that he or others might "open themselves up to demonic forces and allow these things to take place in their lives"[64] remains potent. Against the dual pressures of infiltrating and destructive demonic forces and disintegrating White supremacy (arguably a demonic principality in its own right), the power of the Holy Ghost is invoked through prayer and ritual. Expulsion of the demonic is part of that process. Exorcism—which Allen admits is done with some difficulty—is therefore consonant with the ultimate goal of African primal cosmology of "attain[ing] and preserv[ing] a righteous equilibrium of interdependent relationships."[65] The aimed for result is holistic healing: a *re*-integrating

---

62. Walton, "Prosperity Gospel," 455.
63. Interview with Bishop Joseph Allen, Jan. 14, 2016.
64. Interview with Bishop Joseph Allen, Jan. 14, 2016.
65. Ryan, *Spirituality as Ideology*, 29.

conversion that "represents a counterhegemonic act of reclaiming discredited aspects of self."[66]

A World of Spirit Power and the Abundant Life

What has emerged from the description of the history, beliefs and practices of the ASHC is a foundational primal orientation and belief set that the tangible, sensible realm depends on an intangible world of spirit power full of spiritual entities. This numinous realm impinges on the ordinary world in concrete ways. This may seem a mundane observation, but its importance cannot be overstated. Though all Christians notionally believe in the reality of an unseen realm of spirit powers, "for many if not most, reality in practice is reduced to the physical universe (understood in a modern scientific sense) with God added on."[67] This is decidedly *not* the case for Christians in the ASHC. In the ASHC, as in both spiritual and Pentecostal churches more broadly, the reality of the spirit world and active engagement with it are not theoretical or notional, but actual and active. In Otto's words, "It is one thing merely to believe in a reality beyond the senses and another to have experience of it also; it is one thing to have ideas of 'the holy' and another to become consciously aware of it as an operative reality, intervening actively in the phenomenal world."[68] It is this conscious apprehension that animates the beliefs and practices within this, as in other, Pentecostal churches:

> The human spirit is touched by the divine Holy Spirit from which flows power through the subconscious to the conscious from origins that are cosmic and not merely individual. The experience of the essence of religion ... makes it possible for both the individual and the community to substitute confidence for fear, a sense of security for a life lived on the ragged and vulnerable margins of an oppressive society.[69]

Apart from this belief, much of the ritual activity of the church would be rendered meaningless. The numinous or spiritual realm is both the locus

---

66. Ryan, *Spirituality as Ideology*, 32.
67. Lane, *Unseen World*, ix.
68. Otto, *Idea of the Holy*, 143.
69. Clemmons, *Bishop C. H. Mason*, locs. 1313–16.

of holy power via the Holy Spirit, and the source or abode of other spiritual entities that can and do affect the lives of people in concrete ways.[70]

Kwame Bediako has noted that it is the "primal conception of the universe as a unified cosmic system, essentially spiritual" that is key to the primal imagination.[71] The connection between the natural and supernatural realms that lies at the heart of the primal understanding of reality also lies at the heart of the All Saints Holiness Church. It is this connection that renders comprehensible the origin of the ASHC as a prayer band led by a woman who was animated by a prophecy and a dream; its evolution from a spiritual church to a holiness Pentecostal one; its early and continued embrace of sacred spaces, ecstatic behavior, and ritual practices; its belief in the mediation of spiritual power through physical means—tarrying, blessed oil, laying on of hands; its concern for healing and wholeness; its engagement in spiritual warfare. These all attest to a distinctly Christian congregation fully alive to the primal instincts of the faith.

---

70. Kwame Bediako's insight about the "unresolved multiplicity" within the African worldview may be important here (*Christianity in Africa*, 97).

71. K. Bediako, *Christianity in Africa*, 96.

8

Primal Spirituality in the St Martins Spiritualist Church

The St Martins Spiritualist Church

Physical Description

ON THE NORTH SIDE of a quiet avenue in west-central St. Louis, Missouri, sits the St Martins Spiritualist Church (SMSC). The residential streets heading southward, though ostensibly public, are gated—restricting vehicular access from the evidently poorer environs to the north. These neighborhoods are filled with palatial homes marked by the historic prestige of their proximity to Forest Park, home to the famous 1904 World's Fair. The neighborhood to the north of the church stands in stark contrast. Two-family structures in various stages of decline or renewal predominate. SMSC is housed in one of these—a converted structure with a nicely clipped lawn, differentiated from the houses around only by the painted white exterior and the modest sign.

Inside the SMSC, a quite different aesthetic prevails. The small vestibule containing a small altar with three statuettes and seven candles opens into the small auditorium. At the entry is a small font of water, a mezuzah, and a piece of wood alleged by the pastor to have been taken from the cross upon which Jesus was crucified.¹ Church members dip their fingers in the font, touch the wood, and then make the sign of the cross before entering the chapel. Within the chapel itself, the altar table—located at the front of the room opposite the entry and flanked by chairs—is prominently decorated. Glass and brass bowls, a seven-candle candelabra, a seven-day votive and other candles, a small wicker basket, incense censer, and several small vials of blessed oil are all displayed. One of the bowls and the wicker basket contain small slips of paper. In front of the altar is a cushioned kneeler.

In the pulpit area are several cushioned chairs and another seven-candle candelabra topped with an ornate cross. The rear wall of the pulpit area is mostly covered with plush red curtains, except the portion behind the baptismal pool, which is covered with a mural depicting Jesus as a Black man, with his hands outstretched over a multiracial group of baptismal candidates and onlookers.

The auditorium contains sixteen pews arranged in two columns. The walls are adorned with pictures of the founder, Rev. Ernestina Martin, and the previous pastor, Rev. E. C. McAfee. Displayed prominently along one wall is a hanging in celebration of the church's centennial celebration: 1915–2015. Flat-screen televisions and audio speakers are also found, and boom mics are suspended from the ceiling. A small sound and media room is located in the back at the entrance. The basement of the church contains a small kitchen and fellowship hall, while the upstairs hosts various classrooms, the church office, and the office of the pastor.

The pastor indicates that Rev. Martin had three thousand followers—though he admits that the church building itself has never been large enough to accommodate such a crowd. Today the group is small, with fewer than fifty in attendance when I visited. However, the pastor suggests a larger number of people from other churches and denominations visit, seeking counsel and prayer, than is indicated by the number in attendance. Thus, he refers to the church as "the Nicodemus Church" in reference to those who might be termed clients of the ministry, but out of concern for reputation are unwilling to openly associate with them. This may have been the case in Tyler's time as well, which would account for the larger number the pastor indicates were associated with the church. If so, then SMSC's experience mirrors those of other spiritual groups with "clients [who] do not become

---

1. According to the pastor, in the 1940s some lumber was found that, when chipped away at, began to reproduce itself. Many churches that accepted this miracle obtained pieces of the wood. I have used pseudonyms throughout this chapter.

involved in the public activities of the Spiritual congregation [but] instead engage in a dyadic relationship with one of the several mediums or healers who are commonly found in the Spiritual churches"[2] The congregation is overwhelmingly Black, though one white member was present during my visit in January 2016. Women far outnumber men both in the congregation and among the leadership. Three of the four ministers are women while the pastor is the only male.

History in Brief

The St Martins Spiritualist Church is now over one hundred years old, having celebrated its centennial in 2015. The founder, Ernestina Martin, born in 1888, was one of the many millions of Black Americans who relocated from the agrarian south to urban centers in the South, North, and Midwest during what is termed the Great Migration. She spent much of her life in and around the Mill Creek Valley, a largely Black community whose population had swelled with migrants from the rural South. It was here in 1915 that Rev. Martin reportedly received a vision of Jesus Christ, who commanded her to teach true spiritualism. "In initial disbelief, she asked the figure [Jesus] for a sign of proof. Immediately, the knobs on her stove began to turn by themselves." Convinced by this sign, Martin began meetings in her home for singing, prayer, and sharing about "the wonderful things that JESUS has revealed to her." As she grew in her familiarity with, and ability to, handle spiritual things, Jesus apparently permitted her to be visited by various spirits, and taught her to distinguish the good from the bad. Additionally, she was used by spirit guides who would "take control of her vocal chords and speak to the members [of the church] describing themselves and telling about their condition, so as to be recognized by their friends and relations." According to the church's history, some of these spirits testified that prayers offered by members were beneficial and permitted them to be "lifted to higher spheres." Martin continued pastoring the church until her death in November 1937.

Shortly after her death, leadership of the church passed to her Assistant Pastor, the late Rev. E. C. McAfee. He served as pastor for forty-eight years until his death. He was held to be anointed by God with "the spiritual gifts of Healing, Seer, and being a Voice Medium." After his death, the current pastor, Harold Anderson, assumed the pastorate.

2. Baer, *Black Spiritual Movement*, 48.

Worship at the SMSC

Worship services at SMSC are similar to what might be found in other Christian congregations, yet also evince some differences attributable to its identity as a spiritualist congregation. What follows is a summarized description of services I personally observed, followed by a discussion of how these beliefs and practices inform a dual identity of Christian and spiritualist.

Sunday Morning Worship: Sunday School

Sunday morning worship at SMSC begins, as it does in many churches, with Sunday school. Though only about four people were present at the start of the service (others joined later), the service began promptly at eight thirty with the singing of a hymn, "Never Alone." As the song concluded, the leader—a warm, smartly dressed woman who appeared to be in her mid-forties, and who I later learned is one of the ministers of the church—led the group in a prayer ritual: face east, recite the Twenty-Third Psalm and the Lord's Prayer, followed by the phrase: "Hail Mary, Hail Mary, Hail Mary, the Blessed Mother of Jesus." This was followed by another hymn, during which several congregants went to kneel at the altar to pray, ending their brief prayers by crossing themselves and repeating the threefold Hail Mary, after which they returned to their seats. The leader was the last to kneel, after which she proceeded to begin teaching the Sunday school lesson.

The discussion centered on practical issues of how to live in a Christian manner; people talked freely, and there were frequent references to conflict between the carnal and the spiritual, with carnality also termed "the lower story." The offering bowl was passed around without comment, taken up by the minister who knelt at the altar to pray for the offering; this prayer too ended with making the sign of the cross and a repetition of the threefold Hail Mary. The minutes from the previous week's Sunday school class were read, and the group faced the east and prayed the closing prayer, concluding with the threefold Hail Mary.

Devotional Service

The Sunday morning worship began at ten with the lighting of the candelabra as the choir sang the hymn "Never Alone." The congregation stood and conducted the usual prayer ritual. This was followed by more congregational singing led by the choir. The Scripture reading by one of the women leaders dressed in a white robe and an offering collection—one dollar only—followed. Those who did not give simply touched the bowl as it passed by. The offering, once collected by the usher, was brought to the altar where she knelt, lifting the offering bowl up. Congregational singing— mostly traditional Black gospel choruses—continued throughout this time.

Announcements followed the offering time, and then the choir, who had been seated in the rear of the church, processed down the aisle, single file, to the choir box while singing. Once situated there, they sang another song, the Black gospel song "A Song in the Midst of the Storm." The congregation joyfully clapped and sang along. A brief testimony service followed; different congregants stood to offer thanks to God for various things—good health, divine protection, successful medical interventions, and even for restraining heavy traffic to enable the person to make it to church. Some offered songs or requested for particular songs to be sung for them. The testimonies were personal and forthright, and each person was supported with frequent interjections of "amen" or "alright" from the audience. While the final testimonies were being given, the lights in the chapel were extinguished. The room was illumined now only by candlelight. The sudden smell of incense pierced the air.

Incensing and Prayers

At SMSC, at the conclusion of the testimony service, the woman who earlier led Sunday school appeared at the rear of the auditorium with a large censer attached to a chain. She proceeded in a counterclockwise direction, down the side aisle, through every part of the pulpit area, down the other side aisle, then down the rear stairs into the basement, returning after a few moments to proceed down the center aisle ending at the altar. While this was taking place, the congregation sang the hymn "Come, Ye Disconsolate" in a solemn mood. The censer was placed on the altar, the lights in the auditorium raised, and the congregation stood. Again, they faced the east, and repeated the now-familiar prayer ritual.

The lights were again extinguished while the pastor and other ministers stood and faced the congregation. In turns, different ministers knelt at the altar to pray, while the congregation sang hymns. Each prayer ended with the threefold Hail Mary. Among the congregants, some might be seen singing, others praying quietly, while others still simply observed. When the prayer time concluded the lights were again raised and the pastor came to the podium to begin his sermon for the morning.

The Sermon

The sermon text was Mark 9:1–13, the story of the transfiguration. The preaching was not expository, but rather served as a departure point for Rev Anderson to highlight the importance of sensitivity to the Spirit.[3] According to his presentation, Peter, James, and John were privy to the transfiguration because of their spiritual sensitivity and maturity. The ability to recognize and relate to spiritual reality was a key emphasis in the message. Jesus, according to Rev. Anderson, made Peter, James, and John aware of what the forefathers of SMSC had also taught—the existence and engagement with what he termed the "so-called dead," for Moses and Elijah, if dead, would have been unable to speak with Jesus. He used the occasion of the sermon to rebuke those members who do not come for spiritual development classes to grow their own spiritual sensitivity. Generally, there seems to be no particular pattern in place for the selection of texts, but it is driven more by the preacher's preference and the day: Palm Sunday 2017 featured a sermon drawn on lessons from the palm tree, while the sermon for May 14, 2017, Mother's Day, was drawn from 1 Sam 1 and focused attention on Hannah as a mother. At the close of the sermon, an usher came to light a single candle on the altar.

Offertory

The offertory followed. Ushers led the congregation row by row to bring their offerings to the altar where they were placed in a basket. Immediately prior to this, however, small slips of paper were passed around on which people wrote prayer requests. If the request is for oneself, it is to be folded three times towards you; if for others, then three times away from you. The offering was collected, and the prayer request slips placed in a basket from which they would later be collected and burned as "incense to the Lord."

---

3. During my observations at SMSC, I noted that "spirit" and "father" (as in God the Father) are frequently referred to without the definite article "the," which presents some ambiguity. Given the other Christian referents in the church's practices, and the context of usage, I have chosen to capitalize "Spirit" and "Father" except when used in obvious reference to other spirit entities.

After depositing the prayer request, another slip of paper was collected with a Scripture reference written on it.

After the offertory, the lights were again extinguished. The congregation sang "Sweet Hour of Prayer" as prayer requests were one by one opened and burned at the altar by one of the officiating ministers. The congregation was then asked to hold their hands over their hearts as prayer was offered. At the close of service, one member who had brought candles for distribution announced this fact and offered them for sale.

Monday Prayer Service and Spiritual Development Class

On Monday evening, SMSC hosts a prayer meeting followed by what is termed a spiritual development class. This meeting has fewer attendees and focuses, as the title indicates, much less on worship than on prayer and hearing from the Spirit. The service began with the usual prayer ritual, followed by hymn singing and prayer, in a contemplative mode. The seven-candle candelabra and seven-day votive candle were alight throughout the service. After the opening time of devotional prayer and singing, the pastor mounted the pulpits and informed the congregation that he wanted to "go deeper [into] spiritual awareness."

Spiritual Development Teaching

The teaching during the spiritual development class was wide ranging, though roughly centered on the theme of spiritual warfare based on the Ephesians text. Reference was made to climate change, violent crime, and political corruption, all of which were linked in his teaching, to undertakings in the spiritual realm. Extensive reference was made throughout the session to angels, demons, and principalities, which Rev. Anderson defined as an order of angels "designed to cheat God of his glory; to steal us [Christians] away from God by distracting us." A key concern of the session was the spiritual powers behind natural or material concerns, one example cited being that of the extensive drug trade and gun violence in "ghetto" communities, though neither guns nor drugs are manufactured there. He concluded his teaching by relating a dream he had had in which his spirit reportedly traveled into what he termed a spiritual ghetto, where he observed much chaos and confusion. In the context of this sharing, he mentioned reincarnation as a teaching of the church, the concept of the spirit traveling at night, why someone should not be shaken out of his sleep, and the importance of reconciling oneself to God at night before sleeping because "you don't know if you're waking up."

Prayer and Prophecy

The teaching time was followed by a subdued time of prayer. The auditorium was illumined solely by candlelight. Approximately fifteen people were present for the service. Two chairs were placed flanking the altar in which ministers sat. On this occasion, the pastor called for five prayers. Ministers and congregants alike came to the altar and knelt to offer prayers while the congregation supported with songs. There was a great deal of liberty, it seems, in who raised or led the singing. The mood was warm, spiritual, and anticipatory. After about thirty minutes of prayers and songs, the pastor asked for three minutes of silence before the "prophecy time." After the observed time of silence, he invited people to speak "as the Spirit gave utterance."

Several people shared in turn what they had reportedly received from the Spirit or what they "saw." The prophecies were generally words of encouragement, instructions to perform certain tasks (e.g., drink a little warm water with a bit of salt in it), prayers, or indications that a particular loved one was present "with" someone. At times, the person sharing would request a song they had "received" to be sung—a request that was complied with. Some of the sharing consisted of general admonitions to remain in the faith or not worry, while others had meanings that were unclear or perhaps symbolic. All who desired to share, however, were freely allowed to, and no commentary was made on the validity of what any person received or shared from "the Spirit." The atmosphere was thus very open and accepting. Rev. Anderson concluded the prophecy time with an anecdote about his involvement with the furniture business and the Internal Revenue Service. The upshot of the story was that the church ought to be prepared (as he and his erstwhile business partners had not been) for the challenges that come from growth—the need to be "on one accord" because of the potential attack from Satan.

Christian, Spiritualist, Primal

Currently, SMSC is one of only a few named "spiritualist" congregations in St. Louis. SMSC is one of the churches that resisted the trend of contracting "spiritualist" to "spiritual."[4] Pastor Anderson was aware of only two active spiritualist congregations—his own and another, predominantly White, congregation—though he did indicate knowledge of some "spiritual" churches. He did not draw out the distinction he made between the two, but in light of the history and practices of the spiritual movement, the decision to retain the spiritualist label is a self-conscious effort to redeem a term that has been largely associated with "communication with loved ones, séances, and fortune-telling."[5] SMSC, while not entirely rejecting this association, chooses instead to affirm an explicitly Christian and spiritualist identity. The rituals, prayers, and worship practices here described, as well as what emerges from the history of their founder, affirm this. It is also indicative of resistance to the dualistic, disjunctive "either/or" thinking that predominates in Euro-Western thought. In this regard, SMSC stands firmly in the mainstream of Black American cultural tradition that "prefers the conjunctive 'both/and' of archaic and oral cultures in which ambiguity and multivocity are taken for granted."[6] These are features of the primal imagination that have continued to persist with Black American Christianity. The affirmation of dual identity becomes clearer when their belief and ritual practices are considered. At its core, this duality is a demonstration of the pervasiveness of the primal imagination in the life and ministry of SMSC.

Beliefs

The doctrines of the SMSC are initially appear difficult to ascertain. The website lacks the list of creedal affirmations or Statement of Faith that one

---

4. Baer, *Black Spiritual Movement*, 115. It is also notable that Baer identifies the Redeeming Christian Spiritualist Church as the "first Black Spiritualist or Spiritual congregation established in Nashville," and that this church had been established by "Sister Moore [who] received training from a Spiritualist medium in St. Louis" (30). The name and the connection to Nashville suggest an early organic link between the spiritual movement in St. Louis and in Nashville, and more specifically between the SMSC and spiritual groups in Nashville, one that is later reinforced in the founding of the All Saints Holiness Church discussed earlier.

5. Baer, *Black Spiritual Movement*, 115.

6. T. Smith, *Conjuring Culture*, 143.

typically finds on such sections of church websites. Previous research, when encountering the paucity of such statements, concluded that the belief system of the spiritual Movement was essentially syncretic: "a combination of religious traditions, including elements of orthodox Christianity (Roman Catholicism and mainstream Protestantism), Pentecostalism, voodoo, and Spiritualism."[7] This is, perhaps, a misinterpretation based on the assumption that doctrines are best described using propositional terminology. Instead of this, the "What We Believe" section of SMSC's website is devoted largely to description of their ritual practices. This is instructive, for it suggests that SMSC views doctrine as a way of "living religiously as being in touch with the source and channels of power in the universe"[8] rather than as a set of propositions to which one must assent. One *knows* what is taught through the *practice* of ritual. This reflects a *holistic* and *dynamic* primal epistemology, one born of "relational knowing, from both inner and outer space."[9] In this, one can already begin to discern how the primal imagination pervades the belief and practice of this congregation.

Nevertheless, one does find on the website this opening phrase, from which the outline of the key teachings of the church can be discerned:

> Here at SMSC we do not go against the teachings of the BIBLE. WE acknowledge the fact that the spirit world exists. We believe in Jesus and that the message of salvation is the main message. Our tradition is sacred as our practices are based on the teachings from our founder.

Four things emerge from this: the importance of the Bible, the existence of the spirit world and the concomitant interpenetration of that world with the natural (or carnal) world, the centrality of Jesus and message of salvation, and finally, the importance of keeping faith with ancestral wisdom as embodied in the teaching handed down through Rev. Ernestina Martin.

The Importance of Scripture

"We are *Christian* spiritualists," affirms Rev. Anderson, "there are spiritualists that don't really go to the depth of the Bible, but we are Christian

---

7. Jacobs and Kaslow, *Spiritual Churches*, 58. Cf. Baer, *Black Spiritual Movement*, 151.
8. K. Bediako, *Christianity in Africa*, 106.
9. Kovach, *Indigenous Methodologies*, 57.

because we believe in Christ, we believe in the Trinity." His statement is a positive affirmation of what the opening phrase "we do not go against the teachings of the Bible" states in negative terms. By this, the core distinction SMSC makes between itself and non-Christian spiritualist groups is made clear. The Bible lies at the heart of SMSC's self-understanding as a Christian congregation. That both the website and Rev. Anderson make this assertion so forcefully is, perhaps, a response to the charges of syncretism and sub-Christian identity that have historically been made against those in the spiritual movement. This affirmation goes beyond words, however, and is evidenced in the emphasis placed by the church and the pastor on the importance of Bible study. The study and comprehension of the Bible is an important emphasis of Anderson's teaching. For example, when preaching on Nicodemus's encounter with Jesus, he used Nicodemus's lack of understanding as a springboard to highlight the importance of Scripture study to his members. "You got to know something," he said. "You got to be trained. So where do you get trained? Not on Sunday; Sunday is worship. Bible study, Sunday school is training." Sermons, though not necessarily expository, are biblically focused, and Scripture references are liberally scattered throughout his preaching and that of other ministers I observed. He critiques those members who carry their Bible as a protective charm and who use it only during preaching sessions, challenging them that "this book will tell you how to be successful on earth and get to heaven." The Bible is considered the product of "spiritual inspiration" that came "through the Holy Ghost."

Though the whole Bible is considered essential, certain themes within Scripture emerge as being of particular importance to SMSC. Scriptures centered on what may be termed "spiritual" subjects, or that describe activities relating to spiritual beings (i.e., angels, Satan, demons), loom large. These passages, and indeed the Scriptures, are read in an exemplary way and provide the framework through which SMSC sees and interprets reality. Kwame Bediako has suggested that Scripture is best understood as the interpreter of our tradition and culture. Consequently:

> [It] is more than just a book from which we take ideas ... more than just a holy book from which we take even teachings or biblical principles ... more than a book in which we believe. Rather, *Scripture is a story in which we participate.* When understood like this, Scripture becomes recognised by us as the narrative that explains who we are, and therefore as our narrative.[10]

---

10. K. Bediako, "Scripture as the Hermeneutic," 5; emphasis added.

What Bediako proposes is actualized in the approach that SMSC takes to Scripture. It is not read or preached as a flat text, or a book of doctrine. It exemplifies spiritual reality, and provides the model of SMSC's own participation in that reality.

For example, Anderson mentioned his own preference for Revelation "because it is spiritual, in there we find John in the Spirit on the Lord's day . . . talking with the elders . . . [the] book of Revelation is powerful because it forecast[s] yesterday, today, and tomorrow." John's account thus provides biblical grounding for the reality of participation in the spirit realm and of communication with spiritual beings. The biblical account of the transfiguration appears important as well, again in relation to communication with spirits and with the possibility of reincarnation.[11] Indeed, John the Baptist's identification with Elijah in the Matthean account of the transfiguration was connected by Anderson to reincarnation. More is said on this matter below. In the context of discussing spiritual warfare and principalities based on Eph 6, additional reference was made to the account of Gabriel's battle with Michael in the book of Daniel. Although direct citations of Scripture were not made in the sermon preached by assistant pastor Rev. Ernestina Jester, mention was made of the "ministering spirits" God sent to speak to various women in the Bible, notably Sarah, Rebecca, and Rachel. These women, too, present for SMSC a pattern of participation in and with the spirit realm that is to be actively emulated.

It is important to note that though the Bible is asserted as central, other extra-biblical texts inform their beliefs and practices as well. Rev. Anderson referred to a story from the extra-canonical Book of Adam and Eve in which God promises Adam and Eve that he would bring them back to paradise, and links this promise to Jesus's crucifixion.[12] Anderson's citation of this work need not be interpreted as rejecting or supplanting of the authority of the Bible however, for he referred to it as part of the Apocrypha—"chapters in the Catholic Bible that the Protestant Bible don't have because they are not ready to talk about it." Though his attribution was mistaken, his belief that these books were, in some sense, canonical, demonstrates

---

11. This passage was mentioned not only in our personal interview, but also in his sermons of Jan. 3, 2016, and May 7, 2017.

12. According to the preface, the Book of Adam and Eve is "probably the work of some pious or orthodox Egyptian of the fifth or sixth century" whose aim is "to connect the first Adam with the coming of the second, Christ; five thousand five hundred years after Adam's fall in Eden, and in fulfilment of the promise then made him of a Saviour" (Malan, *Book of Adam and Eve*, v).

a concern that his teaching be rooted in Scripture and reflects a desire to deepen his and his congregation's understanding of the Bible.

The Existence and Primacy of the Spirit World

Perhaps the most noticeable belief that finds expression in the practices of SMSC is belief in the existence and primacy of spiritual reality over the natural one. For the members of SMSC, the distance between this world, and the spirit world is small indeed. It is not "the carnal flesh" that matters, but "the spirit that God has put within us" for it is this spirit that "makes you [who you are]." Indeed it may be reasonably suggested that many of the church's practices center on engagement with the spirit realm. According to the pastor, it is this—"the existence of spirits communicating with man"—that other churches do not address that makes his church distinct. For SMSC, the spirit world is the primary reality from which wisdom and knowledge are derived. It is important therefore to listen to what he calls our "guiding spirit" because such "the spirit forces . . . are more intelligent than we are." Familiarity with the spirit realm, the ability to distinguish good spirits from evil ones, and an overall sense of closeness to the spirit realm all flow from this belief. Consequently, relationship and communication with God are often expressed in very personal ways as, for example, when Rev. Jester related the following: "On January third of this year as I was in my prayer room, Father came to me and said, 'I am pleased with your efforts and I am taking you off the job.'" In the same sermon she expressed gratitude to "father" for allowing "Mother Mary"—who she acknowledged as very special to her—to "be a part of [her] life." A sense of the pervasiveness of spiritual reality comes through clearly in her comments.

The spirit realm, which is so much a part of the belief structure of SMSC, is neither placid, nor passive, but a dynamic reality in which spirit forces of various kinds are active. Rev. Anderson's foray into what he termed a "spiritual ghetto" rife with chaos has already been mentioned. Among these spirit forces are those "forefathers," i.e., the now deceased founder and other leaders of the church, who now exist "on the spirit side of life" where they are believed to be actively "working on our behalf." Though some may attribute this to the influence of American spiritualism, which Baer has suggested served as a "springboard" for the present Black spiritual movement,"[13] echoes of the African primal belief in ancestors and ancestral

---

13. Baer, *Black Spiritual Movement*, 113.

intercession may also be present. Indeed, Judylyn Ryan's observation of the place of the ancestor within the kinship matrices of the Black diaspora as portrayed in Black women's literature and cinema is instructive. She comments: "Kinship matrices consist of several roles that have explicit and extensive sustaining functions and include living relatives, cultural kin, and, most important, *elders and ancestors*."[14] Toni Morrison too notes the foundational place of the ancestor within Black literature, concluding that their presence is of primary importance; "if we don't keep in touch with the ancestor . . . we are, in fact, lost."[15] What these writers have observed is how deeply embedded honoring ancestors is within Black American culture, quite apart from any other influences. A cursory glance at the names of Black churches across the denominational spectrum reveal many that are named for their founders or other prominent persons.[16] Indeed one need only recall that the name of SMSC was changed in 1942 "to give honor and recognition to Rev. Ernestina Martin, founder." It is unsurprising therefore that SMSC would accord such high respect to its founders and departed leaders.

Because of the belief in active engagement with the spirit realm, during the time of prophecy and prayer in the above-mentioned spiritual development class, substantial time was devoted to listening to the Spirit/spirits to receive instruction or messages. Spirits perceived to have especially close relationships to those present were considered somehow "present" to communicate their concerns to the living. For example, one of the messages came from a spirit described as "earthbound," who was full of concern for his living loved ones, and admonished them to "stay in God's will." The service and belief system resembled in this respect what Hans Baer described as "message sessions" within White spiritualist congregations,[17] yet unlike what Baer described, it was not an either/or phenomenon where only the singular Holy Spirit or multiple spirits of the departed were involved in the communication. Moreover, there was no expectation in the service I

---

14. Ryan, *Spirituality as Ideology*, 38–39; emphasis added.

15. Morrison, "Rootedness," 63.

16. Mason Temple Church of God in Christ in Memphis, Tennessee; Allen Temple Baptist Church in Oakland, California (M. Taylor, "History"); and Rogers Memorial Baptist Church in Knoxville, Tennessee (Rogers Memorial Baptist Church, "Church History"), are three example of his trend that come immediately to mind. It is so common an occurrence as to almost escape notice or commentary.

17. Baer, *Black Spiritual Movement*, 117.

observed that the recipient of the message was expected in any way to aid in the interpretation of the content of the message.

Given the historic charges of syncretism and occultism that have been lodged against Black spiritual groups, it is important to clarify what occurs in such sessions, and distinguish it from what may obtain in other, non-Christian, spiritualist settings. As mentioned above, echoes of the African primal belief in ancestors can be discerned in SMSC's approach to their departed dead. Like the African ancestor, these too are believed to exist "on the spirit side of life" where they are actively "working on our behalf." Kwame Bediako has noted the important distinction made within the African primal between nonhuman spirits—divinities—and ancestors, the "somewhat 'apotheosised' spirits of a person's or community's elders," who are therefore "not quite so easily susceptible to demonisation in the Christian consciousness."[18] He further notes that African ancestors "do not become after death what they were not before death."[19] They are human spirits who remain incorporated into the family or community.

Beyond this "family resemblance" between the African primal and Black American practice, which should be kept in mind in any assessment of their practices, SMSC recognizes the potential for accusations of occult practice or witchcraft. They are therefore careful to explicitly disavow any such connection They maintain "we don't engage in calling up spirits or mediumship. Spirits can only communicate with us by permission from GOD. We don't practice nor possess the power to call them up." They cite the negative example of 1 Sam 28, wherein God permitted the spirit of Samuel to communicate with Saul, much to the surprise of the witch, as a caution against communion with "familiar spirits working through false prophets to give messages." Instead, SMSC emphasizes their reliance upon the Holy Spirit "working through our spiritual development (gifts) to help improve the quality of our lives and to help spread the message of SALVATION," the ultimate goal being "to spread the gospel of JESUS CHRIST." Thus while the practices appear similar to those conducted by other, non-Christian, groups, it is their explicitly Christocentric focus that ultimately distinguishes SMSC's practices from those of other spiritualist groups.

A corollary to the belief in the active influence and engagement with the spirit realm is a belief in reincarnation. At the conclusion of his teaching during the spiritual development class, Rev. Anderson asserted

18. K. Bediako, *Christianity in Africa*, 216.
19. K. Bediako, *Christianity in Africa*, 217.

"we believe in reincarnation." Baer noted that a belief in reincarnation was held by some in the spiritual church movement but was suspicious that such a belief could have its roots in African tradition, choosing instead to emphasize the connection of some spiritual groups with "a variety of occult groups other than Spiritualism in the larger society."[20] Yet as has been demonstrated in relation to the place of ancestors within the Black American experience, resemblances to beliefs and understandings of the African primal are numerous. It is therefore unnecessary to attribute belief in reincarnation either to occult influence or to mainstream White spiritualism. Whereas these may have their place, such beliefs would have had difficulty in taking root, were there no cultural readiness for them. In any case, reincarnation in the SMSC appears to be related to the notion that each spirit has a particular assignment to complete, as indicated by Rev. Anderson's plea at the close of his teaching session (in relation to reincarnation), "let me finish my work completely—don't send me back there!" According to him, if a person has failed to fulfil his assignment, God may send them back until they get it right. He also cited the parable of Lazarus and the rich man (Luke 16:19-31) as well as the appearance of Elijah at the transfiguration, who was likened to John the Baptist (Matt 17:9-13), though John had already been beheaded (Matt 14), as evidence of this possibility.

The Centrality of Jesus and the Necessity of Salvation

The centrality of Jesus and the necessity of salvation is another core belief of the SMSC. Unlike belief in the spirit realm, which is so evident, this belief, though no less firmly held, is more subtly expressed. The name of Jesus is, of course, mentioned frequently, but references to "Spirit" and "Father"—which are often used interchangeably with Jesus—are more frequent still. In the worship services and teaching sessions observed during this study, no invitations to church membership, offers of baptism, or explicit calls to discipleship were observed, though this does not, of course indicate anything about SMSC's view of salvation or of Christ. According to Rev. Anderson, however, the basic problem of mankind arises from the disobedience planted by Satan in the heart of Adam and Eve who previously knew no evil. Consequently, man has "[lost] sight of God by corruption, worldly things, and [as] the Bible says, the love of money [that] is the root of all evil." The result of this "corruption" is God's judgment—the destruction of

---

20. Baer, *Black Spiritual Movement*, 119.

man both in Noah's time and potentially in our own. The notion of human sinfulness and consequent divine judgment come through in these statements. Additionally, the statement "we believe in Jesus . . . the message of salvation is the main message" finds expression in phrases scattered in the preaching of Anderson and other ministers of the church. The centrality of faith in Jesus as Savior begins to emerge clearly from statements such as: "The church belongs to Jesus. He died for the church. He died for you!"; "God sacrificed His only begotten son that hung out on Calvary's cross for you and I. He left His heavenly home . . . and came down to earth to save a hard-headed, disobedient people." "The ultimate triumph was when Jesus hung, bled and died for us, so that we can have a right to the tree of life . . . what's our eternal promise? And that is to be with our Lord and Savior Jesus Christ. We know that because he rose from the dead." These examples demonstrate how SMSC understands the place of Jesus's death and resurrection and salvation in and through him as of primary import.

Ancestral Wisdom

As has already been mentioned, honor and respect for ancestors are embedded at least to some degree in Black American culture. Toni Morrison has described ancestors within Black literature as a "sort of timeless people whose relationship to the characters are benevolent, instructive, and protective [who] provide a certain kind of wisdom."[21] There is a resonance here with African primal understanding as well, wherein the ancestor—the righteous dead of a society—are considered "living members of the community . . . responsible for channelling the life force within the community and thus exert(ing) an influence on the vitality of the community."[22] Though the terminology of ancestral wisdom may seem questionable to some, when one considers the way in which SMSC preserves and honors the traditions passed on to the church by their founders and early leaders, particularly in light of Morrison's description and the African understanding of the ancestor, it becomes clear that this is the appropriate terminology.

As with other elements of the belief structure of SMSC, belief in and reliance upon ancestral wisdom is more often demonstrated than explicitly expressed in words. The Catholic elements that pervade their religious worship are, for example, based on the instruction handed down from the

21. Morrison, "Rootedness," 62.
22. Nichols, "African Christian Theology," 27.

church's founders who taught them to be "like unto the Catholics" in their religious services. Rev. Jester reverently referred to the church's founder, Rev. Martin, as one who was "near and dear" because of "all that she went through for the teaching . . . that we would have a place to learn about true Christian spiritualism." Yet the most striking example of the place of ancestral wisdom lies in the church's annual covenant renewal ceremony.

Exodus 12 records the inauguration of the Passover festival of Israel as a sign and commemoration of the preservation of the lives of the firstborn as a prelude to their liberation from Egyptian bondage. SMSC observes a similar ritual enacted annually on the second Monday of October. This ceremony was inaugurated October 12, 1942, during the height of the Second World War, in a service conducted by a Rev. Marcus. During this service, the congregation observed a Passover meal served by the then pastor Rev. McAfee and Daisy McAfee. As the meal was served, those who came to partake brought with them a handkerchief or napkin "that had never been in use" to be sprinkled with lamb's blood, which Rev. McAfee did using an envelope sealer. Though lamb was served as part of this Passover meal, the blood used to sprinkle the handkerchiefs did not come from the same lamb that was eaten, but from another, undisclosed, source.[23] According to Rev. Marcus, the instruction about the handkerchief and the ceremony came from "Father," who also told some of the participants to attend though they had not been invited by anyone else present, but had been led to do so by the "High Powers."[24] The handkerchief, once sprinkled with blood, is to be carried when traveling as an indication of this covenant, because "the blood must be wherever ye are." This ceremony and covenant renewal is observed annually and Rev. Anderson avers that not only can numerous testimonies can be attributed to the covenant of the blood handkerchief, but of the people from the church who went to serve during World War II, none were lost.

23. When I inquired about the source of the blood used for the "blood handkerchief" the pastor pointedly refused to disclose the source, citing concern that there are "many people who would like to see us disappear [and] will do all they can to hinder us." Similar concerns about disclosure of secrets, and suspicion of outsiders, seems to be common among spiritual groups. This may be due to a history of the churches being branded "centers of superstition" (Baer, *Black Spiritual Movement*, 132) and consequently facing "threats from the police and courts" (Jacobs and Kaslow, *Spiritual Churches*, 186). Cf. M. Smith, *Spirit World*, 31.

24. No clear definition can be discerned of who these "High Powers" are, but they are equated in some sense to "Father." It may thus be inferred that High Powers may refer in this case to spiritual beings acting under instruction from God.

The dedication to reenactment and remembrance of this covenant renewal ceremony, as well as in other practices and teachings, by SMSC, demonstrates a commitment to the preservation and perpetuation of ancestral wisdom derived from the founders and early leaders of the church. Much of the belief and practice of the church—though traceable to Scripture and influenced by other Christian groups—is largely inherited from the forefathers of the congregation, men and women believed to have been led by God and instructed by the spirit.

Ritual Practices

In what has described above of the worship service and spiritual development classes, several rituals may be identified. The first, and perhaps most evident from the perspective of an outside observer, is the patterned prayer ritual of facing the east, reciting the Twenty-Third Psalm and the Lord's Prayer, followed by the phrase: "Hail Mary, Hail Mary, Hail Mary, the Blessed Mother of Jesus." The reference to Mary at the end of each prayer is, according to the church's website, "because Jesus told our founder to recognize his mother." Incensing is another such practice. At SMSC, incense is burned on the first Sunday of each month, "because incense is used in all high mass services and always have been from the Old Testament until now." Members are to partake in a daily ritual described as follows:

> When we awake in the morning, we thank God for another day. We start our day on our right foot when getting out the bed and go to our water supply and wash our face in cold water by splashing cold water on our face three (3) times (in the name of the Father, Son, and the Holy Spirit) and we take three (3) swallows of water. Then we go to the east window, door, or wall of our prayer room or home and as we look east, we pray the 23rd Psalms, the Lord's Prayer, and make whatever request to the Lord. Afterwards, we sit with our Father (Jesus) at our altar or table and we meditate, whatever length of time the morning permits. After meditation we light our candle, rap three (3) times on our Bible, then we open it to where the Spirit leads us and read it for our daily message. Now we are ready to begin our day spiritually. All of this should be done before speaking to anyone.

> We pray three (3) times a day (regardless of where we are), 9am, 12pm, and 3pm to further our spiritual growth. For our members with strict schedules we remember, "Lord have Mercy," is a prayer

within itself. When we pray we light our white stick candles as they represent the purity which was Jesus and it draws us high in the holy spirits. We also do our three (3) raps and say three (3) hail Marys at the end of our prayers. Before entering a building or home we do our 3 raps as we were taught. The 3 raps are in the name of the Father, Son, and the Holy Spirit.[25]

On a weekly and monthly basis, other ritual traditions are practiced. As mentioned above, incense is burned on the first Sunday of the month, Monday services are held by candlelight "to block out all carnal distractions in meditation with the holy spirit," and each third Wednesday of the month, a black veil is worn during prayer service, "as a symbol of atonement for the sins of the world and we pray for the passed our [sic] spirits." There are some dietary practices as well: a pinch of salt and teaspoon of cod liver oil daily, fish on Fridays, and baked potatoes on Wednesdays.

These rituals combine elements of explicitly and readily identifiable Christian practices (Bible reading, prayer, meditation) with others that are less so. All of them are, however, considered to be sacred tradition derived from the explicit teachings of the founder, Rev. Ernestina Martin, who reportedly received them, as by revelation, from God. However derived, the Catholic influence on Martin's teaching is undeniable. Rev. Anderson affirmed this when he noted that it was from their fathers (i.e., the founders of the church) that they learned to be "like unto the Catholics" in their religious services. The extensive use of Catholic paraphernalia—statuary, holy water, crucifixes, and the like—and rituals—genuflection, recitation of the Hail Mary, making the sign of the cross upon entering the sanctuary or at other times—are well attested among Black spiritual people. That SMSC practices these as well as other rituals generally associated with Catholicism is therefore unexceptional when considered in light of the broader spiritual movement.

The extent to which Martin was influenced by other spiritualists, Christian or otherwise, in formulating her teachings is unclear. The possibility of such influence cannot, however, be discounted entirely. American spiritualism, a movement which originated in the mid-nineteenth century, and which may be broadly defined as "talking with the dead," had gained "thousands and perhaps millions" of adherents during the mid- to late nineteenth century, during which time St. Louis emerged as a center of

---

25. SMSC's website, "What We Believe."

post–Civil War spiritualism.[26] Although spiritualism had lost some of its cachet by the early twentieth century when Martin began her ministry, it still retained much of its vitality as a movement. Whatever may be said of the movement generally can be applied to the movement in St. Louis. It must, of course, also be admitted that many of the phenomena associated with spiritualism, most notably belief in and the practice of communicating with the dead, are not peculiar to that movement. In any case, the ritual practices of SMSC demonstrate the eclecticism that is characteristic of the Black spiritual movement.

Primal Spirituality and Identity

Black spiritual churches have been described as "thaumaturgical/manipulationist sects" who place great emphasis on "the manipulation of one's present condition through the use of various magico-religious rituals and the acquisition of esoteric knowledge, often referred to as "secrets" or "mysteries."[27] This description leaves little ground for consideration of the group's stated religious identity, or the relationship of that identity to the Christian gospel. Notwithstanding what may obtain among other groups claiming the label "spiritual," the beliefs and practices of SMSC described thus far point towards an identity grounded in the primal imagination. Such an identity is not inherently antithetical to Christianity. Indeed, the primal has been described as the substructure of Christianity—"the universal, basic elements of man's understanding of God and of the world"[28]—elements containing "essential and valid religious insights [that] may be built upon or suppressed, but not superseded."[29]

While there are several ways in which this primal sensibility is evidenced in the life of SMSC—the aforementioned beliefs and ritual practices being the most obvious—at its core, it is the primal spirituality that undergirds and animates these beliefs and rituals that gives SMSC its distinctive identity. This primal perspective considers spirituality to be inseparable from the fabric of daily life, wherein "no distinction can be made between sacred and secular, between natural and supernatural,"[30] as evidenced by the

26. Nartonis, "19th-Century American Spiritualism," 361.
27. Baer and Singer, "Typology of Black Sectarianism," 8, 9.
28. John V. Taylor, *Primal Vision*, 18.
29. G. Bediako, "Primal Religion," 12.
30. John V. Taylor, *Primal Vision*, 64.

daily ritual and dietary restrictions practiced by the congregation. Stated differently, the identity of SMSC as Christian *and* spiritualist derives from its essentially primal orientation—an orientation cultivated and reinforced through the rituals here described. It is this orientation that undergirds the church's understanding of reality and thus self-understanding, and indeed their whole conception of Christianity.

African Parallels

The phenomenon of African Christian independency, which in some respects parallels that of the Black spiritual church, proves helpful in understanding the ministry of SMSC. Spiritual churches in the African context have similarly been derided as unorthodox, syncretistic, or even occult, yet more recently have been acknowledged as prefiguring the "direction in which broad sections of African Christianity were moving,"[31] and thus cannot simply be dismissed as heterodox or outside the mainstream of Christianity. The ministries of William Wadé Harris (1860–1929) of West Africa and Simon Kimbangu (1887–1951) of the Congo, both of whom worked around the same time that Ernestina Martin began her ministry in St. Louis, are exemplars of primal movements that have now been seen as having operated within recognizable Christian parameters. Like Martin, "these two men shared a common fundamental experience: a vision and revelation of God giving them a command to witness, to preach, and to heal."[32]

Wadé Harris in particular has been noted for the primal features of his ministry, and especially his sense of operating under the direction of spirit forces, in his case the angel Gabriel. David Shank notes that "Harris continued to the end of his life to acknowledge the control of the angel, who replaced all the other authorities to whom he had been subject in his life."[33] Harris's ministry is now widely recognized as having brought many thousands to Christian faith. One of the earliest chroniclers of his movement noted that "modern missions supply no case of such multitudes being brought to God in so short a time at the preaching of a single man."[34] Yet Harris accomplished this as an outsider to the Christian missionary

---

31. K. Bediako, *Christianity in Africa*, 66.
32. Sundkler and Steed, *Church in Africa*, 781.
33. Shank, *Prophet Harris*, 129.
34. Walker, *Story of Ivory Coast*, 18.

establishment, was propelled by a spiritual trance-vision, and sustained by an ongoing sense of participation in the spirit, with the angel Gabriel as his guide. He was, in short, a man whose ministry was thoroughly infused with the primal imagination. Given these precedents, one must exercise caution before a too facile dismissal of the beliefs and practices of SMSC can be attempted. Indeed, SMSC may be understood as demonstrating, within a Black American context, an appreciation, understanding, and engagement with spiritual reality similar to what has obtained within the African situation.

Spirituality

Spirituality is a slippery term that frequently obscures as much as it reveals and is sometimes defined as much by what it is not as what it is. It suffices to say that religious activity is not synonymous with spirituality, though there is a connection between the two. Religious activity may coexist and correlate with spirituality, and indeed often does, but is not interchangeable with it. Neither again can theology be correlated with spirituality, though the two cannot, or at least should not, be divorced from one another. Yet despite the slipperiness of the word, *spirituality* is the right term to encompass the relationship between human beings and immaterial, nonphysical reality, a reality that is personal in nature. Rudolph Otto's discussion of encounter with the Other—"that which is quite beyond the sphere of the usual, the intelligible, and the familiar, which therefore falls quite outside the limits of the 'canny', and is contrasted with it, filling the mind with blank wonder and astonishment"[35]—is instructive, for it underscores the relationality that lies at the heart of spirituality. Spirituality therefore has to do with engagement with entities presumed to exist as real, and not with ideas or abstract concepts. John V. Taylor speaks of an African primal "world of presences, of face-to-face meeting not only with the living but just as vividly with the dead and with the whole totality of nature."[36] Taylor wrote in reference to the African situation in the mid-twentieth century, yet his insights are equally applicable to SMSC in the early decades of the twenty-first. The basis for SMSC's self-understanding as a people is underlain by just this kind of spiritual vision.

---

35. Otto, *Idea of the Holy*, 26.
36. John V. Taylor, *Primal Vision*, 189.

When Pastor Anderson declares, "We are Christian spiritualists,"[37] it is a positive affirmation of an identity rooted in participation in the spiritual realm and communion with those entities that abide there. This participation is expressed in many ways. The Monday spiritual development class is one clear example. The service, held by candlelight "to block out all carnal distractions in meditation with the holy spirit," includes time given to silent waiting in anticipation that spirit will speak. The quietude of the service suggests that spirit entities are not invoked by any activity of the members but are believed to be present, able and willing to communicate to those sensitive enough to receive such messages. It is therefore important to develop spiritual sensitivity—to "grow to a level of spiritual understanding [so that] God will begin to reveal things," that is to position oneself spiritually for the acquisition of knowledge and understanding that would not be otherwise obtainable. Knowledge, Anderson affirms, is not generated internally, from within a person, but comes from external sources, from "spirit forces who are more intelligent than we are whether good or evil," and thus it is necessary to learn to "listen to our guiding spirit" rather than to "the one who wants to cloud our judgment," that is, to Satan. In this, Anderson agrees with the insights of indigenous scholars who have asserted knowledge as a relational entity,[38] inseparable from its source in the spirit realm and engagement with the source is an inextricable component of the process of knowledge construction. Such knowledge is not an end in itself, but has functional importance related to the promotion of individual and communal well-being, as indicated by the nature of messages received from the spirit(s) during the prophecy session.[39]

This approach to spirituality may appear to some as occult—the candlelit room, the receiving of messages ostensibly from loved ones, and the talk of spirit forces can seem mysterious, if not evil. Others may be tempted to dismiss it as superstitious because of the prescribed rituals of prayer and Scripture recitation, use of candles and rapping three times as a means of prayer, not to speak of the wearing of white robes worn as spiritual protection and bloodied handkerchiefs carried as tokens of covenant. Yet understood from within the framework of the primal imagination, these may

37. Interview with Rev. Harold Anderson, Jan. 5, 2016.
38. Wilson, "Indigenous Research Methodology," 177.
39. According to Marcus Harvey, a similar perspective on knowledge production may be observed among the Akan of Ghana. Harvey has also suggested that the Akan also believe that "knowledge of the world, or a mode of knowing, ensues from regular contact with the spiritual realm" ("Life Is War," 210).

rather be understood as signs of recognition of the comprehensiveness of spirituality and a response to what Kwame Bediako terms "the rending of the veil, so that the nature of the whole universe as instinct with the divine presence [is] made manifest."[40]

Conclusion

The history, ritual practices, and beliefs of the SMSC present a remarkable case of how the primal imagination has found expression within the context of Black American Christianity. While SMSC appears to be less "mainstream" in its emphases than other congregations, a close examination reveals a profound concern for fidelity to the Bible, reliance upon the Holy Spirit for guidance, and belief in the necessity of salvation through Jesus Christ. These concerns are, however, expressed in deeply primal ways. Their ritual practices—use of incense, candles, and daily prayer rituals, among others—place spirituality and engagement with the spiritual realm as central to their identity as *Christian* spiritualists. For SMSC, participation in Christ opens the way to a greater participation in and with the spirit realm, through whom wisdom, knowledge, and power to contend with the challenges of "carnal" life may be accessed. The Scriptures are a story in which SMSC takes part, providing for them the means to understand their participation not only with Christ, but with angels, the departed "forefathers" of the church, and a variety of spirit forces, as well as defining and interpreting the parameters of that participation. This participation is indeed vital in the truest sense of the word; "the resources and powers of all those who are brought within the community . . . includ[ing] both living and dead,"[41] are brought to bear in a tangible experiential way. Jesus speaks to them as "Father," "Mother Mary" is experienced as close, and the departed forefathers are busily working "on [their] behalf. What emerges from the SMSC is therefore not to be taken as occult, dismissed as superstition, nor even perceived as a quest for esoteric knowledge for its own sake, but rather as an expression of the primal imagination from within the Black Christian context.

---

40. K. Bediako, *Christianity in Africa*, 102.
41. K. Bediako, *Christianity in Africa*, 103.

9

Emerging Theological Matters and Concluding Reflections

"CHRISTIAN FAITH," WRITES ANDREW Walls, "is repeatedly coming into creative interaction with new cultures, with different systems of thought and different patterns of tradition."[1] It is from within the context of this dynamic engagement that new theological reflection is conducted, and out of it, that new insights may emerge. Yet the history of Euro-Western engagement with Black peoples and religions—an engagement marked by pretensions of Euro-Western superiority and normativity, disdain and suspicion of Black peoples, and social, economic, political, and cultural oppression of the same—has largely constrained Black theological reflection within the confines of Euro-Western White supremacy, even as it fights against it. When this is coupled with the Euro-Western suppression of the primal legacies of its own culture, and suspicion and denigration of the primal in other cultures, it is no wonder that Black spiritual and Pentecostal church traditions have largely been overlooked as sources of theological insight, drawing attention primarily from secular anthropologists driven by other concerns. In this concluding chapter, I wish to provide some theological reflection based on what has emerged in the course of this study, indicate

---

1. Walls, *Cross-Cultural Process*, 30.

some possible avenues for further research, and offer some concluding thoughts in relation to the whole project.

Emerging Theological Matters

Examination of and reflection on these traditions in light of the primal imagination that animates them has led to the emergence of some ideas that point to the need for further investigation and deeper theological reflection. These ideas may challenge some of the conventional assumptions of post-Enlightenment evangelical Protestantism, though they cannot be said to be entirely unprecedented. The ideas I offer here are only preliminary, however. Much more can, and should, be said than can be done in the space available, and one may undoubtedly find some scholarly work has already begun in the direction of these musings, though little, I suspect, through the lens of the primal imagination.

Embodied Theology or Bodily Expressed Theology

The first of these is that of embodied theology or alternatively, bodily expressed theology. When I speak of embodied theology, I am not referring to a theology *of* the body in the sense of St. John Paul II's articulation from within the Roman Catholic tradition of an integrated vision of the human person, and more especially around issues of human sexuality.[2] Reflection on and engagement with these series of addresses in light of the primal imagination as refracted through the lens of Black spiritual and Pentecostal tradition would be a valuable study in its own right. Nor do I refer to embodied theology in the sociocultural sense of theology shaped by its cultural embeddedness or by cultural constructions of the body, that is, how the body is perceived, acted upon, or formed by its cultural or historical setting—a definition that has gained currency in some sectors of the academy.[3] I refer, rather, to theology that is articulated via the medium of the human body. This is not a theology per se, but I propose it as a frame or lens through which theology might be comprehended, or an avenue by which the theological enterprise might be undertaken. It is one that takes

---

2. *Theology of the Body* is the popular name given to a series of public addresses given by Pope John Paul II during his Wednesday audiences between 1979 and 1984.

3. See Miller-McLemore, "Embodied Knowing, Embodied Theology," for discussion of this trend. See also Mitchem, "Embodiment."

seriously the full range of human sensory experience and expression in religious matters, including music, art, dance, ritual, and other forms of communication. I offer it in contrast to theology that is word based and word bound, and that operates as a scientific system of ideas that mediate the boundary between the empirical and immaterial realms. It is needful here to recall Kwesi Dickson's observation that "not all theologizing issues in a formal presentation [and] it would be an error if all theologizing were to be constricted into propositional articulation, though some kind of articulation might become necessary in the interests of communication."[4] This is especially so when it comes to the religious, an irreducible category of human experience replete with other modes of communication. The import of this continues to elude the Euro-Western academy. Sam Gill captures it thus:

> Surely compared to religion there is no subject of study more richly textured by images and actions that are not based in words nor adequately captured by words—art, music, architecture, ritual, pilgrimage, landscapes, colors, mountains, trees, dancing, dramatic performances, praying, gesturing, clothing and vestments, hair styles, eating, drinking, animals, fasting, killing, birthing, initiating, dying, marrying, nurturing, loving, laying on of hands, circumcision, tooth extraction, menstruation, sub-incision, singing. Is there an end to this list? Yet, surely there is no academic endeavor more word-bound, headier, more hostile to the senses and emotion, than the academic study of religion.[5]

What Gill asserts about the dissonance between religious experience and expression and the discourse around religious expression within the academy is critical, and especially problematic when it comes to Black American religion, especially in its pneumatic sacramentalist expression. I believe this problem stems from a lack of critical engagement with the primal imagination within religious discourse, or perhaps even a fear of the primal elements in religion, especially Christianity. One is reminded again that the dualistic separation of "form from function, structure from meaning, and style from content" is derived from a Euro-Western epistemological assumption "that favors literate over narrative means of expression."[6] Given this, restricting theological reflection to only what arises in the form

---

4. Dickson, *African Theology*, 5.
5. Gill, "Play and the Future," 3.
6. Matthews, *Honoring the Ancestors*, 10, 11.

of propositional articulation inherently marginalizes those who operate from within the framework of the primal imagination. But this is not all. These assumptions not only "den[y] the legitimacy of non-Western cultural forms,"[7] but significantly impair the relationship of Christian theology with the vast array of nonliterate expressive forms within Euro-Western culture itself, thus impoverishing the theological enterprise on a vast scale. Nonliterate expression may become reduced to its entertainment value or seen as theologically valuable only insofar as it directly references propositional articulations of the implications of faith. This includes the immense amount of religiously inspired music, art, architecture, and other cultural forms in European cultural history. I am not, however, speaking only of religiously *inspired* art forms, valuable though these are, but of theology expressed *through* the various media of art and the body itself.

The tendency towards word-based abstraction and away from concretized body-based expression is particularly pernicious in its impact on interpretations of Black peoples and religion, where style, meaning, and content frequently fused together in a primal synthesis. Because the exigencies of existence within a racist and racialized society severely restricted Blacks' access to literary-based forms of theological communication, while simultaneously denying the validity of their nonliterary forms of expression, their theological insights were invisibilized altogether. This is all the more problematic when one realizes, and as this study illuminates, that this primal synthesis of form and meaning is even more pronounced in the pneumatic sacramentalism of Black Pentecostal and spiritual people—religious groups who have historically been sidelined even within the study of Black religion—existing on the margins of the marginalized. Until quite recently, very few scholars of Black religion had emerged from the Black Pentecostal tradition, and its chief interpreters within Black religious scholarship have frequently been disdainful of the tradition—agreeing tacitly if not overtly with characterizations of Pentecostalism as "sound instead of sense."[8] Over and again such groups have been overlooked or disdained within the theological academy as having little or nothing of value to contribute to the theological enterprise.

Because Black Pentecostals and spiritual people have tended to express their theology through dance, song, shout, and testimony within a

---

7. Matthews, *Honoring the Ancestors*, 14.

8. "Fanatical Worship of Negroes Going on at Sanctified Church," *Commercial Appeal* (May 22, 1907), quoted in Sanders, *Saints in Exile*, 31.

ritual context, they have sometimes been adjudged as having no theology at all, or a deficient one. The overemphasis on conceptual abstraction as determinative of theological validity, to the virtual exclusion of other forms of artistic expression, is one source of this error. Yet as Hurston astutely observed, "All religious expression among Negroes is regarded as art, and ability is recognized as definitely as in any other art. The beautiful prayer receives the accolade as well as the beautiful song."[9] Artistry in music, dance, drama, and other genres is inextricably tied together with the religious. Teresa Reed describes it thus: "[African] music is intrinsically spiritual, the sacred is intrinsically musical, and both music and the divine permeate every imaginable part of life."[10] Of African Christians it is said that "to sing is to theologize, to dance is to witness to his goodness and testify of one's relationship with him, and to dramatize is to make the message clear and understandable."[11] This extends to their Black American counterparts as well. One would do well to remember also that this is the New Testament pattern: "The first Christians did not express their faith in a speculative way.... They responded to the preaching [of the gospel] by worship; they sang the work that God had done for them, in hymns."[12] It is, therefore, time that truncated and myopic perspectives on what counts as legitimate avenues for theological expression be eclipsed by a more expansive vision.

Music as an Exemplary Form of Bodily Expressed Theology

This study is not about music. Music does, however, provide an example of a non-text-based form of communication that is sometimes overlooked in terms of its theological relevance. Though I claim no special expertise on this matter, all too often it seems that it is the song lyrics alone that are deemed to be of theological significance, while the music fades to irrelevance as only a background "canvas" upon which the lyrics are painted—music reduced to performance. When this occurs, the music can be decontextualized and used for any purpose whatsoever, including trivial or sacrilegious ones. Historically, Blacks were not only forbidden access to conventional, literary forms of expression through legal sanctions on education during slavery, and the imposition of legal impediments to quality

---

9. Hurston, *Sanctified Church*, 83.
10. Reed, *Holy Profane*, 5.
11. King et al., *Music in the Life*, 7.
12. Allmen, "Birth of Theology," 41.

education thereafter. The enslaved were also banned from using certain other expressive forms, specifically certain types of musical instruments. The principal African instrument—the drum—was banned in many slaveholding areas in recognition of its communicative potential.[13] Slaveholders were aware that drums could be made to talk—to give expression—to human ideas, and communicate those ideas to those with ears to hear. Such potentially subversive communication could not be permitted to persist. In addition, the various percussive polyrhythms of African music were demonized by Whites as well as by some "blacks who identified more with the genteel classes [and] sought to distance themselves as much as possible from the practices that they considered barbaric."[14] The drums were the devil's instrument and the beats and dance that accompanied them were demonic, and were consequently unacceptable for proper "civilized" Christian practice.[15] It was left to those who would come to be called "sanctified" to maintain these body-centered forms of expression:

> The worship aesthetic that blacks appropriated for their own Pentecostal experience was, to a large degree, retained directly from the bush-meeting and ringshout customs of slavery. And we know that for much of the antebellum period and in many places throughout the South, drumming was specifically prohibited. Blacks, therefore, often resorted to other percussive means—like clapping and stomping—to achieve the desired effect.[16]

The "sanctified" are the descendants, inheritors, and propagators of these traditions; those Zora Neale Hurston would attest were "putting back into Negro religion those elements which were brought over from Africa and grafted onto Christianity."[17] The music performed in the ritual context of these churches serves as a primary link back to these African elements.

---

13. Reed, "Shared Possessions," 10. Reed points out that slaveholders were aware of how drum language was used to facilitate communication among the enslaved, and sought to eliminate it.

14. Reed, "Shared Possessions," 9.

15. Roberta King has noted the inseparability of music, dance, and spectacle within African music. This extends to the Black American context as well (King et al., *Music in the Life*, 137).

16. Reed, "Shared Possessions," 13.

17. Hurston, *Sanctified Church*, 105.

New Testament Basis for Embodied Theology

The primal vision of "God and man in an abiding relationship which is the divine destiny of humankind"[18] reveals the transcendent as involved in the full spectrum of human existence and human affairs, an involvement concretized in the incarnation, and fully manifest in the life and ministry of Jesus as expressed in the New Testament. Further, the bodily resurrection and ascension of Jesus mean that humanity has been permanently taken up into the abiding presence of the transcendent, a reality expressed in Eph 2:6, "And God raised us up with Christ and seated us with him in the heavenly realms in Christ Jesus" (NIV). The resurrection and ascension are both bodily events, not "spiritual" ones, so the language cannot be taken as merely metaphorical or figurative. The primal imagination, which integrates the physical and nonphysical/spiritual realms of existence, particularly as expressed in the Black spiritual and Pentecostal traditions, places the body, and thus the full range of bodily expression, as a locus of theology. The jumping, dancing, and shouting common in the Black Pentecostal church—these bodily expressions should not be dismissed as simply emotion laden cathartic exercises, but considered "a reproduction of... the moral universe where abundant life is not an external commodity, but an internal fountain experienced in the company of the faithful."[19] The "shout" and the "holy dance" therefore may be understood as a kind of theological articulation, affirming the present reality of the biblical hope: "Behold, the dwelling place of God is with man. He will dwell with them, and they will be his people, and God himself will be with them as their God" (Rev 21:3 ESV).

The Pentecostal emphasis on being filled with the Holy Spirit further confirms the physical body as an instrument of theological expression. First Corinthians 6:19 indicates that the Christian's body is "the temple of the Holy Spirit" (NKJV), therefore the movement of the body under the direction of the Spirit may be read as a form of reciprocal communication between God, the individual, and the community of which he or she is part. It is true, of course, that dance and other nonliterary forms of communication lack the precision of the written or spoken word, but language is itself limited as a form of expression. This does not mean that they are therefore to be a priori excluded from consideration as vehicles of theological

---

18. K. Bediako, *Christianity in Africa*, 101.
19. Scandrett-Leatherman, "Can't Nobody Do Me," 237.

communication. As Dickson notes concerning the theological process, "There is the level at which reflection upon one's faith may not issue in the expression of one's thinking in coherent language. The reflection may be done in song, or in prayer, in action or in mediation,"[20] or, I may add, in dance, testimony, or various forms of visual and performance art. Scripture itself asserts that the intercession of the Holy Spirit occurs in "groaning too deep for words" (Rom 8:26 ESV). In a similar way in the spiritual church, the pinpoint light of burning candles, the repetitive patterns of recited prayers, and the smells of incense and oils engage the sensory organs of the human body, simultaneously evoking a sense of otherness and holiness and yet nearness of the spirit realm. This is a theological articulation of a different kind, but one no less potent for its locative imprecision. Thus, whether in the tarrying services of the All Saints Holiness Church, or the rituals practiced by members of St Martins Spiritualist Church, "bodily expression is a bodily participation in the Spirit,"[21] articulating, in a primal way, the theology of the churches.

Christ as Exemplar of Embodied Theology

This concern for embodied theology does not emerge only from the context of the Black Pentecostal and spiritual churches; it extends beyond ethnic and denominational categories, and may also be considered as inherent in Christian theology itself. Theology can be defined as the attempt to communicate something about God. Within the Christian understanding, Jesus is not simply the bearer of a message about God, which would make him a prophet, but is *himself* the definitive communication of God in bodily form. He is therefore a living communication about God, an embodied theology, as it were, proclaiming through his actions and inactions, as much as in his words, who and what God is. Apart from his miraculous conception, Jesus's life was that which any common first-century Palestinian Jewish peasant might experience. Much of what is recorded of his life is anchored by bodily referents; he eats, sleeps, becomes weary, hungers, and thirsts. He extends his hands to touch the afflicted. Tears stain his cheeks in grief. He undoubtedly lifted up his hands in prayer, and perhaps even sang and danced at wedding feasts and festivals. The bodily suffering, bodily death, bodily resurrection, and bodily ascension of Jesus Christ are central

20. Dickson, *African Theology*, 13.
21. Scandrett-Leatherman, "Can't Nobody Do Me," 236.

to the great creeds of Christianity and belie the subtle, though generally unstated, primacy accorded to abstract articulation in the Euro-Western academy—something more likely owed to Greek influence than to the biblical accounts. The most enduring ritual inaugurated by Jesus—the Lord's Supper—is a bodily exercise of eating and drinking, his body and blood, the food and drink of the new covenantal community. The bread/body and wine/blood are smelled, touched, tasted, ingested—the sense organs of the body fully engaged in a ritual meal that Scripture hems about with warnings of taking "in an unworthy manner," lest judgment be incurred, resulting in bodily sickness or even bodily death (1 Cor 11:27–30 ESV). The Pentecost event as well, so fundamental in the self-understanding and theology of Pentecostals generally, is one that places the body as central. The English rendering of *glossolalia* as tongues—a body referent—combined with auditory and visual stimuli of rushing wind and flames of fire, present the picture of sensory overload, every part of the body is taken by the Spirit with the effect that onlookers suspect drunkenness, yet this is an ordered intoxication, impelled by the Spirit. The body, filled with the Spirit is not disorderly, but becomes properly ordered because of its reorientation to God through the Spirit. As mentioned above, the process of apprehension of the Spirit causes the body itself to be apprehended by the Spirit in a mutually reinforcing embodied way. The body/bodies gathered in the upper room become filled with and placed at the disposal of the Holy Spirit so that the human body/bodies express the wondrous works of God in diverse tongues. All of these point to the centrality of the physical body within the ministry of Jesus and the early life of the church as portrayed in the New Testament.

Taken together—the body-focused spirituality of Black spiritual and Pentecostal tradition, with music as a key example, the New Testament witness, and Jesus's embodied communication about God—point towards a need for a deeper theological engagement with the primal sense of appreciation of the physical as a sacrament of the spiritual. They further highlight the need for more substantive interaction between theology and nonliterate forms of human expression so as to extend the range of both theological inquiry and theological insight.

Multiplicity in the Spiritual Realm

In his reflection on African theology, Kwame Bediako noted that it "has answered to only part of the total spiritual universe of African primal religions."[22] By this, he referred to the multitude of spiritual entities that occupy the transcendent realm of African religious thought and which had been, in his view, inadequately accounted for by African theology. That world is "a universe of distributed power, perhaps even of fragmented power,"[23] a multipolar world, as it were, and one in which simply positing the transcendent God, known from afar in African traditions, but now brought near in Jesus Christ, atop a hierarchy of spiritual beings imperfectly addressed the very this-worldly orientation of African primal religions. Bediako's proposed solution arises from the primal understanding, and calls for recognition that "at the heart of the universe and of religion is a divine-human relationship for the fulfilment of man's divine destiny," and that "God is abidingly involved in a relationship with man, and for man; God has never left men and never been far removed from man."[24] Such an understanding makes possible the further recognition that the participation in the transcendent that has been made possible by Christ's death, through the Holy Spirit, likewise entails participation "in the resources and powers of all those who are also brought within the community . . . both living and dead."[25] This is for Bediako primarily linked to the predominant place of ancestors within African cosmology (thus his reference to "both living and dead"), though is not restricted to it.

Bediako's proposal is preliminary, and while he points towards a probable resolution to the problem of unresolved multiplicity, he does not, in this volume, flesh out the full implications of his proposal, nor does he address the full spectrum of spiritual beings that must be contended with. His primary concern, given the African context, is ancestors. In the Black American Pentecostal and especially spiritual church traditions, which are removed from direct interaction and engagement with their African antecedent traditions, ancestors play a much less prominent role than in the African, though they are still important, as has been demonstrated above. Nevertheless, the problem Bediako identifies is present within these

22. K. Bediako, *Christianity in Africa*, 99.
23. K. Bediako, *Christianity in Africa*, 99.
24. K. Bediako, *Christianity in Africa*, 101.
25. K. Bediako, *Christianity in Africa*, 103.

traditions as well. As the case of the SMSC shows in a specific way, and other churches exhibit more broadly, reference to the importance of ancestors either formally or informally still occurs. The vital participation in the transcendent realm of which he speaks, and which draws within its orbit both living and dead, does not fully address the question of who and what are the entities that animate that realm, if even one lays aside ancestors—whose ontic reality is itself an area in dire need of further theological reflection and analysis.

The varying and complex ways in which the dead are presented within the New Testament further complicates the picture. As demonstrated earlier, in the primal world of the New Testament, the dead seem not to be fully dead, but appear again and again in ways that defy conventional assumptions. I have mentioned, for example, the recitation of ancestors in Jesus's genealogy in the birth narratives, which I likened to the recitation of the ancestors that takes place during the pouring of libation in traditional Akan religious practice. Like the latter, the former recitation may also be read as an invocation—inviting the attendance of these living dead as witnesses and participants in Jesus's birth. In reference to these biblical ancestors, Paul John Isaak asserts, "God says that he is still in a relationship with [the ancestors], then they must still in some sense be alive."[26] The theological implications of this claim are tremendous, and the soteriological implications are unavoidable. If the patriarchs of Israel, whose relationship to God was prior to the giving of the law, and was mediated solely on the basis of faith in the living God apart from any knowledge of the person of Jesus, nor any conception of the need for a Messiah at all—if they can be said to be alive and in communion with God, then cannot the same can be argued for the ancestors of other peoples who have related on the same basis of faith in the living God? It may be possible to consider them in the same category as Moses and the other Old Testament saints who lived in a manner consistent with faithfulness to Christ though they did not know him.[27] This possibility is strengthened when coupled with the biblical account of Jesus's descent into the realms of the dead where he "preached to the spirits in prison" (1 Pet 3:19 NKJV). This passage need not be considered time-bound and applicable to only the people of Israel since Christ's work relates to cosmic realities that transcend the particularities of time and space. After all, "not all who are descended from Israel are Israel" (Rom 9:6 NIV);

---

26. Isaak, "Luke," 1244.

27. Nichols, "African Christian Theology," 30.

the Israel of faith is not coterminous with the Israel of blood descent. If the ancestor Christology proposed by Bediako and others aims to "[make] room among the 'living-dead' for the Lord, the judge of both the living and the dead,"[28] then the question as to whether the converse is true naturally follows, that is, whether room can be made in the Lord for the living dead. The answer to this question lies on the borderlands of Christology, soteriology, and ecclesiology that it is not my intention to address. However, I note with provisional approval O. Samuel Nichols's commentary in relation to the question of African ancestors:

> One must grant that the ancestors, like the saints, are fellow disciples in the community of disciples. They are not situated between Christ and us; they are with us, in Christ, as sisters and brothers with whom we share a common humanity, a common faith, and a common eternal destiny. Hence we can pray for one another, insofar as we accept that it is Christ as Mediator who makes it possible. The church is a community in itself, and the ancestors are a part—in so far as they lived exemplary lives.[29]

Beyond Ancestors

Within the Black Pentecostal, and especially spiritual church traditions, there is a profound appreciation of multiplicity within the spiritual sphere that goes beyond the issue of ancestors. They believe in a diversity of spiritual powers that are not easily bifurcated into the categories of good and evil, but whose influence on life can be significant. When, for example, the forefathers of SMSC referred to "High Powers" during the institution of their covenant renewal/Passover ceremony,[30] it is not immediately apparent what spiritual forces are being referenced, though it is implied that they are good. What is one to make of Ernestina Martin, the church's founder, who was said to be used by spirit guides who would "take control of her vocal chords and speak to the members [of the church] describing themselves and telling about their condition, so as to be recognized by their friends and relations," and yet in the process was taught by Jesus to distinguish the

---

28. K. Bediako, *Christianity in Africa*, 217.

29. Nichols, "African Christian Theology," 31.

30. "Covenant Ceremony" (photocopy of typed transcript of meeting held Oct. 12, 1942, at SMSC).

good from the bad?[31] Bishop Allen's mention of "demons that are set out to destroy people" can be rather straightforwardly linked to New Testament descriptions of evil spirits, but the reference in his mother's ordination papers to "Divine Mediumship" is rather more obscure. Who or what was to be mediated from the realm of the divine, and how were these to be discerned? Dismissing these as either demonic counterfeits or superstitious imaginations is too facile, and does not resolve the issue theologically, especially when one considers these experiences in light of similar manifestations of the primal around the world, throughout Christian history, and within the Bible itself.

Multiplicity in the New Testament

The New Testament presents a more complicated picture of spiritual reality than is commonly recognized, a reality that goes beyond easy, bifurcated categories of angels and demons. The Pauline reference in Eph 6 to "rulers . . . authorities . . . cosmic powers . . . spiritual forces" (RSVCE) and the Johannine admonition, "do not believe every spirit, but test the spirits to see whether they are from God" (1 John 4:1 RSVCE),[32] are examples of this. In both cases, the simplistic binary category of the "good" angelic and the "evil" demonic seem inadequate.[33] John implies a significant amount of ambiguity about the nature of the spirits that might be encountered. Spirits may be either good, bad, or possibly even neutral in some sense; discernment is needed, and he offers guidelines for this. The guidance he offers though, says nothing of the intrinsic nature of the spirits; they are "of God" or "not of God" in relation to their confession concerning Jesus Christ (vv. 2–3). Furthermore, these spirits are associated with prophets, some of whom are false, others of whom are presumably true. Surprisingly, John does not mention the Holy Spirit at all, except in reference to how a believer may recognize God's abiding presence within himself (1 John 3:24), which suggests at least a possible multiplicity of "good" or God-sent spirits. More complex interpretations have been offered, Walter Wink's trilogy on the

---

31. SMSC's website, "About Us."

32. This Scripture was frequently cited or alluded to in my church during my youth, and was often paraphrased, "try the spirit by the Spirit." Jacobs and Kaslow report a similar usage among spiritual people in their research in New Orleans (*Spiritual Churches*, 128).

33. See, for example, S. Noll, *Angels of Light*.

powers most notable among them. Walter Wink's "naming" of the powers, which are predominantly associated with bad or with evil, represents an effort from within the Euro-Western theological academy to take seriously the issue of spiritual beings. Yet aside the fact that Wink does not deal with possible multiplicity of "good" spiritual beings or forces, his naming of the powers as the "*inner aspect of material or tangible manifestations of power*" that do not "have a separate, spiritual existence"[34] is, in the end, unsatisfactory. His interpretation of the powers is reductionist and depersonalizing, to the end that Satan himself is reduced to "a function in the divine process, a dialectical movement in God's purpose which becomes evil only when humanity breaks off the dialectic by refusing creative choice."[35] Such an analysis cannot be reconciled with the biblical view without doing damage to the text, nor with the totality of human experience. Nevertheless, Wink's recognition of the simultaneity of spiritual and earthly reality is to be commended, as is his recognition that within the primal biblical framework, potentially, "there is more to events than what appears."[36] These insights should not be overlooked, despite my critique. The Black Pentecostal and spiritual traditions have much to contribute to a deeper engagement and understanding of these issues.

The Cosmos as a Single, Spiritual System

Wink's insight accords well with Bediako's observation of the place of the transcendent in primal understanding. This brings us to one of the most compelling and important theological matters emerging from this study of Black spiritual and Pentecostal traditions: a deep sense of the essential unity of the cosmos, which is spiritual, with the consequence that the whole of life, and the whole of one's being—material and immaterial—are brought under the ambit of spirituality, nothing apart. If all of life is spiritual, then every dimension of that life is an avenue for the expression of spirituality, and all of life is included in the sweeping scope of God's saving grace. I do not intend to suggest that this is unique to the experience and expression of Black American Pentecostal and spiritual traditions. Yet the spirituality of these traditions prioritizes this sense, leaving the door open, as it were, for diverse experiences of transcendence in ordinary life. Inspired

34. Wink, *Naming the Powers*, 104–5; emphasis original.
35. Wink, *Unmasking the Powers*, 33.
36. Wink, *Naming the Powers*, 140.

"transcendent" happenings like visions, prophecies and healings occur, but others, less spectacular and less extraordinary do as well. The Spirit may direct a particular choice of clothing or indicate that a different route should be taken to work, which may lead to a fortuitous meeting, or the averting of an accident or traffic on the road. The Spirit may descend as readily in a shower stall as in a tarrying service, making each place a sanctuary, an altar where the divine rains down upon human weakness. The primal spiritual vision of Black Pentecostals and spiritual people offers nothing less than the resacralization of the world. I identify three manifestations of this vision.

The Good Life

One manifestation of this perspective is the abiding concern for a life that is characterized by a holistic and integrated sense of well-being, in and through the Spirit, with rituals of physical healing being the most prominent example. Yet the concern for healing is not the only way that this is expressed. That all of life is potentially included within the scope of salvation also explains the apparent openness to teachings that emphasize material prosperity, as seen in Rev. Anderson's contention that the Bible is to give us both eternal life and prosperity: "If you're not prosperous, you're missing something." His assertion gives voice to an enduring and deeply felt concern among Black Americans for both physical and spiritual well-being, and the deep sense of connection between them. This sense was heightened by the need to confront the reality of a perilous existence on the margins of American life, though not precipitated by it. There is, therefore, in much of Black religion a pervasive "theological accent on ascertaining and critical engagement with allaying the sources of black suffering and practical concern with securing *eudemonia*, what the Greeks defined as the 'good life.'"[37] The problematic aspects of this tendency when stretched to extremes are well noted elsewhere.[38] I have no intention of disputing them; any gospel proclamation that decenters Jesus and marginalizes the cross is no gospel at all. Even so, the pursuit and acquisition of the "good life" as a component of spirituality cannot be dismissed simply as a response to impoverished circumstances, or sociocultural disenfranchisement as some observers would

---

37. Walton, "Prosperity Gospel," 455.

38. Cheryl Sanders, among others, has noted with concern the rise of such teachings ("Pentecostal Ethics").

have it;[39] that is an overly reductive view, unsupported by the evidence. It is not at all apparent that this perspective on spirituality is held only by poor, or otherwise socially and economically deprived people.

With the aforesaid as a necessary caveat, and notwithstanding the errors of the so-called "prosperity gospel," simply dismissing the underlying framework that conceives of salvation as encompassing the whole of life including the spiritual, physical, *and* material well-being of the believer is problematic. Facile dismissal fails to take seriously the full spectrum of the beliefs and the practices of the traditions covered in this study, but more importantly, neglects the witness of Scripture, in which these churches ground their theology and practice. As mentioned above, much of Jesus's ministry involved holistic restoration through exorcism and physical healing, actions that are frequently linked together based on a sense of humans as whole, integrated persons. The story of the healing of the paralytic man in Mark 2:1–12 (cf. Matt 9:1–8, Luke 5:17–26) wherein Jesus makes explicit the connection between spiritual and physical wholeness, reinforces this idea. This connection is seen in other places as well Paul ties sickness and premature death to unworthy partaking of the Lord's Supper (1 Cor 11:27–30), while James links confession of sin to bodily healing (Jas 5:14–16). Canon 22 of the Fourth Lateran Council calls for spiritual intervention to precede medical treatments, "so that after spiritual health has been restored to them, the application of bodily medicine may be of greater benefit, for the *cause* being removed the effect will pass away,"[40] the cause indicated here being sin. The connection made by Black Pentecostal and spiritual people between the physical and spiritual well-being of a person, indeed the essential reliance of the former upon the latter, is clearly not an esoteric concept with no basis in Scripture or precedent in Christian theology. Indeed, is appears that it is the latter—salvation conceived solely in "spiritual" terms—that is more unusual.

The Abiding Relationship: Salvation and Worship as Vital Participation

Black American Christian traditions have frequently been evaluated and interpreted primarily in relationship to the sociocultural realities of the surrounding society.[41] Consequently, the implications of their primal sen-

39. Baer, *Black Spiritual Movement*, 168.
40. Leclercq, "Fourth Lateran Council (1215)," canon 22; emphasis added.
41. Baer and Singer's schematization of Black Pentecostals as conversionist, and of

sibilities on Christian theology as a whole have frequently been obscured. Specifically, the primal assertion that all of reality is one, without a firm demarcation between the material and immaterial, physical and nonphysical reality, challenges, in a profound way, much of the thinking that underlies post-Enlightenment Euro-Western epistemology. Arguably, much of Euro-Western theology is premised on a transcendent realm separate and apart from the earthly realm and assumes a more or less unbridgeable gap between the earthly realms of the humanity and the heavenly realms of divinity. To assert, as Bediako states, and as Black Pentecostals and spiritual people implicitly affirm, that "God and man [are] in an abiding relationship which is the divine destiny of humankind"[42] is to call into question theologies premised upon belief in a foundational severance of that relationship. The key word here is "abiding," for it suggests continuity rather than discontinuity of relationship. Paul, in bearing witness of Christ among the Athenians, draws on the prior, primal wisdom of the Greek philosopher Epimenides. In doing so, he implicitly acknowledges the covenant God of his ancestors as the single source of that insight—a not insignificant acknowledgement given the strict severity of Judaic monotheism—but not only that. He acknowledges also that circumcised Jew and unbelieving gentile, are both in an *abiding* relationship with the God and Father of our Lord Jesus Christ. God is near to them both, and both might "grope for him and find him" (v. 27). The relationship, though impaired, is not entirely severed and it is on the basis of that existing relationship that Paul calls for his Athenian audience to repent. "We are so close to the spirit world," says Rev. Anderson, echoing Paul. Both he and Paul draw from the same deep wells of the primal imagination though with slightly different emphases.

---

spiritual groups as thaumaturgical/manipulationist sects is exemplary in this regard. Baer and Singer's typology is now nearly forty years old, but what it holds in common with other, more recent, interpretations is the prioritization of the sociocultural location of Black peoples in interpretations of their religious experience instead of spiritual and theological approaches (Baer and Singer, "Typology of Black Sectarianism," 5–10). For example, Frederick Ware criticizes Church of God in Christ Bishop George McKinney's employment of demonology as a means to identify and address social issues facing the Black community by suggesting that McKinney's approach amounts to "a form of morality grounded in middle class values and centered on improving and normalizing family relationships," an approach Ware holds to be "an impediment to the achievement of social justice" ("Compatibility/Incompatibility of Pentecostal Premillennialism," 199). This approach prioritizes the sociocultural, while consigning the spiritual/theological to an apologetic that either does, or does not support what Ware takes to be more important.

42. K. Bediako, *Christianity in Africa*, 101.

Proximity to the spirit realm, and reality of an abiding relationship mean that participation ranks much higher than belief—cognitive assent to certain doctrines—as an indicator of salvation. One's participation in the Spirit, along with attendant manifestations in the physical realm, are the means by which salvific status is ascertained. The biblical model for this is found in Acts 10, where Cornelius's salvific status was made evident to Peter and his companion not because of anything Cornelius confessed concerning Jesus—after explaining the circumstances of his invitation to Peter, he is not heard from again (vv. 30–33)—but because of the manifestation of the Spirit's presence (v. 46). The physical manifestation of the Spirit's presence presented sufficient evidence of God's acceptance of Cornelius's faith commitment to Christ—his verbal communication of that faith was far less significant, and based on the scriptural evidence, was not inquired about. Salvation is not construed to be *primarily* about adherence to a certain creed, though belief in and adherence to creed is important, but about vital participation in Jesus Christ through the Holy Spirit, leading to transformation.

The creation of sacred time and space wherein manifestation and participation in and with the Spirit can occur is therefore not ancillary but is a central focus of Black American Christian spirituality. Where the evangelical Protestant would assert that "preaching lies at the heart of worship" because it "present[s] Jesus Christ as Saviour and Lord"[43] leading to a response of worship, Black Pentecostals might reverse the order. It is out of the sacred space of worship that preaching is expected to occur; it is the manifestation of the Spirit's presence in worship that leads to a response of preaching. The creation of sacred space and time is, therefore, the integrating center of worship and of the Christian life. Kwame Bediako attests to the same expectation in worship settings among African Christians, noting that "in the interplay between spontaneity and order, it is spontaneity, by and large, that is prior, more important and becomes the renewer of order."[44] This is a spontaneity born of the leadership of the Holy Spirit in worship, who may order or reorder the worship as he wishes. Bediako wrote this from within the context of a "church that uses set liturgies"[45]—in his case, the Presbyterian Church of Ghana—so his identification of this phenomenon is an indication of the persistence of a primal perspective

---

43. Clowney, *Church*, 130.
44. K. Bediako, "Worship as Vital Participation," 6.
45. K. Bediako, "Worship as Vital Participation," 7.

shared by Black American and African Christians and cannot be attributed to sectarian attitudes.

Power Lord

The final manifestation of the cosmos as a single, spiritual system that I wish to identify here, is a focus on spiritual power as integral to salvation. Given the history of Black American *dis*-empowerment under Eurocentric White supremacy, some may be tempted to consider this concern with power as a counter-hegemonic means of resorting to "spiritual" forms of power in the absence of sociocultural and political power. This interpretation is explicit in anthropological approaches like Hans Baer and Merrill Singer's typology of Black religion, and Baer's assessment of women's empowerment within the Black spiritual movement.[46] It is implicit in much of the methodology of Black American theology which Frederick Ware notes "assigns priority to addressing the suffering of black people, highly values and links freedom with equality and justice, and emphasizes the role of the church in the transformation of society."[47] However, the roots of concern for power lie deeper, in the primal resources drawn from African antecedents. It arises from the primal apprehension of the cosmos as a realm of diffuse and differentiated power, with God as both the highest/supreme power and the source of all other power(s). Power is the currency of the cosmos, operative in both the material and immaterial realms, and success in either realm relies upon access to it. It was this apprehension that linked conjure with Christianity, and it is this recognition that continues to place empowerment at the forefront of the Christian life for Black Pentecostal and spiritual people. Kwame Bediako speaks of "being in touch with the source and channels of power in the universe"[48] as a touchstone of theological expression of the primal imagination. To extend this theological insight further, one must understand that the power focus of Black Pentecostalism is an affirmation that Christianity is not, at base, an ethical system, though there are moral and ethical implications for the individual as well as for the society. These, however, are not primary. Christianity is rather a way of living supernaturally by the power of the Holy Spirit. Consequently, the

---

46. Baer and Singer, "Typology of Black Sectarianism"; Baer, "Limited Empowerment of Women."
47. Ware, "Methodologies," 129.
48. K. Bediako, *Christianity in Africa*, 106.

key responsibility of the Christian is to acquire and maintain the "inward conditions of attitude and receptivity [to the Spirit]" so that "heightened insight, self-control, strength, poise, and revolutionary patience" might result.[49] In Bishop Allen' words the believer must "allow the Holy Spirit to perfect [him] in areas of [his] imperfection . . . to allow the Spirit of God to help them to overcome issues and problems."[50] It is a dynamic spirituality, blown by the wind of the Spirit, whose fixed compass is the word of God.

Pointers towards Future Inquiry

In identifying some areas of theological reflection that have emerged from my examination of the New Testament and the Black Pentecostal and spiritual churches through the lens of the primal, I have already begun to point towards areas in need of deeper research and reflection. Though there are many possible areas of inquiry, I identify two that I believe will expand and deepen both our understanding of Black religion and our understanding and engagement with Christian faith.

First, the range of expressive forms within Black American Christianity, present the opportunity for a broader and deeper engagement with these practices as avenues of theological expression. Marcus Harvey's extensive use of Zora Neale Hurston's work *Their Eyes Were Watching God* to illumine heretofore obscured aspects of Black religion is one example of how this engagement is taking place utilizing Black literature.[51] My own use of Judylyn Ryan's positive vision of Black spirituality is in a similar vein. These are developments that broaden the "source texts" of theology, but they remain bound by written texts. Inasmuch as Black theology takes Black religion as its subject matter and has usefully employed oral and written black sources in the formation of that theology,[52] this needs to be extended to other sources such as dance, music, art, architecture, and other artistic forms. The rationalist, text-centered, "scientific" systematizing approach to theology that has dominated the Euro-Western academy since the Enlightenment has its place, but its limitation in the matter of interpreting what is essentially a nonrational phenomenon—religion—must be admitted. As Camille Paglia presciently observes, "Rationalists have their place, but their limited

---

49. Clemmons, *Bishop C. H. Mason*, locs. 1321–23.
50. Interview with Bishop Joseph Allen, Jan. 14, 2016.
51. Harvey, "Life Is War," 55.
52. Ware, "Methodologies," 129.

assumptions and methods must be kept out of the arts. Interpretation of poem, dream, or person requires intuition and divination, not science."[53] I contend that this extends to religious ritual as well, which may be considered a form of art, and perhaps even the origin of art. Testimony, shouting, dance, and the ritual aesthetics of worship in the St Martins Spiritualist Church, in the All Saints Holiness Church, and in other such churches are all forms that embody theological meaning—communication to and by the participants about the nature of God and God's relationship with creation, through Jesus Christ mediated through the Holy Spirit. What is true of these churches is true more broadly and serious theological inquiry must not exclude engagement with these forms.

Second, a more robust interaction with African sources, theologies, and concepts is needed to illuminate the Black American religious experience more fully and to enrich Christian theology. The debate over the presence or absence of African retentions in the Black American cultural consciousness seems to me to be beside the point. The quest for specific evidence of so-called African retentions among Black Americans has been muted by the realization of the continuity of common ritual systems which evince a primal orientation. For example, I have, drawn upon the religious experience of Africans like William Wadé Harris and Simon Kimbangu, as well as from an array of African Christian theology as a means of shedding greater light on Black American Christianity. Much more can be done that would prove to be mutually enriching. Harvey's use of Yorùbá and Akan, religious grammars of knowledge to illuminate aspects of Black religious experience.[54] Scandrett-Leatherman likewise draws upon the ancient African healing institution known as *ngoma*, which he views as having "provided the ritual foundation for both Africans and Africans in the diaspora,"[55] as a route to deeper understanding of the ritual aesthetics of the Church of God in Christ, the largest Black Pentecostal denomination. Though separated by distance and hampered by the exigencies of the slavery system, the "abiding influence of [the] ancient African tradition [Ngoma] on American soil"[56] remains and continues to shape Black American religious experience. Sadly, Christian theology still suffers from aversion to engagement with "non-Christian," that is, primal, religious thought.

53. Paglia, *Sexual Personae*, 222.
54. Harvey, "Life Is War," 21.
55. Scandrett-Leatherman, "Can't Nobody Do Me," 75.
56. Scandrett-Leatherman, "Can't Nobody Do Me," 83.

Recognition of the abiding links arising from the primal substrata that underlies much of both African and Black American religious understanding, and the New Testament itself, provides a great opportunity to remedy the divide between African Christian theology and Black American religious scholarship typified by John Mbiti's early rebuff of the efforts of Black theology to find common ground with African Christian theology.[57] The primal resources of African thought provide a way for Black American religious scholarship to escape its teleological limitations, which are in great measure based on its captivity to "white racism and the culture of survival."[58] African anthropocentricity and the primal recognition that "God is abidingly involved in a relationship with man, and for man,"[59] decenters race and race-based oppression as the core of the religious experience of Black people, thus opening the door for a more robust and comprehensive theological reflection.

Concluding Reflections

The serial expansion of Christianity has again and again brought the gospel of Jesus Christ into contact with peoples whose primal imagination has enabled them to apprehend the gospel on their own terms, and in the process, raising and answering new theological questions, finding new ways of expressing their experience of God revealed in Jesus Christ, and ultimately reinterpreting Christianity itself such that any one expression of the faith might appear entirely alien to Christians of another era.[60] The indigenization of Christian faith in diverse ethno-cultural contexts, an outgrowth of the gospel principle that "God accepts us as we are, on the ground of Christ's work alone, not on the ground of what we have become or are trying to become," has meant that Christianity has been "at home" among diverse peoples of various ethnicities and cultures without losing its essence.[61] Yet this same principle carries with it the risk that the peoples among whom Christianity found a home would come to regard it as something like a personal possession, with a right to set for themselves and for all others the normative parameters of faith. It is into this error that Euro-Western

---

57. Mbiti, "American Black Theology."
58. V. Anderson, *Beyond Ontological Blackness*, 87.
59. K. Bediako, *Christianity in Africa*, 101.
60. Walls, *Missionary Movement*, 3–15.
61. Walls, *Missionary Movement*, 7.

"Christian" civilization fell, assuming that since they belonged to Christ, Christ—and the Bible through which he was revealed—belonged to them. So it is that even at the beginning decades of the twenty-first century, when there is no longer any serious doubt about the shift in the center of gravity of Christianity to the non-Western world, for many, Christianity *is* White, Western religion. It is defined and delimited by Euro-Western cultural norms, divorced from and superior to the primal, and, due to the centuries-long oppression of Black peoples by "Christian" Euro-Western civilization, viewed by some to be complicit in that oppression and ultimately inimical to the full flourishing of Black humanity. This presents both a theological and missiological problem that the resources of Black theology have been unable to satisfactorily resolve. This belief is the culmination of a long process of cultural development that is inextricably tied to the suppression of the primal imagination in Euro-Western civilization and a concomitant denial of the primal features of Christianity itself.

Historical and Cultural Survey

In the first part of this book, I traced the early origins of the idea of Christianity as White Euro-Western "civilized" religion from its roots in the alignment of Christian faith with Greco-Roman civilization, through the establishment of Christendom which solidified Christianity as *the* faith of European peoples, with the emergence of the idea of Christian Europe sharpened by the Crusades. These trends eventuated in the establishment of the United States as the exemplary White Christian civilization. I also trace the gradual evolution of beliefs about Black people as the exotic, mysterious and erotic "other"; beliefs that were reinforced by negative cultural and religious association of the color black with the evil and the erotic, and bolstered by dubious travel accounts. These beliefs primed Europeans in the early modern era to view Black people in a negative light, and to interpret both them and their religious practices as inherently deficient. These perceptions were amplified through the slave trade and justified by the curse of Ham myth, even as the labor of enslaved African peoples increased the wealth and power of Europe and her North American offshoot, the United States. Quasi-scientific ideas about physiological differences increasingly congealed into racial theories that assigned Black people to the lowest rungs of human existence, while Whites were positioned at the top. A multidimensional Euro-Western conceptual framework slowly emerged that helped Europeans make sense of their world and understand their place in it. In all its dimensions, however, Euro-Western "Christian" civilization, increasingly defined not only in geographic, but also in racial terms, was believed to represent the apex of human development. Religious scholarship in general and Christianity in particular were shaped to fit into this framework and co-opted to bolster its claims.

As Euro-Western civilization distanced itself from its own primal heritage, the Euro-Western academy increasingly looked to scientific rationalism to order the cosmos. To retain its relevance, Christian theology had to contend with the increasing pressures of Enlightenment rationalism, with some opting for Deism as the appropriate response. Others, more orthodox, applied rational principles to Christian faith. The Bible was subjected to rigorous scientific analysis, giving birth to the historical critical method, while Christian scholars, in an effort to make sense of a new world of religious diversity, applied the same hierarchical schemes to religious development as had been applied to race. All the while, the primal elements of Euro-Western culture were suppressed, though not altogether eliminated. In an ironic twist, Euro-Western interpretation of the Bible became a tool for the suppression and delegitimization of the very primal setting from which it is derived, "an instrument of domination" wielded in the conquest and colonization of indigenous peoples,[62] including Africans transported to the Americas as slave labor. That the biblical authors were people operating from within a primal worldview, no less in the New Testament than in the Old, was downplayed. The troubling primal features of the Old Testament were dismissed as vestiges of a primitive era, now surpassed by the higher, ethical religion of the New Testament. The primal features of the New Testament—miracles, prophecy, supernatural manifestations of spiritual power, healings, and the like—were either demythologized, safely locked away in the confinement of the apostolic era, explained away as metaphor or ignored altogether. There was now no longer room in high Euro-Western thought for the messy irruptions of the supernatural into everyday life. By the turn of the twentieth century, Christianity was understood to not only be coterminous with White, Euro-Western culture and civilization—the pinnacle of human cultural, religious, and racial development with the United States as its exemplar—but also a reasoned and rational faith in which the primal had no place.

62. Tamez, "Bible and Five Hundred Years," 18.

Finally, attention is turned to the New Testament itself as the foundational text of Christian faith. With Turner's six-feature analysis as a guide, the study explores how the text of the New Testament is grounded in the primal imagination even in the process of canonization and implicitly in the Christian doctrine of inspiration. From there, selected passages of New Testament Scripture are assessed with the aim of bringing to light the primal assumptions that underlie them. The primal is especially apparent in the dynamism ascribed to the spiritual realm as it interpenetrates the material realms of existence through dreams, and magic. The study also attends to the beings that animate the spirit realm, with particular attention given to the ambiguous position of the dead vis-à-vis certain narratives. An exploration of exorcism, healing and spiritual warfare concludes the section on the New Testament.

The Primal Made Manifest

I then move from the external lens of historical and cultural development to listen for the voice of the primal imagination from within Black American Christianity. I trace the historical development of Black American Christianity, with particular attention given to the Pentecostal and spiritual church traditions, what I term the *pneumatic sacramentalist tradition*. The primal conjure tradition and its interplay with mainstream Christian belief and practice and the way that interplay uniquely shaped Black American Christianity is shown. Using a chronological history, the study describes how enslaved Blacks came to gradually embrace Christian faith, yet not altogether on the terms and in the ways that according with Euro-Western Christian sensibilities. This is followed by a description of the emergence of Pentecostalism, with a focus on William Seymour and the Azusa Street Revival, in which the primal imagination played a key role. The parallel emergence of the spiritual movement, with its roots planted firmly in the primal soil of the conjure tradition is also traced.

In this part of the book I highlight two churches, the first a Pentecostal church with origins in the spiritual movement. The manifestation of the primal imagination within the belief system and practices of the church are identified from the history, physical features, and descriptions of ritual practices. Particular attention is drawn to three key areas of this manifestation—sacred times and holy places, the mediation of power, and holistic salvation—with the conclusion that the primal imagination in the All

Saints Holiness Church displays itself most in a focus on a world of spirit power and the abundant life.

A similar approach is taken with the second church, St Martins Spiritualist Church, though a less familiar and consequently more easily questionable tradition (from the perspective of mainstream Christianity) necessitated lengthier descriptions of worship services and more attention to easily missed indications of the church's essential orthodox beliefs. The primal core of SMSC is most clearly observed in its multifaceted identity—Christian and spiritualist—held together in tension without any sense that one take precedence over or negates the other. This the church holds in common with African parallels such as Wade Harris, who have been recognized as evincing a fundamentally Christian, yet thoroughly primal faith.

Throughout this study, the fundamental unease with which the primal imagination has been regarded emerges as a clear feature of Euro-Western Christianity in its post-Enlightenment, Protestant expression. What is also clear is the extent to which color consciousness, transmuted into race consciousness, was married to that unease, with Black people and Black religion together representing the antithesis of all that Christianity was supposed to be—Black instead of White, ritualistic rather than refined, seething with primal energies, and ever open to irruptions from the numinous realm, instead of constrained within the bounds of Euro-Western cultural norms. Nevertheless, the primal persists, and it was the recognition and apprehension by enslaved Blacks of the primal features of the gospel that enabled them to welcome Christ as their own and on their own terms and to find in Christianity an affirmation of their own primal imagination.

The pneumatic sacramentalist strand of Black American Christianity resisted the siren call of assimilation to Euro-Western norms and by their persistence, rejected Euro-Western value setting for the Christian faith, insisting that they were no less Christian for embracing and expressing their faith in a manner consistent with the primal imagination. In so doing, they presaged the shift in the center of gravity to the non-Western world by demonstrating the validity and vibrancy of an essential non-Western expression of faith within the context of a racially hostile and oppressive environment. The churches covered in this study are exemplary of other churches, many of which have closed their doors, or declined into irrelevance, but who kept the flame of primal Africa alight, in the process giving lie to the pretension of Euro-Western ownership of Christianity. As I began with Kwame Bediako's assessment of Tatian, who rejected the presumptive superiority of Greco-Roman culture, and "[bade] farewell to the arrogance of Romans and the idle talk of Athenians, and all their ill-connected opinions [and] embraced [the] barbaric philosophy,"[63] so I end with him. Just as "Tatian understood very well that the Christian faith was in direct historical continuity with a 'Barbarian' tradition,"[64] so too I, and others of the pneumatic sacramentalist strands of Black American Christianity, know that Christianity is a faith thoroughly informed and sustained by the resources of the primal imagination, and that Black American expressions of that faith are no less authentically Christian for being primal.

---

63. Tatian, "Address to the Greeks," locs. 23968–69.
64. K. Bediako, *Theology and Identity*, 67.

Bibliography

Aaron, David H. "Early Rabbinic Exegesis on Noah's Son Ham and the So-Called 'Hamitic Myth.'" *Journal of the American Academy of Religion* 63 (1995) 721–59. http://www.academicroom.com/article/early-rabbinic-exegesis-noahs-son-ham-and-so-called-hamitic-myth.

Achtemeier, Paul, et al. *Introducing the New Testament: Its Literature and Theology.* Grand Rapids: Eerdmans, 2001.

Adeyemo, Tokunboh, ed. *Africa Bible Commentary.* Nairobi: WordAlive, 2006.

———. "Dreams." In *Africa Bible Commentary,* edited by Tokunboh Adeyemo, 993. Nairobi: WordAlive, 2006.

Alexander, Estrelda Y., and Amos Yong. "Introduction: Black Tongues of Fire: Afro-Pentecostalisms Shifting Strategies and Changing Discourses." In *Afro-Pentecostalism: Black Pentecostal and Charismatic Christianity in History and Culture,* edited by Amos Yong and Estrelda Y. Alexander, 1–19. Religion, Race, and Ethnicity. New York: New York University Press, 2011. Kindle.

Allmen, Daniel von "The Birth of Theology: Contextualization as the dynamic element in the formation of the New Testament." *International Review of Mission* 64 (1975) 37–52.

Anderson, Allan. "The Dubious Legacy of Charles Parham: Racism and Cultural Insensitivities among Pentecostals." *Pneuma* 27 (2005) 51–64.

Anderson, Douglas W. "The Origin and Purpose of Matthew 27:51b–53." PhD diss., University of Otago, 2013. http://hdl.handle.net/10523/4962.

Anderson, Victor. *Beyond Ontological Blackness: An Essay on African American Religious and Cultural Criticism.* New York: Continuum, 1995.

Anonymous. "On Charles White's *Account of the Regular Gradation in Man*." In *Race: The Origins of an Idea, 1760–1850,* edited by Hannah Franziska Augstein, 51–55. Key Issues Series. Bristol: Thoemmes, 1996.

Anyabwile, Thabiti M. *The Decline of African American Theology: From Biblical Faith to Cultural Captivity.* Downers Grove, IL: IVP Academic, 2007.

Asamoah-Gyadu, J. Kwabena. *African Charismatics: Current Developments within Independent Indigenous Pentecostalism in Ghana.* Studies in Religion in Africa 25. Leiden: Brill, 2005.

———. "Drinking from Our Own Wells: The Primal Imagination and Christian Religious Innovation in Contemporary Africa." *JACT* 11 (2008) 34–42.

Athanasius. *Life of Antony.* In $NPNF^2$, edited by Philip Schaff, 4:530430–31337. Edinburgh: T&T Clark, 1852. Kindle.

BIBLIOGRAPHY

Augstein, Hannah Franziska, ed. *Race: The Origins of an Idea, 1760–1850*. Key Issues Series. Bristol: Thoemmes, 1996.

Augustine. "A Treatise Concerning the Correction of the Donatists." In *NPNF*[2], edited by Philip Schaff, 4:275971–6607. Edinburgh: T&T Clark, 1892. Kindle.

Baer, Hans A. "An Anthropological View of Black Spiritual Churches in Nashville, Tennessee." *Central Issues in Anthropology* 2 (1980) 53–63.

———. "Black Spiritual Churches: A Neglected Socio-Religious Institution." *Phylon* 42 (1981) 207–23. http://www.jstor.org/stable/274918.

———. *The Black Spiritual Movement: A Religious Response to Racism*. Knoxville: University of Tennessee Press, 1984.

———. "The Limited Empowerment of Women in Black Spiritual Churches: An Alternative Vehicle to Religious Leadership." *Sociology of Religion* 54 (1993) 65–82. http://www.jstor.org/stable/3711842.

———. "The Metropolitan Spiritual Churches of Christ: The Socio-Religious Evolution of the Largest of the Black Spiritual Associations." *Review of Religious Research* 30 (1988) 140–50. http://www.jstor.org/stable/3511351.

Baer, Hans A., and Merrill Singer. *African American Religion: Varieties of Protest and Accommodation*. 2nd ed. Knoxville: University of Tennessee Press, 2002.

———. "Toward a Typology of Black Sectarianism as a Response to Racial Stratification." *Anthropological Quarterly* 54 (1981) 1–14. http://www.jstor.org/stable/3317481.

Bailey, Kenneth. *Jesus through Middle Eastern Eyes: Cultural Studies in the Gospels*. Downers Grove, IL: InterVarsity, 2008.

Bailey, Michael D. "The Disenchantment of Magic: Spells, Charms, and Superstition in Early European Witchcraft Literature." *American Historical Review* 111 (2006) 383–404. http://www.jstor.org/stable/10.1086/ahr.111.2.383.

Bailey, Ronald. "The Slave(ry) Trade and the Development of Capitalism in the United States: The Textile Industry in New England." *Social Science History* 14 (1990) 373–414. http://www.jstor.org/stable/1171357.

Bainton, Roland. *From the Birth of Christ to the Reformation*. Vol. 1 of *Christendom: A Short History of Christianity and Its Impact on Western Civilisation*. New York: Harper & Row, 1964.

Barrett, C. K. *The New Testament Background: Selected Documents*. London: SPCK, 1987.

Baylis, Philippa. *An Introduction to Primal Religions*. Edinburgh: Traditional Cosmology Society, 1988.

Bediako, Gillian M. "Changing the Centre of Gravity: Reflections on Christian Mission from the Vantage Point of Contemporary Africa." *Rethinking Mission* 26 (2004) 17–23.

———. "Editorial: Thoughts on the Background to the Project." *JACT* 11 (2008) 1–4.

———. "Old Testament Religion as Primal Substructure of Christianity: Questions and Issues." *JACT* 12 (2009) 3–7.

———. "Primal Religion and Christian Faith: Antagonists or Soul-Mates?" *JACT* 3 (2000) 12–16.

———. *Primal Religion and the Bible: William Robertson Smith and His Heritage*. Sheffield: Sheffield Academic, 1997.

Bediako, Kwame. "Christian Faith and African Culture—An Exposition of the Epistle to the Hebrews." *JACT* 13 (2010) 45–57.

———. *Christianity in Africa: The Renewal of a Non-Western Religion*. Studies in World Christianity. Akropong-Akuapem, Ghana: Regnum, 2014.

———. "Gospel and Culture: Some Insights from the Experience of the Early Church." *JACT* 2 (1999) 8–17.

———. *Jesus and the Gospel in Africa: History and Experience*. Theology in Africa. Maryknoll, NY: Orbis, 2004.

———. "Scripture as the Hermeneutic of Culture and Tradition." *JACT* 4 (2001) 2–11.

———. *Theology and Identity: The Impact of Culture upon Christian Thought in the Second Century and in Modern Africa*. Regnum Studies in Mission. Oxford: Regnum, 1992.

———. "Toward a New Theodicy: Africa's Suffering in Redemptive Perspective." *JACT* 5 (2002) 47–52.

———. "Understanding African Theology in the 20th Century." *Themelios* 20 (1994) 14–20.

———. "Understanding the Unity of the Church." Lecture at Zondervan, Grand Rapids, May 7, 2008.

———. "'Why Has the Summer Ended and We Are Not Saved?': Encountering the Real Challenge of Christian Engagement in Primal Contexts." *JACT* 11 (2008) 5–8.

———. "Worship as Vital Participation: Some Personal Reflections on Ministry in the African Church." *JACT* 8 (2005) 3–7.

Betz, Hans Dieter, ed. *The Greek Magical Papyri in Translation, including the Demotic Spells*. Chicago: University of Chicago Press, 1986.

Blackburn, Robin. "The Old World Background to European Colonial Slavery." *William and Mary Quarterly* 54 (1997) 65–102. http://www.jstor.org/stable/2953313.

Bloesch, Donald G. *Holy Scripture: Revelation, Inspiration & Interpretation*. Downers Grove, IL: InterVarsity, 1994.

Bolt, Peter G. "Jesus, the Daimons and the Dead." In *The Unseen World: Christian Reflections on Angels, Demons and the Heavenly Realm*, edited by Anthony N. S. Lane, 75–102. Tyndale House Studies 6. Grand Rapids: Baker, 1996.

Bosch, David J. *Transforming Mission: Paradigm Shifts in the Theology of Mission*. American Society of Missiology Series. Maryknoll, NY: Orbis, 1991.

Boyce, Mary. *The Early Period*. Vol. 1 of *A History of Zoroastrianism*. Leiden: Brill, 1996.

Brauch, Manfred T. *Hard Sayings of Paul*. Downers Grove, IL: InterVarsity, 1989.

Braude, Benjamin. "The Sons of Noah and the Construction of Ethnic and Geographical Identities in the Medieval and Early Modern Periods." *William and Mary Quarterly* 54 (1997) 103–42. http://www.jstor.org/stable/2953314.

Brettler, Marc. "Cyclical and Teleological Time in the Hebrew Bible." In *Time and Temporality in the Ancient World*, edited by Ralph M. Rosen, 111–28. Philadelphia: University of Pennsylvania Museum of Archaeology and Anthropology, 2004.

Brown, William Wells. "Black Religion in the Post-Reconstruction South." In *Afro-American Religious History: A Documentary Witness*, edited by Milton C. Sernett, 239–43. C. Eric Lincoln Series on the Black Experience. Durham: Duke University Press, 1985.

Bruce, F. F. "Myth & History." In *History, Criticism & Faith: Four Exploratory Studies*, edited by Colin Brown, 79–100. Leicester: Inter-Varsity, 1976.

Buell, Denise Kimber. *Why This New Race? Ethnic Reasoning in Early Christianity*. New York: Columbia University Press, 2005.

Carlston, Charles E. "Transfiguration and Resurrection." *JBL* 30 (1961) 233–40. http://www.jstor.org/stable/3264779.

Carter, J. Kameron. *Race: A Theological Account*. Oxford: Oxford University Press, 2008. Kindle.

Chireau, Yvonne P. *Black Magic: Religion and the African American Conjuring Tradition*. Berkeley: University of California Press, 2003.

Church of God in Christ. "What We Believe." Church of God in Christ, n.d. https://www.cogic.org/about-us/what-we-believe/.

Clemmons, Ithiel C. *Bishop C. H. Mason and the Roots of the Church of God in Christ*. N.p.: Pneuma Life, 1996. Kindle.

Clowney, Edmund P. *The Church*. Contours of Christian Theology. Downers Grove, IL: InterVarsity, 1995.

Cone, James H. *Black Theology and Black Power*. Maryknoll, NY: Orbis, 1989.

Conniff, Michael L., and Thomas J. Davis. *Africans in the Americas: A History of the Black Diaspora*. New York: St Martins, 1994.

Copeland, M. Shawn. "African American Religious Experience." In *The Oxford Handbook of African American Theology*, edited by Katie G. Cannon and Anthony B. Pinn, 40–67. Oxford Handbooks. New York: Oxford University Press, 2014.

Cornelius, Janet Duitsman. *Slave Missions and the Black Church in the Antebellum South*. Columbia: University of South Carolina, 1999.

Cotter, Anthony C. "*Non Gustabunt Mortem*." *CBQ* 6 (1944) 444–55. http://www.jstor.org/stable/43723786.

Cox, Harvey. *Fire from Heaven: The Rise of Pentecostal Spirituality and the Reshaping of Religion in the 21st Century*. Cambridge, MA: Da Capo, 2009. Kindle.

Cragg, Gerald R. *The Church and the Age of Reason: 1648–1789*. London: Penguin, 1960.

Curtin, Philip D. *British Ideas and Action, 1780–1850*. Vol. 1 of *The Image of Africa*. Madison: University of Wisconsin Press, 1964.

Daniels, David D., III. "Navigating the Territory: Early Afro-Pentecostalism as a Movement within Black Civil Society." In *Afro-Pentecostalism: Black Pentecostal and Charismatic Christianity in History and Culture*, edited by Amos Yong and Estrelda Y. Alexander, 43–63. Religion, Race, and Ethnicity. New York: New York University Press, 2011. Kindle.

Datiri, Dachollom. "1 Corinthians." In *Africa Bible Commentary*, edited by Tokunboh Adeyemo, 1377–98. Nairobi: WordAlive, 2006.

DeSilva, David A. *Honor, Patronage, Kinship & Purity: Unlocking New Testament Culture*. Downers Grove, IL: IVP Academic, 2000.

Dickson, Kwesi. *African Theology*. London: Darton, Longman & Todd, 1984.

Digg, S. H. "Relation of Race to Thought Expression." *Journal of Philosophy, Psychology and Scientific Methods* 12 (1915) 346–58. http://www.jstor.org/stable/2013771.

Dulles, Avery. "Church, Ministry, and Sacraments in Catholic-Evangelical Dialogue." In *Catholics and Evangelicals: Do They Share a Common Future?*, edited by Thomas P. Rausch, 101–21. Downers Grove, IL: InterVarsity, 2000.

Dunbar-Ortiz, Roxanne. *An Indigenous Peoples' History of the United States*. Boston: Beacon, 2014.

Elkins, Stanley M. *Slavery: A Problem in American Institutional and Intellectual Life*. 3rd ed. Chicago: University of Chicago Press, 1976. Kindle.

Eltis, David. "Free and Coerced Transatlantic Migrations: Some Comparisons." *American Historical Review* 88 (1983) 251–80. http://www.jstor.org/stable/1865402.

Eve, Eric. *The Healer from Nazareth: Jesus' Miracles in Historical Context*. London: SPCK, 2009.

Gill, Sam. "Play and the Future of the Study of Religion . . . and the Academy." Sam Gill, July 2009. http://sam-gill.com/PDF/Play%20&%20Future.pdf.

Gilsdorf, Joy. *The Puritan Apocalypse: New England Eschatology in the Seventeenth Century*. New York: Garland, 1989.

Felder, Cain Hope, ed. *Stony the Road We Trod: African American Biblical Interpretation*. Minneapolis: Fortress, 1991.

Ferdinando, Keith. "Screwtape Revisited: Demonology Western, African, and Biblical." In *The Unseen World: Christian Reflections on Angels, Demons and the Heavenly Realm*, edited by Anthony N. S. Lane, 103–32. Tyndale House Studies 6. Grand Rapids: Baker, 1996.

Fletcher, Richard. *The Conversion of Europe: From Paganism to Christianity 371–1386 AD*. London: Fontana, 1997.

France, R. T. "The Authenticity of the Sayings of Jesus." In *History, Criticism & Faith: Four Exploratory Studies*, edited by Colin Brown, 101–43. Leicester: Inter-Varsity, 1976.

Friesen, J. Stanley. *Missionary Responses to Tribal Religions at Edinburgh, 1910*. New York: Lang, 1996.

Frey, Sylvia R., and Betty Wood. *Come Shouting to Zion: African American Protestantism in the American South and British Caribbean to 1830*. Chapel Hill: University of North Carolina Press, 1998.

Gibbon, Edward. *The Decline and Fall of the Roman Empire*. Edited by Hans-Friedrich Mueller. Modern Library Classics. New York: Modern Library, 2005.

Gijswijt-Hofstra, Marijke, et al. *Witchcraft and Magic: The Eighteenth and Nineteenth Centuries*. London: Athlone, 1999.

Gottlier, Alma. "Non-Western Approaches to Spiritual Development among Infants and Young Children: A Case Study From West Africa." In *The Handbook of Spiritual Development in Childhood and Adolescence*, edited by Eugene Roehlkepartain et al., 150–62. Thousand Oaks, CA: Sage, 2005.

Green, Joel B., et al. *Dictionary of Jesus and the Gospels*. IVP Bible Dictionary. Downers Grove, IL: InterVarsity, 1992.

Harrison, Ira. "The Storefront Church as a Revitalization Movement." In *The Black Church in America*, edited by Hart Nelsen et al., 240–50. New York: Basic, 1971.

Harvey, Marcus Louis. "'Life Is War': African Grammars of Knowing and the Interpretation of Black Religious Experience." PhD diss., Emory University, 2012. https://etd.library.emory.edu/concern/etds/sf26855ob?locale=en.

Hawthorne, Gerald F., et al., eds. *Dictionary of Paul and His Letters*. IVP Bible Dictionary. Downers Grove, IL: InterVarsity, 1993.

Hay, Denys. *Europe in the Fourteenth and Fifteenth Centuries*. 2nd ed. General History of Europe. Harlow: Longman, 1989.

Haynes, Stephen R. *Noah's Curse: The Biblical Justification for American Slavery*. Religion in America. New York: Oxford University Press, 2002.

Hays, J. Daniel. *From Every People and Nation: A Biblical Theology of Race*. New Studies in Biblical Theology 14. Downers Grove, IL: IVP Academic, 2003.

Henke, Frederick G. "The Gift of Tongues and Related Phenomena at the Present Day." *AmJT* 13 (1909) 193–206. http://www.jstor.org/stable/3155190.

Herodotus. *The Histories*. N.p. Wilder, 2014. Kindle.

Hesselgrave, David J. *Communicating Christ Cross-Culturally: An Introduction to Missionary Communication*. 2nd ed. Grand Rapids: Zondervan, 1991.

Heward-Mills, Dag. *How to Pray*. Accra: Parchment, 2013.

Hiebert, Paul G., et al. *Understanding Folk Religion: A Christian Response to Popular Beliefs and Practices*. Grand Rapids: Baker Academic, 1999.

Hollinger, David A. "The Accommodation of Protestant Christianity with the Enlightenment: An Old Drama Still Being Enacted." *Dædalus* 141 (2012) 1–13. http://history.berkeley.edu/sites/default/files/narrative-daedalus12.pdf.

Holsey, Lucius H. "The Colored Methodist Episcopal Church." In *Afro-American Religious History: A Documentary Witness*, edited by Milton C. Sernett, 234–38. C. Eric Lincoln Series on the Black Experience. Durham: Duke University Press, 1985.

Home, Henry. "Preliminary Discourse, Concerning the Origin of Men and of Languages." In *Race: The Origins of an Idea, 1760–1850*, edited by Hannah Franziska Augstein, 10–23. Key Issues Series. Bristol: Thoemmes, 1996.

Hood, Robert E. *Begrimed and Black: Christian Traditions on Blacks and Blackness*. Minneapolis: Fortress, 1994.

Horsman, Reginald. *Race and Manifest Destiny: The Origins of American Racial Anglo-Saxonism*. Cambridge, MA: Harvard University Press, 1981.

Hoyt, Thomas. "Interpreting Biblical Scholarship for the Black Church Tradition." In *Stony the Road We Trod: African American Biblical Interpretation*, edited by Cain Hope Felder, 17–39. Minneapolis: Fortress, 1991.

Hume, David. *Essays Moral, Political, Literary*. Edited by Eugene F. Miller. Rev. ed. Indianapolis: Liberty Fund 1987. http://oll.libertyfund.org/titles/704#lf0059_label_332.

Hurston, Zora Neale. "Hoodoo in America." *Journal of American Folklore* 44 (1931) 317–417. http://www.jstor.org/stable/535394.

———. *The Sanctified Church*. New York: Marlowe & Company, 1981.

Inikori, Joseph. "The Slave Trade and the Atlantic Economies, 1451–1870." In *Caribbean Slavery in the Atlantic World: A Student Reader*, edited by Verene Shepherd and Hilary McDonald Beckles, 290–308. Kingston: Randle, 2000.

Isaac, Benjamin. "Proto-Racism in Graeco-Roman Antiquity." *World Archaeology* 38 (2006) 32–47. http://www.jstor.org/stable/40023593.

Isaak, Paul John. "Luke." In *Africa Bible Commentary*, edited by Tokunboh Adeyemo, 1203–50. Nairobi: WordAlive, 2006.

Jacobs, Claude F., and Andrew J. Kaslow. *The Spiritual Churches of New Orleans: Origins, Beliefs, and Rituals from and African-American Religion*. Knoxville: University of Tennessee Press, 1991.

Jahoda, Gustav. *Images of Savages: Ancient Roots of Modern Prejudice in Western Culture*. Routledge: London, 1999.

Jefferson, Thomas. *The Jefferson Bible: The Life and Morals of Jesus of Nazareth*. Jefferson Bible, 1904. http://www.thejeffersonbible.com/.

Jennings, Willie James. *The Christian Imagination: Theology and the Origins of Race*. New Haven: Yale University Press, 2010. Kindle.

Jerome. "Homily 80 (VI) on Mark 9.1–7." In *The Homilies of Saint Jerome*, 2:159–68. Translated by Marie Liguori Ewald. Fathers of the Church 57. Washington, DC: Catholic University of America Press, 1966. http://www.jstor.org/stable/j.ctt2853tn.24.

Johnson, Aaron P. "The Blackness of Ethiopians: Classical Ethnography and Eusebius's Commentary on the Psalms." *HTR* 99 (2006) 165–86. http://www.jstor.org/stable/4125292.

Johnson, Sylvester. "The African American Christian Tradition." In *The Oxford Handbook of African American Theology*, edited by Katie G. Cannon and Anthony B. Pinn, 68–84. Oxford Handbooks. New York: Oxford University Press, 2014.

Jones, Jacqueline. *A Dreadful Deceit: The Myth of Race from the Colonial Era to Obama's America*. New York: Basic, 2013.

Joyce, Timothy. *Celtic Christianity: A Sacred Tradition, a Vision of Hope*. Maryknoll, NY: Orbis, 1998.

Kabasélé, François. "Christ as Ancestor and Elder Brother." In *Faces of Jesus in Africa*, edited by Robert Schreiter, 116–27. Maryknoll, NY: Orbis, 1991.

Kapolyo, Joe. "Matthew." In *Africa Bible Commentary*, edited by Tokunboh Adeyemo, 1105–70. Nairobi: WordAlive, 2006.

Keener, Craig S. *The Gospel of Matthew: A Socio-Rhetorical Commentary*. Grand Rapids: Eerdmans, 2009.

Keillor, Steven J. *This Rebellious House: American History & the Truth of Christianity*. Downers Grove, IL: InterVarsity, 1996.

Kellerman, James, trans. *Incomplete Commentary on Matthew (Opus imperfectum)*. Edited by Thomas C. Oden. 2 vols. Ancient Christian Texts. Downers Grove, IL: IVP Academic, 2010.

Kidd, Colin. *The Forging of Races: Race and Scripture in the Atlantic World, 1600–2000*. Cambridge: Cambridge University Press, 2006.

King, Roberta, et al. *Music in the Life of the African Church*. Waco: Baylor University Press, 2008.

Kovach, Margaret. *Indigenous Methodologies: Characteristics, Conversations, and Contexts*. Toronto: University of Toronto Press, 2009.

Kraft, Charles H. *Anthropology for Christian Witness*. Maryknoll, NY: Orbis, 1996.

———. *Christianity in Culture: A Study in Dynamic Biblical Theologizing in Cross-Cultural Perspective*. Maryknoll, NY: Orbis, 1979.

Kratz, Reinhard G. "Eyes and Spectacles: Wellhausen's Method of Higher Criticism." *JTS*, n.s., 60 (2009) 381–402. http://jts.oxfordjournals.org/.

Kuper, Adam. *The Invention of Primitive Society: Transformations of an Illusion*. New York: Routledge, 1988.

Landau, Brent. "The Sages and the Star-Child: An Introduction to the Revelation of the Magi, an Ancient Christian Apocryphon." PhD diss., Harvard Divinity School, 2008. https://www.academia.edu/207510/The_Sages_and_the_Star_Child_An_Introduction_to_the_Revelation_of_the_Magi_An_Ancient_Christian_Apocryphon.

Lane, Anthony N. S. *The Unseen World: Christian Reflections on Angels, Demons and the Heavenly Realm*. Tyndale House Studies 6. Grand Rapids: Baker, 1996.

Larkin, William J., Jr. "The Recovery of Luke-Acts as 'Grand Narrative' for the Church's Evangelistic and Edification Tasks in a Postmodern Age." *JETS* 43 (2000) 405–15. http://www.etsjets.org/files/JETS-PDFs/43/43-43/43-43-pp405-415_JETS.pdf.

Leclercq, H[enri]. 'Fourth Lateran Council (1215)." EWTN, 1996. From *Catholic Encyclopedia*, 1913. https://www.ewtn.com/catholicism/library/fourth-lateran-council-1215-10584.

Lee, Blewett. "The Conjurer." *Virginia Law Review* 7 (1921) 370–77. http://www.jstor.org/stable/1064358

———. "Spiritualism and Crime." *Columbia Law Review* 22 (1922) 439–49. http://www.jstor.org/stable/1112490.

Le Jau, Francis. "Slave Conversion on the Carolina Frontier." In *Afro-American Religious History: A Documentary Witness*, edited by Milton C. Sernett, 24–32. C. Eric Lincoln Series on the Black Experience. Durham: Duke University Press, 1985.

LeMarquand, Grant. "New Testament Exegesis in (Modern) Africa." In *The Bible in Africa: Transactions, Trajectories, and Trends*, edited by Gerald O. West and Musa W. Dube, 72–102. Leiden: Brill, 2000.

Lovejoy, Arthur O. *The Great Chain of Being: A Study in the History of an Idea*. Cambridge, MA: Harvard University Press, 1936.

Macquarrie, John. *Principles of Christian Theology*. London, SCM, 1966.

Maggay, Melba Padilla. "The Persistence of the Old Gods: Some Inter-Cultural Dimensions." *JACT* 11 (2008) 23–33.

Malan, S. C., trans. *The Book of Adam and Eve, Also Called The Conflict of Adam and Eve with Satan: A Book of the Early Eastern Church*. London: Norman and Sons, 1882. https://archive.org/details/bookofadamevealsoomalaiala.

Markus, R. A. *Christianity in the Roman World*. London: Thames and Hudson, 1974.

Marshall, P. J., and Glyndwr Williams. *The Great Map of Mankind: British Perceptions of the World in the Age of Enlightenment*. London: Dent & Sons, 1982.

Martin, Ralph P., and Peter H. Davids, eds. *Dictionary of the Later New Testament and Its Developments*. Downers Grove, IL: IVP Academic, 1997.

Martínez, María Elena. "The Black Blood of New Spain: Limpieza de Sangre, Racial Violence, and Gendered Power in Early Colonial Mexico." *William and Mary Quarterly*, 3rd ser., 61 (2004) 479–520. http://www.jstor.org/stable/3491806.

Martínez, Florentino García, and Eibert Tigchelaar. *The Dead Sea Scrolls Study Edition*. 2 vols. Leiden: Brill, 1997.

Matthews, Donald H. *Honoring the Ancestors: An African Cultural Interpretation of Black Religion and Literature*. Oxford: Oxford University Press, 1998.

Mbiti, John S. *African Religions and Philosophy*. Oxford: Heinemann, 1969.

———. "An African Views American Black Theology." In *Black Theology: A Documentary History*, edited by James H. Cone and Gayraud S. Wilmore, 1:477–82. Maryknoll, NY: Orbis, 1979.

"The Men and Brutes of South Africa." *North American Review* 68 (1849) 265–300. http://memory.loc.gov:8081/ammem/ndlpcoop/moahtml/title/nora_vols.html#V68.

Miller-McLemore, Bonnie J. "Embodied Knowing, Embodied Theology: What Happened to the Body?" *Pastoral Psychology* 62 (2013) 743–58.

Milne, Bruce. *Know the Truth: A Handbook of Christian Belief*. 2nd ed. Leicester: IVP Academic, 1998.

Mitchem, Stephanie. "Embodiment in African American Theology." In *The Oxford Handbook of African American Theology*, edited by Katie G. Cannon and Anthony B. Pinn, 308–18. Oxford Handbooks. New York: Oxford University Press, 2014.

Monrad, H. C. *A Description of the Guinea Coast and Its Inhabitants*. Translated by Selena Axelrod Winsnes. Vol. 2 of *Two Views from Christiansborg Castle*. Accra: Sub-Saharan, 2009.

Morrison, Toni. "Rootedness: The Ancestor as Foundation." In *What Moves at the Margin: Selected Nonfiction*, edited by Carolyn C. Denard, 56–64. Jackson: University Press of Mississippi, 2008.

Murphy, Joseph M. *Working the Spirit: Ceremonies of the African Diaspora*. Boston: Beacon, 1994.

Myers, William. "The Hermeneutical Dilemma of the African American Biblical Student." In *Stony the Road We Trod: African American Biblical Interpretation*, edited by Cain Hope Felder, 40–56. Minneapolis: Fortress, 1991.

Nartonis, David K. "The Rise of 19th-Century American Spiritualism, 1854–1873." *JSSR* 49 (2010) 361–73. http://www.jstor.org/stable/40664707.

Neyrey, Jerome H. "The Apologetic Use of the Transfiguration in 2 Peter 1:15–21." *CBQ* 42 (1980) 504–19. http://www.jstor.org/stable/43718838.

Nichols, O. Samuel. "African Christian Theology and the Ancestors Christology, Ecclesiology, Ethics and Their Implications beyond Africa." *JACT* 8 (2005) 27–33.

Niles, Lyndrey A. "Rhetorical Characteristics of Traditional Black Preaching." *Journal of Black Studies* 15 (1984) 41–52.

Nkansah-Obrempong, James. "Angels, Demons and Powers." In *Africa Bible Commentary*, edited by Tokunboh Adeyemo, 1454–55. Nairobi: WordAlive, 2006.

Nock, A. D. *Conversion: The Old and the New in Religion from Alexander to Augustine of Hippo*. Oxford: Oxford University Press, 1933.

Noll, Mark A. *The Rise of Evangelicalism: The Age of Edwards, Whitefield and the Wesleys*. History of Evangelicalism 1. Downers Grove, IL: IVP Academic, 2003.

Noll, Stephen F. *Angels of Light, Powers of Darkness: Thinking Biblically about Angels, Satan & Principalities*. Downers Grove, IL: InterVarsity, 1998.

O'Connell, James. "The Withdrawal of the High God in West African Religion: An Essay in Interpretation." *Man* 62 (1962) 67–69. http://www.jstor.org/stable/2796426.

Opoku, Kofi Asare. *West African Traditional Religion*. Accra: FEP, 1978.

Otto, Rudolph. *The Idea of the Holy*. Translated by John W. Harvey. London: Oxford University Press, 1950.

Packer, J. I. "Revelation and Inspiration." In *New Bible Commentary*, edited by Donald Guthrie et al., 12–18. 3rd ed. Leicester: Inter-Varsity, 1970.

Paglia, Camille. *Sexual Personae: Art and Decadence from Nefertiti to Emily Dickinson*. New Haven: Yale University Press, 1990. Kindle.

Paris, Peter J. *The Spirituality of African Peoples: The Search for a Common Moral Discourse*. Minneapolis: Fortress, 1995.

Patzia, Arthur G. *The Making of the New Testament: Origin, Collection, Test & Canon*. Downers Grove, IL: IVP Academic, 1995.

Pelikan, Jaroslav. *Christianity and Classical Culture: The Metamorphosis of Natural Theology in the Christian Encounter with Hellenism*. Gifford Lectures. New Haven: Yale University Press, 1993.

Pfeifer, Theresa H. "Deconstructing Cartesian Dualisms of Western Racialized Systems: A Study in the Colors Black and White." *Journal of Black Studies* 39 (2009) 528–47. http://www.jstor.org/stable/40282581.

Pfleiderer, Otto. "The National Traits of the Germans as Seen in Their Religion." *International Journal of Ethics* 3 (1892) 1–39. http://www.jstor.org/stable/2375465.

Pieris, Aloysius, SJ. *An Asian Theology of Liberation*. Maryknoll, NY: Orbis, 1988.

Pinn, Anthony B. *The Black Church in the Post-Civil Rights Era*. Maryknoll, NY: Orbis, 2002.

———. "Black Spiritual Churches." In *The African American Religious Experience in America*, 29–46. American Religious Experience. Westport, CT: Greenwood, 2006.

Placher, William C. *A History of Christian Theology: An Introduction*. Philadelphia: Westminster, 1983.

Quarshie, Benhardt Y. "Paul and the Primal Substructure of Christianity: Missiological Reflections on the Epistle to the Galatians." *JACT* 12 (2009) 8–14.

———. "The Significance of Biblical Studies for African Christian Theology." *JACT* 3 (2000) 17–26.

Raboteau, Albert J. *Slave Religion: The "Invisible Institution" in the Antebellum South*. New York: Oxford University Press, 1978.

Ratzinger, Joseph (Pope Benedict XVI). *From the Baptism in the Jordan to the Transfiguration*. Vol. 1 of *Jesus of Nazareth*. New York: Doubleday, 2007. Kindle.

———. *The Infancy Narratives*. Vol. 3 of *Jesus of Nazareth*. New York: Doubleday, 2012. Kindle.

Reed, Teresa L. *The Holy Profane: Religion in Black Popular Music*. Lexington: University Press of Kentucky, 2003.

———. "Shared Possessions: Black Pentecostals, Afro-Caribbeans, and Sacred Music." *Black Music Research Journal* 32 (2012) 5–25. http://www.jstor.org/stable/10.5406/blacmusiresej.32.1.0005.

Rietbergen, Peter. *Europe: A Cultural History*. London: Routledge, 1998.

Robeck, Cecil M., Jr. *The Azusa Street Mission & Revival: The Birth of the Global Pentecostal Movement*. Nashville: Thomas Nelson, 2006.

Rodney, Walter. "How Europe Became the Dominant Section of World-Wide Trade System." In *Caribbean Slavery in the Atlantic World: A Student Reader*, edited by Verene Shepherd and Hilary McDonald Beckles, 2–10. Kingston: Randle, 2000.

Rogers Memorial Baptist Church. "Church History." Rogers Memorial Baptist Church, n.d. http://rogersmemorialbc.org/churchhistory/.

Ryan, Judylyn S. *Spirituality as Ideology in Black Women's Film and Literature*. Charlottesville: University of Virginia Press, 2005.

Sanders, Cheryl. "Pentecostal Ethics and the Prosperity Gospel: Is there a Prophet in the House?" In *Afro-Pentecostalism: Black Pentecostal and Charismatic Christianity in History and Culture*, edited by Amos Yong and Estrelda Y. Alexander, 141–52. Religion, Race, and Ethnicity. New York: New York University Press, 2011. Kindle.

———. *Saints in Exile: The Holiness-Pentecostal Experience in African American Religion and Culture*. Religion in America. New York: Oxford University Press, 1996.

Sanneh, Lamin. *Whose Religion Is Christianity? The Gospel beyond the West*. Grand Rapids: Eerdmans, 2003.

Scandrett-Leatherman, Craig. "'Can't Nobody Do Me Like Jesus': The Politics of Embodied Aesthetics in Afro-Pentecostal Rituals." PhD diss., University of Kansas, 2005.

Schaff, David S. *The Middle Ages: From Boniface VIII, 1294 to the Protestant Reformation, 1517*. Edited by Philip Schaff. Vol. 6 of *History of the Christian Church*. N.p.: Plantagenet, 2011. Kindle.

Scott, Mark S. M. "Shades of Grace: Origen and Gregory of Nyssa's Soteriological Exegesis of the 'Black and Beautiful' Bride in Song of Songs 1:5." *HTR* 99 (2006) 65–83. http://www.jstor.org/stable/4125253.

Senior, Donald. "The Death of Jesus and the Resurrection of the Holy Ones (Mt 27:51–53." *CBQ* 38 (July 1976) 312–29. http://www.jstor.org/stable/43715149.

Settles, Joshua D. "Engaging Issues of Primal Spirituality and Identity: An Analysis of Short-term Mission Training." *JACT* 17 (2014) 25–36.

Shank, David A. *Prophet Harris, the "Black Elijah" of West Africa*. Abridged by Jocelyn Murray. Studies of Religion in Africa 10. Leiden: Brill, 1994.

Sharp, Douglas R. *No Partiality: The Idolatry of Race and the New Humanity*. Downers Grove, IL: IVP Academic, 2002.

Sheehan, Jonathan. *The Enlightenment Bible: Translation, Scholarship, Culture*. Princeton, NJ: Princeton University Press, 2005.

Sinclair, Andrew. *The Savage: A History of Misunderstanding*. London: Weidenfeld & Nicolson, 1977.

Smith, Adam. *Lectures on Jurisprudence.* Vol. 5 of *Glasgow Edition of the Works and Correspondence of Adam Smith, 1762–1766.* Edited by R. L. Meek et al. Indianapolis: Liberty Fund, 1982.

Smith, Edwin W., ed. *African Ideas of God: A Symposium.* London: Edinburgh, 1950.

Smith, Linda Tuhiwai. *Decolonizing Methodologies: Research and Indigenous Peoples.* 2nd ed. London: Zed, 2012.

Smith, Michael P. *Spirit World: Pattern in the Expressive Folk Culture of Afro-American New Orleans.* New Orleans: New Orleans Urban Folklife Society, 1984.

Smith, Theophus H. *Conjuring Culture: Biblical Formations of Black America.* Religion in America. New York: Oxford University Press, 1994.

Stein, Robert H. "Is the Transfiguration (Mark 9:2–8) a Misplaced Resurrection-Account?" *JBL* 95 (1976) 79–96. http //www.jstor.org/stable/3265474.

Stott, John R. W. *The Baptism and Fullness of the Holy Spirit.* Downers Grove, IL: InterVarsity, 1964.

Stronstad, Roger. *The Charismatic Theology of St. Luke: Trajectories from the Old Testament to Luke-Acts.* 2nd ed. Grand Rapids: Baker Academic, 2012.

Sundkler, Bengt, and Christopher Steed. *A History of the Church in Africa.* Cambridge: Cambridge University Press, 2000.

Sweet, James H. "The Iberian Roots of American Racist Thought." *William and Mary Quarterly* 54 (1997) 143–66. http://www.jstor.org/stable/2953315.

Tacitus, Cornelius. *The Histories.* Translated by W. Hamilton Fyfe. Oxford: Clarendon, 1912. Kindle.

Tamez, Elsa. "The Bible and the Five Hundred Years of Conquest." In *Voices from the Margin: Interpreting the Bible in the Third World,* edited by R. S. Sugirtharajah, 13–26. 3rd ed. Maryknoll, NY: Orbis, 2006.

Tannenbaum, Frank. *Slave and Citizen.* New York: Knopf Doubleday, 1946. Kindle.

Tatian. "Address to the Greeks." In *ANF,* edited by Alexander Roberts and James Donaldson, 2:65–83. Edinburgh: T&T Clark, 1892. Kindle.

Taylor, John V. *The Primal Vision: Christian Presence amid African Religion.* London: SCM, 1963.

Taylor, Martha C. "History." Allen Temple Baptist Church, 2019. https://www.allentemple.org/about-atbc/history.

Tertullian. "On Prayer: 22." In *ANF,* edited by Alexander Roberts and James Donaldson, 3:681–91. Repr., Edinburgh: T&T Clark, 1993.

———. "The Prescription against Heretics." In *ANF,* edited by Alexander Roberts and James Donaldson, 3:243–65. Edinburgh: T&T Clark, 1892. Kindle.

Thielman, Frank. *Ephesians.* BECNT. Grand Rapids: Baker Academic, 2010.

Thiselton, Anthony C. *The First Epistle to the Corinthians* NIGTC. Grand Rapids: Eerdmans, 2000.

Thomas, Robert L. "The Hermeneutics of Noncessationism." *MSJ* 14 (2003) 287–310. http://stage.tms edu/m/tmsj14k.pdf.

Thompson, Lloyd. "Roman Perceptions of Blacks." *Electronic Antiquity* 1 (1993). http://scholar.lib.vt.edu/ejournals/ElAnt/V1N4/thompson.html#1.

Trakakis, Nick. "Does Hard Determinism Render the Problem of Evil Even Harder?" *Ars Disputandi* 6 (2006) 239–64. http://www.tandfonline.com/doi/abs/10 1080/15665399.2006.10819932#.

Turner, Harold W. "New Religious Movements in Primal Societies." In *Australian Essays in World Religions*, edited by Victor Hayes, 38–48. Bedford Park, Aus.: Australian Association for the Study of Religions, 1977.

———. "The Primal Religions of the World and Their Study." In *Australian Essays in World Religion*, edited by Victor Hayes, 27–37. Bedford Park, Aus.: Australian Association for the Study of Religions, 1977.

Turner, Victor. *The Ritual Process: Structure and Anti-Structure*. Ithaca, NY: Cornell University Press, 1969.

Twelftree, Graham H. *Jesus the Miracle Worker: A Historical and Theological Study*. Downers Grove, IL: IVP Academic, 1999.

Van der Walt, B. J. *The Liberating Message: A Christian Worldview for Africa*. Potchefstroom, S. Afr.: Institute for Reformational Studies, 1994.

Vaughan, Alden T., and Virginia Mason Vaughan. "Before *Othello*: Elizabethan Representations of Sub-Saharan Africans." *William and Mary Quarterly* 54 (1997) 19–44. http://www.jstor.org/stable/2953311.

Walker, F. Deaville. *The Story of the Ivory Coast*. London: Cargate, n.d.

Walls, Andrew F. "Christian Scholarship in Africa in the Twenty-First Century." *JACT* 4 (2001) 44–52.

———. "Converts or Proselytes? The Crisis over Conversion in the Early Church." *International Bulletin of Missionary Research* 28 (2004) 2–6.

———. *The Cross-Cultural Process in Christian History*. Maryknoll, NY: Orbis, 2002.

———. *The Missionary Movement in Christian History: Studies in the Transmission of Faith*. Maryknoll, NY: Orbis, 1996.

———. "World Christianity, Theological Education and Scholarship." *Transformation* 28 (2011) 235–40.

Walton, Jonathan L. "Prosperity Gospel and African American Theology." In *The Oxford Handbook of African American Theology*, edited by Katie G. Cannon and Anthony B. Pinn, 453–68. Oxford Handbooks. New York: Oxford University Press, 2014.

Ware, Frederick L. "Methodologies in African American Theology." In *The Oxford Handbook of African American Theology*, edited by Katie G. Cannon and Anthony B. Pinn, 124–35. Oxford Handbooks. New York: Oxford University Press, 2014.

———. *Methodologies of Black Theology*. Eugene, OR: Wipf and Stock, 2008.

———. "On the Compatibility/Incompatibility of Pentecostal Premillennialism with Black Liberation Theology." In *Afro-Pentecostalism: Black Pentecostal and Charismatic Christianity in History and Culture*, edited by Amos Yong and Estrelda Y. Alexander, 191–206. Religion, Race, and Ethnicity. New York: New York University Press, 2011. Kindle.

Washington, Joseph R., Jr. *Black Religion: The Negro and Christianity in the United States*. Repr., Lanham, MD: University Press of America, 1984.

Waters, Kenneth L. "Matthew 27:52–53 as Apocalyptic Apostrophe: Temporal-Spatial Collapse in the Gospel of Matthew." *JBL* 122 (2003) 489–515. http://www.jstor.org/stable/3268388.

Weathers, Robert A. "Leland Ryken's Literary Approach to Biblical Interpretation: An Evangelical Model." *JETS* 37 (1994) 115–24. http://www.etsjets.org/files/JETS-PDFs/37/37-31/JETS_37-1_115-124_Weathers.pdf.

Wehmeyer, Stephen C. "'Indians at the Door': Power and Placement on New Orleans Spiritual Church Altars." *Western Folklore* 66 (2007) 15–44. http://www.jstor.org/stable/25474844.

Wenham, J. W. "When Were the Saints Raised? A Note on the Punctuation of Matthew XXVII. 51–53." *JTS*, n.s., 32 (1981) 150–52. http://www.jstor.org/stable/23959915.

Wilmore, Gayraud S. *Black Religion and Black Radicalism: An Interpretation of the Religious History of African Americans*. 3rd ed. Maryknoll, NY: Orbis, 1998.

Wilson, Shawn. "What Is an Indigenous Research Methodology?" *Canadian Journal of Native Education* 25 (2001) 175–79. http://www.researchgate.net/publication/234754037.

Wink, Walter, *Naming the Powers: The Language of Power in the New Testament*. Philadelphia: Fortress, 1984.

———. *Unmasking the Powers: The Invisible Forces That Determine Human Existence*. Philadelphia: Fortress, 1986.

Yannoulatos, Anastasios. "Growing into an Awareness of Primal World-Views." In *Primal World-Views: Christian Involvement in Dialogue with Traditional Thought Forms*, edited by John B. Taylor, 72–78. Ibadan: Daystar, 1976.

Yorke, Gosnell L. O. R. "The Bible in the Black Diaspora: Links with African Christianity." In *The Bible in Africa: Transactions, Trajectories, and Trends*, edited by Gerald O. West and Musa W. Dube, 127–49. Leiden: Brill, 2000.

Zahan, Dominique. "Some Reflections on African Spirituality." In *African Spirituality: Forms, Meanings, and Expressions*, edited by Jacob K. Olupona, 3–25. New York: Crossroad, 2000.

www.ingramcontent.com/pod-product-compliance
Lightning Source LLC
Chambersburg PA
CBHW071247230426
43668CB00011B/1622